Projects in Computing and Information Systems

A Student's Guide

Second Edition

CHRISTIAN W. DAWSON

 ADDISON-WESLEY

An imprint of Pearson Education

Harlow, England • London • New York • Boston • San Francisco • Toronto • Sydney • Singapore • Hong Kong
Tokyo • Seoul • Taipei • New Delhi • Cape Town • Madrid • Mexico City • Amsterdam • Munich • Paris • Milan

For Jacob and Ben

Pearson Education Limited
Edinburgh Gate
Harlow
Essex CM20 2JE
England

and Associated Companies throughout the world

Visit us on the World Wide Web at:
www.pearsoned.co.uk

First published 2005
Second edition 2009

ISBN 978-0-273-72131-4

British Library Cataloguing-in-Publication Data
A catalogue record for this book is available from the British Library

Library of Congress Cataloguing-in-Publication Data
Dawson, Christian W.
    Projects in computing and information systems : a student's guide / Christian W. Dawson.
—2nd ed.
        p. cm.
    Includes bibliographical references and index.
    ISBN 978-0-273-72131-4 (pbk. : alk. paper)
    1. Electronic data processing. 2. Information technology. I. Title.

QA76.D3333326 2009
004—dc22   2009006227

10 9 8 7
13

Typeset in 9.75/12pt Galliard
Printed in Great Britain by Henry Ling Limited., at the Dorset Press, Dorchester, DT1 1HD.

Projects in Computing and Information Systems

We work with leading authors to develop the
strongest educational materials in computing
bringing cutting-edge thinking and best learning
practice to a global market.

Under a range of well-known imprints, including
Addison-Wesley, we craft high-quality print and
electronic publications which help readers
to understand and apply their content, whether
studying or at work.

To find out more about the complete range of our
publishing, please visit us on the World Wide Web at:
www.pearsoned.co.uk.

Contents

Preface

Projects are a major component of virtually all undergraduate and postgraduate computing and information science courses within universities. They require students to draw on a number of separate but highly important skills; surveying literature, report writing, developing and documenting software, presentational skills, time management, project management skills and so on. For students to excel in all of these areas is a major accomplishment, yet it is something that academic institutions have come to expect as part of the independent learning process.

While there are books available that cover *some* of these topics in great detail, there are none that draw **all** these skills together and which are aimed specifically at students on computing and information systems courses of one kind or another. This text fills this gap and provides a foundation in the skills both undergraduate and postgraduate students require to complete their projects successfully.

This book is structured in a chronological fashion so that the main stages through which projects progress are discussed in sequence. It is split into the following five main sections:

The background. This section provides a general introduction to projects, the different degree structures that are in place and the stakeholders involved. It also provides a useful introduction to research in the context of computing projects.

Setting your project's foundation. This section describes the skills you will need during the initial stages of your computing project. It covers such topics as choosing a project, writing a project proposal and planning your project.

Conducting your project. This section covers the skills you will need while you are actually working on your project – from doing your literature survey to managing your time and any information and data that you collect, as well as how to liaise effectively with your supervisor. It also includes a chapter on software development for those undertaking projects of this nature.

Presenting your project. The final stage of your project is to present it as a written report and, possibly, an oral presentation. This section will cover the skills you will need to present your project in the best light and to the best of your abilities.

The future. The book concludes with some valuable information on how your project might be assessed, how you can take your project further in the future and how you might consider publishing your work.

Acknowledgements

The author and publishers would like to express their thanks to the following reviewers for their invaluable feedback throughout the development of this book:

Professor Darren Dalcher, Middlesex University
Peter Morris, University of Greenwich
Mikael Berndtsson, University of Skövde
Wamberto Vasconcelos, University of Aberdeen

Microsoft, PowerPoint, Visual C++ and Windows are registered trademarks of Microsoft Corporation.

Reference Manager is a registered trademark of the Institute for Scientific Information.

Publisher's acknowledgements

Figure 9.10 from Yanning Yang, Loughborough University; Figure 9.11 from Rachael Lindsay, Loughborough University; Figure 9.12 from Martin Sykora, Loughborough University.

In some instances we have been unable to trace the owners of copyright material, and we would appreciate any information that would enable us to do so.

The background

CHAPTER

1

Introduction

Aims:

To introduce academic computing projects and the structure of this book.

Learning objectives:

When you have completed this chapter, you should be able to:

- Understand what projects are.
- Understand the different types of academic projects in computing and information sciences.
- Understand different degree structures and project requirements.
- Describe the roles different people have in academic projects.
- Understand how this book is arranged.

1.1 Introduction

Pursuing a project within academia is not the same as performing a project within industry. As a student on a computing degree course of one kind or another, you will be expected to look at things much more critically and more deeply than you would elsewhere. In industry, for example, your line manager might ask you to develop a piece of software to solve a particular problem or improve productivity in a particular area – a database, a production control system, or whatever. You could write this program satisfactorily and install it within a few weeks or months and everyone would be satisfied.

However, although this program might be perfectly adequate and work very well in practice, this project would be lacking *academically*.

Why is this the case? Academic projects should provide evidence of a much deeper understanding of what you are doing. They require some form of justification and contextualisation. You are not expected to do merely what you are told to do; you are expected to develop your own thoughts, arguments, ideas, and concepts. You are expected to question things and look at things in new ways and from new angles. Merely 'turning the handle' or doing what you are told does not lead to intellectual discovery or contributions to world thinking. Importantly, as a degree student you are expected to **think.** This 'deeper' understanding of situations, problems, and events is supported by your *research* skills – skills that are vitally important within academic projects.

Academic projects are usually a critical component of your degree course. Sometimes they make up a significant component of your final year (for example, 30% or more), and sometimes, particularly at postgraduate level, they may represent *all* of your degree. There are a number of reasons universities include project work as part of their courses:

- Assessment across a number of disciplines simultaneously. Your project will require you to apply things you have learnt from lots of different areas of your course – both technical and personal skills. The project will provide evidence of how much you have developed across a wide range of disciplines. It will also show your ability to draw together your knowledge and apply what you have learnt. This might be the first time that the importance of apparently different skills taught on your course may become clear.

- Allows you to develop new skills. The project will also enable you to develop skills you might not have covered explicitly in your course so far. These new skills might be technical (learning a new programming language, development method, design technique, research, etc.) and personal (time management, discipline, communication skills, report writing, etc.).

- Work independently. Your project might be the first time that you have had to work mainly on your own on a project that is primarily your own work, ideas, and responsibility.

- Make a contribution. A project will allow you to make some form of contribution. Previously you might have been doing directed coursework, examinations, etc. The project will allow you to produce something that may be used by or benefit others.

This book aims to help you with this critical component of your course – be it at under-graduate or postgraduate level.

● 1.2 What are (computing) projects?

1.2.1 Introduction

Projects can be defined as 'something which has a beginning and an end' (Barnes, 1989 cited by Turner, 1993: 4). Unfortunately, this rather broad definition of projects does not encapsulate their underlying purpose which is to bring about some form of beneficial change. This change takes you from an existing situation to a desired situation sometime in the future. This can be represented by the *Meliorist Model* shown in Figure 1.1. In this figure a project is represented by a set of actions that you perform. A project thus enables

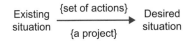

Figure 1.1 The Meliorist Model

you to move from one situation to another. Your movement towards the desired situation might stem from dissatisfaction with your current situation, a lure towards a situation which appears more satisfactory, or some combination of the two.

The desirable situation in this case represents some form of contribution to knowledge – perhaps representing the development of a new tool, technique, discovery, and so on. The term 'contribution' in this context necessarily implies the uniqueness of the project and novelty of its outcomes.

So far, projects have been identified as having a beginning and an end (i.e., they occur within a specified **time frame**) – with a **purpose** being to bring about a beneficial change by making some kind of contribution. Another important aspect of projects that must be discussed is that they are made up of a series of **considered** activities. In other words, projects are broken down into a sequence of **planned** activities that are controlled as the project progresses – they do not simply occur in an *ad hoc* manner. Chapter 4 looks in detail at this aspect of projects – project planning and risk management. We should also consider the fact that projects consume a number of **resources** in order to achieve their purpose. What resources are consumed in your project is introduced in Chapter 4. How these resources are managed is discussed in Chapter 7.

Computing projects come in all different shapes and sizes, as the field they are drawn from is immense. However, these days it is more widely recognised, within academic institutions, that computing projects need to do more than develop a piece of software. The project that you pursue must involve an element of research, it must justify its context and you must evaluate and discuss its results. Merely developing a tool or algorithm with no evaluation or contextualisation may well be acceptable in industry, where commercial solutions are required. However, within the academic world, this is not the case and, depending on the nature of your project, to some extent it must contain an element of research.

Berndtsson *et al.* (2008) point out that the nature of computer science and information systems means that projects are drawn from both the 'hard' sciences (natural science) and the 'soft' sciences (social science). As a result, projects cover a vast range of topics, from highly technical software development projects to (equally difficult) case studies within information science. Figure 1.2 (adapted from Dawson, 2004) shows the extent of the computer science and information science field. At the left-hand side of this scale are the theoretical areas of computer science, encompassing such areas as mathematics, logic, formal methods, artificial intelligence, etc. Moving towards the

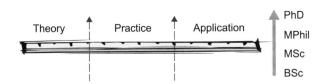

Figure 1.2 The landscape of computing (adapted from Dawson, 2004)

centre of the scale we find practice-based computing, which focuses less on theory and more on the development of software systems – for example, software engineering, software project management, design, development processes, requirements capture and so on. At the right-hand side of the scale are the softer issues in the field, concerned with the application and use of computers and information technology, and the influence and impact they have on organisations and society at large. This area looks at how organisations are structured and operate, how data are stored and processed, knowledge management, and how information is disseminated throughout organisations. This might involve systems beyond software and hardware – for example, paper-based systems, processes, procedures, and more. A vertical scale at the right of Figure 1.2 displays the levels of project work that this book covers – from undergraduate projects to doctoral degrees. These levels are discussed in Section 1.3.

In terms of university degree courses, you will *probably* find that courses entitled 'Computer Science' or 'Artificial Intelligence' tend to fall more towards the left-hand side of this scale. 'Software Engineering', 'Computing', and 'E-business' courses probably fall more towards the centre (with 'Software Engineering' to the left and 'E-business' to the right). Courses entitled 'Information Science', 'Information Technology', 'Business and Information Technology', 'Business Information Systems' and 'Information Systems' will fall more towards the right-hand side. Some courses might fall anywhere along the scale depending on their content – for example, 'Multimedia' and 'Computer Studies' can mean different things in different institutions.

This list is not intended to be exhaustive and you may find that your course falls somewhere else along this line. However, you should have some idea of where your course lies on this scale as this will influence the type of project that is appropriate for you to undertake. This book will address the issues surrounding all of these areas.

The computing project you embark upon gives **you** an opportunity to make your **own** contribution. There is little point in doing a project that merely regurgitates the work of others. Your own thoughts, ideas, and developments **are** important and these are what people reading your report are interested in. Through your project you will develop not only your own skills, but also the ideas and work of others. In Section 5.1 we consider in more detail the level of contribution undergraduate and postgraduate projects make.

The following section introduces the different kinds of project you are likely to encounter in the field of computing. In each case, the project's academic contribution is identified. The projects do not merely follow a simplistic process to develop a product at the end of the day.

1.2.2 Computing project types

This section introduces five categories of computing projects. These categories are not intended to be discrete; you may well find your own project falls into two or even more of these classes (or perhaps falls distinctly into one category but draws on approaches that are identified in others). In addition, the nature of your project will have an effect on the methods you will use to tackle it. Chapter 2 discusses the research methods that you might employ within your project.

■ **Research-based.** 'Many good dissertations do no more than review systematically and impose some structure on, a field of interest' (Sharp *et al.*, 2002: 27). A research-based project involves a thorough investigation of a particular area; improving your understanding of that area, identifying strengths and weaknesses within the field, discussing how the field has evolved, and acknowledging areas suitable for further development and investigation. This kind of project will involve some form of literature search and review, and would be suitable for taught bachelor's or taught master's courses.

So far, the definition of research-based projects has been 'backward looking' rather than 'forward looking' (Cornford and Smithson, 2006: 71). A research-based project may well have to do more than establish the field of study. For example, having established the field (backward looking), a student in a doctoral program (a PhD, for example) would then be expected to *contribute* to that field (forward looking). This contribution might be achieved by addressing a research question, developing something new, solving a problem, and so on. These additional steps are addressed in the following sections in which other project types are defined.

- **Development.** This category includes the development of, not only software and hardware systems, but also of process models, methods, algorithms, theories, designs, requirement specifications, and other interim documents. Examples of software development projects include database systems, multimedia systems, information systems, and web-based systems. For some developments (notably software) you will be required to include requirements documentation, designs, analyses, and fully documented test results along with user manuals or guides.

  Depending on the nature of your course, the focus for a development project may vary. For example, for software engineering courses, emphasis may be placed on the development and evaluation of a piece of software, following particular process models that generate interim evaluatory documentation. Information systems courses may require you to focus more on the development of broader systems using 4GLs, CASE tools, and/or database systems. In this case, evaluation of HCI (human computer interaction), customer issues, requirements capture problems, and the impact of the implemented system and working practices may be more your focus.

  Whichever kind of development project you tackle, it is unlikely that the development of a product would be acceptable on its own. In addition, you would normally be expected to include a critical evaluation of the product as well as the development process used. Critical evaluation emphasises the distinction between the academic qualities of your work from technical ability alone. Figure 1.3 illustrates this point, and contrasts a student project and an industry-based project both attempting to develop a software

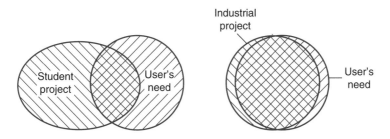

Figure 1.3 Comparison of student development project and industrial development project

system to meet a user's need. While the student project goes some way toward meeting the user's needs, the project includes much more than that (and hence may only partly fulfil the user's need). In contrast, the industrial-based project focuses primarily on solving the user's problem and little else. Consequently, the industrial project develops a system that is close as possible to meeting the user's requirements (although it is never perfect), whereas the student project does not.

- **Evaluation.** This category encompasses all projects that involve some form of evaluation as their main focus. For example, such a project might involve comparing several approaches to a particular problem; evaluating two or more programming languages (applied in different contexts or to different problems); analyzing an implementation process within a particular industry; assessing different user interfaces; analyzing a particular concept; considering alternative and new technological approaches to a problem; appraising development methodologies to a problem; and so on. Projects in this category may well include case studies as a vehicle for evaluating the issue under consideration.

- **Industry-based.** An industry-based project involves solving a problem within either an organisation or another university department. Industry-based projects might be any of the other kinds of projects identified in this section. The difference in this case is that you undertake the project for an actual client, which carries with it a number of benefits as well as drawbacks. Section 3.2 discusses in more detail the advantages and disadvantages of choosing an industry-based project. The most important point is that the sponsor does not 'hijack' the project – that is, force it into a direction the company wishes it to go, regardless of whether it is suitable for your academic work or your course. You will probably find that an industry-based project employs the action research method, which is discussed in Section 2.4.

- **Problem solving.** A problem-solving project can involve developing a new technique to solve a problem, improving the efficiency of existing approaches or an evaluation of different approaches or theories in different situations. It might also involve applying an existing problem-solving technique or theory to a new area. In these cases, some form of evaluation would be expected: for example, did your new approach work well or did you discover reasons why it was unsuitable for problems of this nature? Why does one approach or theory work better in some situations than in others?

1.2.3 Programming in computing projects

Although you are on a computing course of one kind or another, you may or may not be expected to write a program. As noted earlier, the broad field of computing encompasses many topics, such as information systems, software engineering, knowledge engineering, human computer interaction, data communications, networks, computer systems architecture, and much more. Not all of these fields involve programming; to write a program for its own sake is clearly ill-advised.

Sometimes programming is the main emphasis of your project, for example, if you are on a software engineering course. At other times, you may need to write a program as a 'vehicle' for testing and demonstrating one thing or another, for instance, to test out some ideas, demonstrate a technique or algorithm, or evaluate some human computer interaction concepts.

Whatever the case, as a computing student you will naturally be expected to produce code that is of acceptable *quality*. Although you may not be expected to produce a fully documented piece of software with test plans, designs, and evaluation, any code that you do produce should be satisfactory for your aims. Your supervisor should be able to advise you on the breadth and depth of any software you produce as part of your project, so make sure you liaise with him or her closely. Chapter 6 provides some useful material on the approaches you can use to develop software systems; Chapter 8 includes ways of documenting software; and Chapter 9 explains how you can demonstrate your program effectively.

● 1.3 Degree requirements

1.3.1 Degree structures

Educational institutions throughout the world have many different degree structures that take students from school/college level education through undergraduate study to doctoral degrees (sometimes referred to as *higher education*). However, not only do countries have different interpretations of *undergraduate* and *postgraduate* study (for example, would you classify a master's degree as an undergraduate or postgraduate course?), they also have a number of different titles for degrees that are essentially the same (PhD and DPhil, for example).

At the 'undergraduate' level, some countries have a *single tier* of higher education leading to the start of doctoral studies; for example, five years of study leading to the award of a master's degree. Other countries have a *two-tier* structure in place that leads, first, to a bachelor's degree (after around three, four, or even five years of study) and *then* to a master's degree (after a further one or two years of study). There is also diversity at doctoral level, with some countries recognising an intermediate doctoral degree (one could argue the UK's MPhil falls into this category), and some countries having 'higher' doctorates (particularly in Central and Eastern Europe). Although a number of countries have signed up to the *Bologna Declaration* (an initiative intended to harmonise higher education structures in Europe), there is still a long way to go to producing a common degree structure. At the time of writing, 45 countries are involved in the Bologna process. For more information on this process, see Fearn (2008), which provides an interesting discussion on how negotiations are progressing.

In order to avoid confusion and to provide some consistency and a common framework for this book, we will avoid using the terms *undergraduate* or *postgraduate study* except where their meaning is clear or unimportant. Where necessary, a differentiation will be made between *taught* degrees (such as bachelor's and master's degrees – BScs and MScs for example) – which are predominantly based around taught courses that include some project element – and *research* degrees (such as MPhils and PhDs), which are primarily research-based projects that lead to some contribution to knowledge. In this case, although an MPhil and an MSc are both master's courses, an MPhil is viewed at a higher level than an MSc because it involves a much more substantial project component, which is, after all, the focus of this book (see Figure 1.2). In this book, the MPhil is understood to mean a research degree normally completed after about two years of study.

In this model, students can enter higher education to study for a bachelor's degree or a master's degree. Before undertaking a research degree, they must have completed a taught degree to a required standard or equivalent prior learning. This sequence of higher education is shown in Figure 1.4.

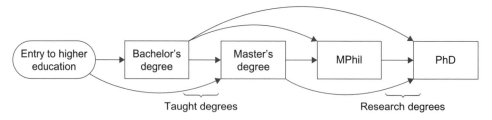

Figure 1.4 Higher education

1.3.2 Degree requirements for projects

 As this book is aimed at students on both taught degrees and research degrees, it is worth spending a little time looking at the differences between the projects undertaken at these different levels. These are general guidelines – your own department and university (and country) can offer specific guidance on what is and what is not appropriate for your own level of study.

A project undertaken as part of a taught course (bachelor's or master's degree) does not need to make great breakthroughs in science. It might involve the development of some software, it could be an extended case study, or it might be research-based. However, generally speaking, you would not be expected to produce work at a level that could be published in an academic journal or presented at an international conference. This is not the case for research degrees, however. An MPhil should produce work that could be published (perhaps with some reworking), whereas students pursuing a PhD will probably be expected to have published some of their work before completing the final thesis (and, in some European countries, this is compulsory). At the research degree level, Chinneck (1999) contrasts master's (in this case, research-based postgraduate study) with PhD-level work in the following way: 'The contribution of knowledge of a Master's thesis can be in the nature of an incremental improvement in an area of knowledge, or the application of known techniques in a new area. The PhD must be a substantial and innovative contribution to knowledge'. The University of Derby (1999) notes the following abilities a student is expected to demonstrate at research degree level:

■ an ability to work independently with minimum supervision;
■ an ability to draw on existing knowledge and identify additional knowledge needed for your study;[*]
■ an ability to critically evaluate advanced literature (journal papers);[*]
■ 'an ability to conceive original ideas';
■ an ability to plan your work effectively;[*]
■ an ability to select and use appropriate hardware, software, tools, methods and techniques;[*]
■ an ability to present your work effectively in written and oral forms;[*]
■ an ability to critically evaluate your own work and justify all aspects of it;[*]
■ an ability to identify areas of further research in your chosen area.

Abilities marked with an asterisk (*) are those that should be evident in taught degree projects as well. What sets research degree work apart is, mainly, an ability to 'conceive original ideas'. This emphasises that for a research degree you are expected to make some kind of contribution to knowledge, not just repeat the work of others. This is discussed in more detail in Chapter 5.

1.4 Stakeholders

1.4.1 Overview

Stakeholders are any individuals who are involved with your project. The most important person in your project is *you*. You are responsible for the overall completion of your project, meeting milestones, achieving objectives, satisfying users, satisfying the examiners, and so forth. Your project has many other stakeholders, and they all have significant roles to play. They include your *supervisor(s)*, your *user(s)*, your *client(s)*, your *examiner(s)* and any software *testers/evaluators* you might employ as part of your system evaluation (if you have one in your project).

1.4.2 Your supervisor

Imagine your project as a large boulder. At the start of your project, this boulder is quite difficult to push (stationary objects like to remain stationary). Getting a project started is always difficult. However, once the project is underway (the boulder is rolling), it becomes much easier to push and gathers momentum as the project unfolds. Now, picture your supervisor alongside you. It is that person's role to encourage you as you push this boulder (your project) along. Your supervisor will encourage you at the start as you try to get the boulder moving. They are also there to ensure you are pushing in the right direction. The supervisor will have an eye on the route you are taking and provide the occasional prod to keep you (and the boulder) on course. Your supervisor is also there to provide encouragement. If you feel yourself flagging at any stage, your supervisor should be there to support you and give you the help you need. In Chapter 3, we look at ways in which you might be able to choose your supervisor and, in Chapter 7, how to use your supervisor effectively as your project progresses.

Sometimes (particularly for research degrees), you may have more than one supervisor. This is especially common where the area of study straddles two fields of expertise. In addition, research degrees often have a supervisor (someone who is responsible for the student overall) and a *director of studies* or *director of research*. The director of research is sometimes a more senior member of academic staff who is interested in the strategic (rather than week-to-week) direction of the project. You may see your supervisor once every one or two weeks, but you would see your director of research only every six months or perhaps once a year.

1.4.3 Client(s) and user(s)

If your project involves the development of a software system or involves action research or case studies, you will probably be working with a client and/or a user. It is important to realise the distinction between these two stakeholders. A client is usually the project's sponsor – the one who has requested the system be developed or study undertaken. The user, on the other hand, will be the one who eventually uses the system or the results of the project. Sometimes the client and the user are one and the same but often, if you are developing a system for a company, for example, they are not. For instance, you might be asked to develop a web site for a company to sell its products. The client is your contact within the company, but your user(s) is anyone who will access that site.

Conflicts usually arise when the client and the user are different: for example, should you provide something the client requests that you know the user won't like? How do you persuade the client that the user needs a particular piece of functionality when the client feels it is unnecessary?

In other cases your supervisor may be your client and/or user as they may have proposed the project you are undertaking. In this case, your supervisor will be acting in all three roles. This can cause conflicts as their advice as a supervisor may not tally with their needs as a user (for example, as a user they may request certain features from your software system, but as a supervisor may recommend that you do not include that feature as it may take too much effort for little reward).

1.4.4 Examiners

 The number and type of examiners you will encounter on your course will largely depend on the level of project you are undertaking (undergraduate or postgraduate) and the regulations your institution has in place (these vary by institution and country). At the undergraduate level, for example, your supervisor may be the only person to mark your project. However, it is more likely that another academic in your department (or perhaps another department within your university) will be involved. Moving to postgraduate projects, external examiners (those from other departments and usually other universities) will be involved. Any number of examiners can be involved in project assessment – from individual examiners to panels of examiners that act as a committee to evaluate the contribution of your work. The examiner(s) will look for a number of things in your project, from the contribution a PhD project makes, for example, to the use of appropriate processes, methods, and techniques for an undergraduate software development-type project. Chapter 10 discusses the criteria examiners look for when evaluating projects.

Depending on the nature of your course, examiners can also be involved at different stages as your project progresses. For example, an examining committee may be involved early on to evaluate your project's requirements or proposal. Or, an examiner may need to see an annual report or other information.

You should be aware of the regulations regarding the evaluation and examination of your project and follow any procedures closely. Institutions are quite strict when it comes to examinations and insist that procedures are followed to the letter. Make sure that your supervisor is aware of the current procedures at your institution and obtain the institution's advice on the requirements for the examination of your project.

1.4.5 Evaluators and testers

If you are developing a software system as part of your project, you will need to test and evaluate this system at some point. It would be wrong to complete all the testing and evaluation on your own, and so others will be involved. These people can range from your client, who has requested the software, the user(s) who will actually use the software, to people (either expert or not – for example, colleagues from your course) who are not involved with the project but can nevertheless provide useful feedback.

Chapter 6 discusses the issues surrounding software evaluation and testing in more detail. It also describes those involved with the evaluation and raises some issues you will need to consider when using others in this capacity.

 ## 1.5 How this book is arranged

1.5.1 Overview

This book is split into five main sections that approximate chronologically to your project's progress. Section 1 includes this chapter and covers some preliminary background material on the types of projects you might pursue and the nature of research. Section 2 covers the skills necessary to set your project's foundation. It covers topics such as choosing a project, planning how to undertake the project, and literature searching and reviewing. Section 3 looks at how to manage your project as it is progressing. This section also includes ways of developing software systems if this is relevant to your own project. Section 4 covers completing and submitting your project – writing reports, giving presentations, viva voce examinations, etc. Section 5 looks into the future – for example, taking your project further after it is completed.

Figure 1.5 depicts how this book is arranged. While sections are designed to be read in order as your project progresses, the chapters within each section can be read in the order that suits your needs. Note that Chapter 3 (Choosing a project and writing a proposal) should be read before Chapter 4 (Project planning and risk management) while Chapter 5 (Literature searching and literature reviews) can be read before, after, or even between both of these.

> **Note**
>
> It is advisable to read Section 10.2 in Chapter 10 before you proceed any further with your project. It describes what examiners will ultimately be looking for and evaluating within your project. Knowing what you need to aim for now is useful as it will guide you in the way you undertake your project and provide a focus for your effort. In addition, for those in need of instant help, Section 10.7 provides the top ten tips for successful projects based on other sections within the book.

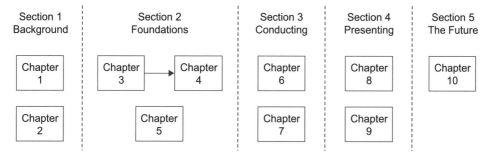

Figure 1.5 How this book is arranged

1.5.2 Taught degree projects versus research degrees

The *mortarboard and certificate* symbol (left) highlights areas in the book where differences between taught degree (BSc, BEng, etc.) and research degree (PhD, DPhil, MPhil, etc.) projects are discussed. MScs may straddle the boundary between the two depending on how they are taught and assessed – for example, some require a significant research component (potentially leading to publishable work), while others may accept less research-oriented software development projects.

Not all sections in this book are relevant to PhD students, although they may provide some useful background reading. Similarly, some sections may go into more depth than a particular taught degree project requires but, for other taught degree projects (research-based projects, for example), the text may be highly relevant. Use these symbolised sections to decide which portions of the book are suitable reading for your own project.

● 1.6 Summary

- The field of computing ranges from 'hard' theoretical computer science, through practical software implementation, to 'softer' areas of information systems concerned with the use and the effect of IT.

- Computing projects tend to fall into one of the following five categories: *research-based, developments, evaluation, industry-based* or *problem solving.*

- This book covers projects that are undertaken as part of *taught* degrees (bachelor's and master's degrees such as BScs and MScs) and *research* degrees (from MPhils to PhDs).

- Your project will have a number of *stakeholders,* the most important of which is **you.** Others include your supervisor(s), client(s), user(s), examiner(s), software testers and evaluators.

- This book is arranged chronologically into the following five sections: *Background, Foundations, Conducting, Presenting,* and *The Future.*

● 1.7 Action points

- Consider where your own course and project lie on the computing scale shown in Figure 1.2.

- Classify your own project into one of the categories identified in Section 1.2.2.

- Identify the stakeholders in your project. Do you know them all yet? What is your relationship with them?

- Read Section 10.2 in Chapter 10 to see what your project must achieve in order to satisfy the examiners. Think about what you will need to do to meet these criteria.

CHAPTER 2

Research

Aims:

To introduce research in the context of computing projects.

Learning objectives:

When you have completed this chapter, you should be able to:

- Discuss what research means.
- Understand the research process.
- Classify research and understand the different research methods available.
- Understand the issues surrounding interviews, questionnaires and observational studies.

- This chapter is highly relevant for research degrees.
- This chapter is highly relevant for research-based taught degree projects and provides useful reading for other taught degree projects.

2.1 What is research?

The good researcher is not 'one who knows the right answers' but 'one who is struggling to find out what the right questions might be'.

Phillips and Pugh (2005: 48)

2.1.1 A definition

A useful starting point from which to discuss research is to examine a seminal definition of the term. Research is defined by the Higher Education Funding Council for England (HECFE) as '*original* investigation undertaken in order to *gain knowledge and understanding*' (RAE, 2008). Three key terms in this definition have been italicised for emphasis; *original, gain* and *knowledge and understanding*. These terms are essential to the definition of research and will be discussed in turn.

2.1.2 Originality

There is no point in repeating the work of others and discovering or producing what is already known. Quite simply, *originality* is doing something that has not been done before. While this remains a relatively simplistic definition, it is important to discuss how originality relates to projects. What can **you** do that is original? What type of things can **you** produce that are original?

You can be original in two ways. First, you can be original in the way you do things – for example, doing something someone has done before but using a different technique or approach. Second, you can be original by producing or developing something that has not been produced before.

In terms of originality in the way you do things, Cryer (2006: 193–195) identifies a number of areas in which your project can be original:

■ **Tools, techniques, procedures and methods.** You may apply new tools and techniques to existing problems or try new procedures and methods in contexts where they have not been applied before. Whether these investigations prove successful or not, you will still be doing something that is original and discovering why these approaches are suitable in certain circumstances or why they aren't.

■ **Exploring the unknown.** Although rare, you may investigate a field that no one has thought to investigate before. Recent discoveries in scientific fields may open up new possibilities and unexplored avenues of research to pursue.

■ **Exploring the unanticipated.** Although you may investigate a field of research that has been looked at many times before, you may come across unexpected results or exciting new directions as yet unexplored. Investigating these 'side tracks' may prove fruitful, but take care that they don't lead to dead ends. You might also be able to contribute to these fields by further developing original work.

Exploring a field that has already been investigated does not necessarily fail to be original. You may be able to improve on something that already exists, provide a new perspective or interpretation, or produce a unique in-depth study of the field.

■ **The use of data.** You can interpret data in different ways, use them in new ways or apply them in alternative areas that have not yet been investigated.

In terms of your project's outcomes, Cryer (2006: 196) identifies originality from the perspective of the results themselves and, also, any original by-products of the research. Thus, original outcomes might include a new product, theory, model or method. Where the intended outcomes are not achieved, by-products might still represent originality – for example, an understanding of why a particular experiment failed or why a particular technique did not work in a new area.

2.1.3 Gain/contribution

'Gain' is, perhaps, an unfortunate term in the HEFCE definition because it does not allude to the fact that research should actually lead to a *contribution* to knowledge. It is all very well performing an exclusive piece of research and learning something new for ourselves, but unless you can disseminate this knowledge to others, the results of your research are somewhat wasted. With this in mind, the following discussion will focus on the term 'contribute', which gives the much clearer message that research should add to world knowledge so that it is accessible to all and not just yourself.

Figure 2.1 depicts the world's body of knowledge and how contributions can be made to it. This body of knowledge represents world understanding, theories, concepts, models, the sciences, the arts and so forth. This knowledge is stored in books, journal articles, conference proceedings, documents, reports, the Internet, art, peoples' minds and more. Your own knowledge, portrayed as the shaded region, is shown as subsumed within this domain. You can obviously learn things that others already know; shown as expansion to your own knowledge 'cloud'. Likewise, you can make contributions to world knowledge from your research, such as inventions, new theories and so on. These are shown as expansions to the world's body of knowledge by the dashed lines. Thus, 'contribution' refers to a sharing of new ideas, theories and results with the rest of the world and expanding what is already known.

2.1.4 Knowledge and understanding

To explain what is meant by knowledge, it will be discussed in terms of a hierarchy consisting of *data, information, knowledge* and *wisdom*. Post and Anderson (2006: 5) identify the meaning of these terms as:

■ **Data.** Data are the factual elements that describe objects or events. They represent the raw numbers and raw text you gather from your investigations. For example, as

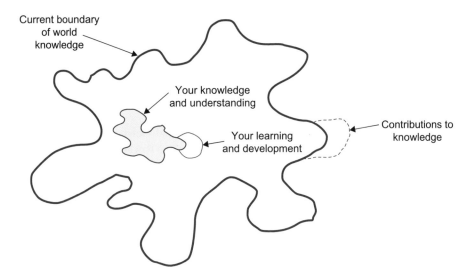

Figure 2.1 Contributions to knowledge

part of your research project, you may need to gather rainfall data from various sites around the country. These data, providing daily rainfall totals at 50 sites, are gathered as raw numbers that mean virtually nothing as they stand.

■ **Information.** Information represents data that have been processed in order to provide you with some insight into their meaning. In other words, the data have been analysed, summarised and processed into a more understandable and useful format. In this form, information can be passed to other people; for example, in books, articles, recordings, speech and so on (Orna and Stevens 1995: 36).

Converting your rainfall data into information may lead to graphs summarising monthly totals, charts presenting seasonal fluctuations and text or tables summarising average daily rainfall at different sites. In these formats the data have some meaning and you now have some insight into what these data represent.

■ **Knowledge.** Knowledge is your higher-level understanding of things. While information provides you with an idea of the 'what' (i.e., what is happening in the real world), knowledge represents your understanding of the 'why'. Knowledge is your personal interpretation of what you gain from information as rules, patterns, decisions, models, ideas and so on. According to Orna and Stevens (1995: 35), knowledge represents the 'results of experience organised and stored inside each individual's own mind'.

While your information about rainfall provided you with an overview of **what** was happening to weather over a period of time, knowledge represents your understanding of **why** rainfall might have changed during this period. For example, your knowledge would be your understanding of why rainfall had increased in particular parts of the country since 1900.

■ **Wisdom.** Wisdom represents your ability to put your knowledge into practice. It represents your ability to apply your skills and experiences to create new knowledge and adapt to different situations.

With reference to the rainfall data example, wisdom would represent your ability to predict likely changes to rainfall and climate in the future or enable you to understand why rain falls at particular levels in entirely different parts of the world.

One more category that is worth mentioning here is **theory.** While data, information, knowledge and wisdom represent a relatively 'firm' understanding of what is going on and how things can be applied, *theory* represents ideas, opinions and suppositions based on your observations of the world. A theory is not necessarily true but, at the moment, it represents the best explanation of what you observe.

Although knowledge has been defined from a personal viewpoint, *world knowledge* can be defined along much the same lines. In this case, world knowledge relates to world understanding, wisdom and interpretation by everybody and everything that is recorded or documented somewhere and somehow.

Collecting data and information on their own is termed as 'intelligence-gathering' by Phillips and Pugh (2005: 47). These data are used to answer what Phillips and Pugh term the 'what' questions – i.e., what is happening in the world, what don't we know and what can we find out? Research, however, must go beyond merely gathering data and describing what you see. It must make a contribution to **knowledge**. It looks for 'explanations, relationships, comparisons, predictions, generalisations and

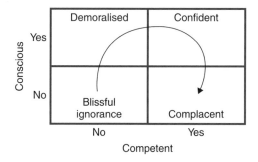

Figure 2.2 Self-awareness of a research field

theories'. Research thus addresses what Phillips and Pugh term the 'why' questions – why do things happen the way they do? Why is the situation the way it is? And so on. While data and information on their own can only answer the 'what?', knowledge and wisdom address the 'why?'.

Finally, it is worth discussing how we interpret our understanding of our own knowledge. At the start of the research process, we have no real understanding of how little we know about our subject – we are not conscious of our own incompetence (*blissful ignorance*). As our research progresses, we move into a (perhaps somewhat demoralising) phase when we become conscious of our incompetence – we become aware of just how little we know about the subject area we are investigating and can become overwhelmed by how vast that area is (*demoralised*). As our research progresses and we begin to understand the field, we move into the next phase – becoming competent in our subject and aware of this understanding (conscious of our competence – *confident*). Finally, we move into a phase in which we lose sight of just how much we do know – we become unconscious of our competence (*complacent*). Figure 2.2 illustrates this development in terms of competence and consciousness.

2.1.5 Summary

Now that the three main aspects of research have been looked at in detail, one other definition of research is presented to see if it encapsulates the essence of the term. As an example, take the definition of research by Sharp *et al.* (2002: 7), which is:

> 'seeking through *methodical processes* to *add* to one's own body of *knowledge* and to that of others, by the *discovery* of *non-trivial facts* and *insights*'.

Once again, the important terms within this definition have been italicised, a number of which relate directly to those that have been discussed already. 'Add', for example, relates to the discussion of 'contribution', and 'discovery' appears to imply some form of 'originality'. 'Non-trivial facts' and 'insights' relate to 'knowledge' and 'wisdom', not data or information.

One element that this definition contributes, that the HEFCE definition did not, is the idea of a 'methodical process'. This points out that research is not something done in an *ad hoc* manner but is something that is planned and pursued in a considered way. Thus, the process of performing research, which is discussed in the following section, is *methodical.*

Drawing these points together results in the following succinct definition of research, which encapsulates all the elements discussed so far – consideration, originality, contribution and knowledge:

> *Research is a considered activity, which aims to make an original contribution to knowledge.*

● 2.2 The research process

2.2.1 Overview

One thing that the above definition of research recognised is that research must be a considered activity. In other words, your research activity should not be performed as and when you feel like it, but it should follow a recognised process. Blaxter *et al.* (2006: 8–9) identify four common views of the research process: *sequential, generalised, circulatory* and *evolutionary.*

■ **Sequential.** The sequential process is the simplest view of all. In this process a series of activities are performed one after another as a 'fixed, linear series of stages'. An example of such a process is the systematic process model of Sharp *et al.* (2002: 17). This process consists of seven unique, sequential steps:

1. Identify the broad area of study.
2. Select a research topic.
3. Decide on an approach.
4. Plan how you will perform the research.
5. Gather data and information.
6. Analyse and interpret these data.
7. Present the results and findings.

Although this model appears entirely sequential, Sharp *et al.* admit that repetition and cycles may take place during this process. However, how and when this repetition takes place is not explicitly identified. Another, perhaps simpler, example of a sequential research process is that defined by Greenfield (1996: 7). Greenfield breaks the research process into four steps:

1. Review the field – i.e., perform a literature survey.

2. Build a theory – based on your understanding and interpretations of the field.

3. Test the theory – does it work?

4. Reflect and integrate – i.e., update your ideas based on your 'tests' and contribute your newfound knowledge to others.

■ **Generalised.** The generalised research process is identical to the sequential process in that a defined sequence of activities is performed one after the other. However, the generalised model recognises that not all stages are applicable and some steps may require performing in different ways depending on the nature of the research. Thus, the generalised model identifies alternative routes that may be taken at different stages depending on the nature and outcomes of the research. An example of such a model is that of Kane (1985: 13), which has 11 distinct stages and a number of alternative research methods.

■ **Circulatory.** The circulatory approach recognises that any research is really only part of a continuous cycle of discovery and investigation. Quite often, research will uncover more questions than it answers and, hence, the research process can begin again by attempting to answer these newfound questions. Experiences of research might lead you to revisit or reinterpret earlier stages of your work (Blaxter *et al.*, 2006: 9). The circulatory interpretation also permits the research process to be joined at any point and recognises that the process is never-ending.

   An example of a circulatory process is Rudestam and Newton's *Research Wheel* (2007: 5), which suggests a 'recursive cycle of steps that are repeated over time'.

■ **Evolutionary.** The evolutionary concept takes the circulatory interpretation one step further and recognises that research must evolve and change over time, not necessarily following a defined circulatory pattern or repeating the same forms of analysis and interpretation that were performed before. The outcomes of each evolution impact on later ones to a greater or lesser extent.

Perhaps one of the more appropriate examples of the research process is that defined by Orna and Stevens (1995: 11). They define a process that is circulatory at the top level and evolutionary within the main search/investigation stage of the process. Figure 2.3 is an adapted interpretation of this model.

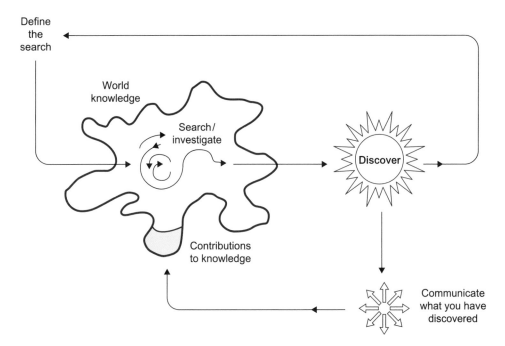

Figure 2.3 The real research process

Figure 2.3 shows a circulatory research process that begins in the top left-hand corner with a definition of your search. Orna and Stevens *(loc. cit.)* identify this search definition as an attempt to answer the following questions:

- 'What am I looking for?'
- 'Why am I looking for it?'
- 'How shall I set about it?'
- 'Where shall I start looking?'

Following on from this stage you begin your *evolutionary* investigation of the chosen research area. This investigation will take place within the current boundaries of world knowledge as you search through, digest and evaluate the material available. This search/investigation is not clear-cut and will evolve over time. It will take time for your ideas to mature, you may find yourself pursuing dead ends and you might create more questions than answers. Eventually your diligence will hopefully pay off and you will discover something of value.

This discovery must then be disseminated to others through your reports, conference and internal presentations, journal articles and discussions. There is no point in keeping discoveries to yourself as to do so ignores a fundamental purpose of the research process – that of disseminating your new-found ideas and results to others. Through this communication you are able to make a contribution to world knowledge and understanding – shown by the shaded area in Figure 2.3.

However, although you may have discovered something of value and contributed it to world knowledge, the research process might be only just beginning. These discoveries might lead to new questions, new avenues of research and so on. Thus, the research cycle is entered once again as you redefine your search and continue your voyage of discovery.

2.2.2 Intellectual discovery

While the research process can be represented by a model of one kind or another, your own reasoning processes and intellectual discoveries are often much more complex and personal. When you are looking for questions to answer and answers to those questions, you will often follow a complex process of *inductive* and *deductive* reasoning.

- **Inductive reasoning.** You start with your observations of the world and come to general conclusions about it. In other words, you build models and theories based on your interpretation of the world. Clearly, this interpretation will depend on the data and information you can draw from the world, the subject/problem you are studying and, importantly, what you already know and believe.

    The knowledge that you can obtain from what you are studying is referred to as *epistemology* (Cornford and Smithson, 2006: 61). You can either draw general conclusions from what you observe and from what you are studying and apply them to other things (*positivism*), or you can only induce knowledge unique to yourself and the particular situation under study (*anti-positivism*).

- **Deductive reasoning.** You start with your knowledge and understanding of the world and predict likely observations within it, even though you might not have encountered them before.

Deductive reasoning is affected by your theory of reality, your own personal understanding of the world and your underlying assumptions about what you are investigating. This is referred to as *ontology*. Different people might deduce different things as their understanding differs from your own and they see things in different ways.

To solve complex problems you might need to follow a complex chain of inductive and deductive reasoning. As discussed earlier, knowledge is what you derive from inductive reasoning. In other words, you build your ideas, models, theories and understanding based on your inductive reasoning about the world. Wisdom, on the other hand, is evident from your abilities of deductive reasoning – applying what you know to other situations and problems you haven't yet encountered.

There is more to intellectual discovery than inductive and deductive reasoning alone. If you are having difficulty solving a problem, two interesting methods of intellectual discovery listed by Greenfield (1996: 5) that might help are:

'*The method of* **Pappus:** *assume the problem is solved and calculate backwards*'

'*The method of* **Terullus:** *assume a solution is impossible and try to prove why*'

In addition, Greenfield also suggests trying techniques such as:

- **Random guesses.** This is a similar technique to *brainstorming* whereby you try to solve a problem by generating a number of potential solutions at random. Hopefully one of them will make sense and work.
- **Analogy.** Is the problem similar to anything else that already has a solution or explanation?
- **Inversion.** Try to look at things from the opposite angle. For example, instead of asking 'which computer language should I use?' ask 'why shouldn't I use Java?'.
- **Partition.** Break the problem or situation down into smaller, more manageable and understandable parts.

It is also worth considering where you are heading with your research before you spend several months pursuing it. For example, quite often research students will get an idea for their investigation and pursue it enthusiastically. However, when they finally obtain the 'answer' they realise that it was of little value in the first place. Try to think of where you are going, assume you have obtained the answer already, and ask yourself 'so what use is this to me?'

2.3 Classifying research

2.3.1 Introduction

Research can be classified from three different perspectives; its *field*, its *approach* and its *nature*. These three categories are adapted from the four categories discussed by Sharp *et al.* (2002:13) and Herbert (1990:1). These authors identify an additional category called *purpose*. However, as the purpose of research is arguably to contribute to knowledge, the way that research achieves this contribution has been identified here subsumed within its *nature*.

■ **Field.** The field of research is 'little more than a labelling device which enables groups of researchers with similar interests to be identified' (Sharp *et al., loc. cit.*). For example, in the topic of computing you might identify research fields in areas such as information systems, artificial intelligence, software engineering and so on. These topics may be further sub-divided into more specific topics to aid the more specialist researcher or expert distinguish aspects of the field.

■ **Approach.** Approach represents the research methods employed as part of the research process – for example, case study, experiment and survey. These methods are discussed in more detail in the following section.

■ **Nature.** The type of contribution that research makes to knowledge depends upon its nature. Sharp *et al.* (2002: 15–16) identify three categories that can be used to classify the nature of research:

Category 1. Pure theoretical development.
Category 2. Research that reviews and assesses pure theory and evaluates its potential for practical application.
Category 3. Applied research that has some practical application or outcome.

The nature of research can also be identified according to the following common classifications, which are adapted from Sharp *et al.* (*loc. cit.*), Herbert (*loc. cit.*) and Saunders *et al.* (2007: 133–135):

■ Pure theory – developing theories to explain things without necessarily linking them to practice. This can be based on your own inductive reasoning which leads you to make conclusions and theories about the world as you see it.

■ Descriptive studies – reviewing and evaluating existing theory and knowledge in a field or describing particular situations or events. This might include testing existing theories, describing the state of the art, or looking for limits in previous generalisations.

■ Exploratory studies – exploring a situation or a problem. These studies are useful for finding out 'what is happening; to seek new insights; to ask questions and to assess phenomena in a new light' (Robson, 2002: 59 cited by Saunders *et al.*, 2007: 133). Exploratory studies can be performed through literature searches, open questionnaires and interviews. These studies can start out by exploring particularly broad areas, concepts and ideas, before focussing in and narrowing down to specifics as the research progresses. The process is thus an iterative and flexible one that seeks new information and ideas.

■ Explanatory studies – explaining or clarifying something or some phenomena and identifying the relationships between things.

■ Causal studies – assessing the effects that one or more variables have on another. The independent variables are those which might be having an influence on the dependent variable in which you are interested. In these studies you would manipulate the independent variables and monitor changes to the dependent variable. For example, does the size of software product (independent variable) affect how difficult it is to maintain (dependent variable which is measured in some way)?

In these studies it is important to ensure that extraneous factors do not influence your results. For example, software size appears to be influencing maintainability but, in fact, maintainability might be due to a range of other factors you were unaware of and did not control.

- Resolving a problem with a novel solution and/or improving something in one way or another.
- Developing or constructing something novel.

2.3.2 What is *good* research?

You should now have an idea of what research is about and how to classify it, but what is meant by *good* research? Phillips and Pugh (2005: 48–49) identify three characteristics of good research:

- **Open minds.** You should work with an 'open system of thought'. Be open minded to the questions posed. 'Conventional wisdom and accepted doctrine... may turn out to be inadequate'.
- **Critical analysis.** Examine data critically. Are these figures correct? Have they been affected in some way? What do these data *really* mean? Are alternative data available? Can these data be interpreted differently?
- **Generalisations.** Researchers generalise and specify limits on the generalisations they identify. Generalisation allows research to be interpreted and applied to a wide variety of situations. However, researchers must know the limitations of these generalisations. Generalisations stem from your own wisdom and evolve from your deductive reasoning which leads you to develop ideas about things you have not encountered before with certain caveats.

Failure to apply these characteristics perpetuates the status quo – everything remains unchallenged and stays the same. Without an open mind to things, without a critical eye and without an ability to generalise your understanding to different things, you will not make a contribution to knowledge. This is, after all, the main aim of your research.

● 2.4 Research methods

2.4.1 Overview

Berndtsson *et al.* (2008: 13) identify two main classes of research methods – *quantitative* and *qualitative*. Quantitative research methods are associated with measuring things on numeric scales. According to Berndtsson *et al.*, these methods stem from the natural sciences and are concerned with understanding 'how something is constructed/built/works'. In the natural sciences one is usually concerned with testing hypotheses and Berndtsson *et al.* point out that 'repeatability of the experiments and the testing of hypotheses are vital to the reliability of the results'.

Qualitative methods, on the other hand, have their origins in the social sciences. Berndtsson *et al.* state that these methods are 'primarily concerned with increasing understanding of a substantive area, rather than producing an explanation for it'. Qualitative methods are more common within the field of information science and involve methods such as case studies and surveys. These methods, along with a number of others, are discussed in the following section.

2.4.2 Research methods

Four of the most common research methods that you might use (either individually or combined) are *action research, experiment, case study* and *survey.*

Action research   Involves 'the carefully documented (and monitored) study of an attempt by you...to actively solve a problem and/or change a situation' (Herbert, 1990: 29). Sometimes referred to as *participant observation*, it involves working on a specific problem or project with a subject or, more usually, an organisation and evaluating the results. With action research you must ensure that you do not become too obsessed with completing the action itself and neglect the real reason for doing it – i.e., evaluating it as part of your academic project.

Experiment   Involves an investigation of causal relationships using tests controlled by yourself. Quite often quasi-experimental research will have to be performed due to problems of insufficient access to samples, ethical issues and so on. According to Saunders *et al.* (2007: 137), experiments typically involve:

- defining a theoretical hypothesis;
- selecting samples from known populations;
- allocating samples to different experimental conditions;
- introducing planned changes to one or more variables;
- measuring a small number of variables;
- controlling all other variables.

Experiments are usually performed in *development, evaluation* and *problem-solving* projects.

Case study   A case study is 'an in-depth exploration of one situation' (Cornford and Smithson, 2006: 71). It involves the investigation of a particular situation, problem, company or group of companies. This investigation can be performed directly, for example, by interviews, observation, etc.; or indirectly by studying company reports or company documentation. Berndtsson *et al.* (2008: 62) point out that you should not merely report on the outcome of the case study investigation, but also attempt to 'generalise from the specific details of the examined setting, attempting to characterise the situation for which the studied organisation is typical'.

Case studies usually generate a large amount of subjective data – data that you must sift, analyse and interpret in order to produce meaningful, accurate and fair conclusions. You should also be aware of your own influence on the case study if it is performed directly. For example, when you interviewed staff within a local company, did they tell you what they felt you wanted to hear rather than the facts of the situation? Is there any means of 'triangulating' your data – i.e., obtaining the data from two or three different sources to confirm the truth in what you are told (and thus eliminating the possible influence you might be having on the data capture)?

For more information on case study research refer to texts such as Gerring (2006) and Yin (2008), which are entire books, devoted to this issue.

Survey   This is usually undertaken through the use of questionnaires or interviews. It allows 'the collection of a large amount of data from a sizable population in a highly economical way' (Saunders *et al.*, 2007: 138). As part of a survey you might have to identify samples and sample sizes, design questionnaires and define interviews as appropriate. While questionnaires and interviewing are covered in the following sections, Czaja and Blair (2005) and Groves *et al.* (2004) are two texts that cover the survey research method in detail.

Research methods can also be classified according to their 'time frame'. In other words, does the study result in a snap shot of what you have observed or do your data provide an insight into events over a *period of time*? A snap shot of a situation or event is referred to as *cross-sectional* study. A long-term picture, on the other hand, in which data are gathered continually over a period of time, is called a *longitudinal* study. Which kind of study you use will depend on the nature of your research and what you hope to achieve. For more information on these kinds of study refer to texts such as Saunders *et al.* (2007: 135–145) and Cornford and Smithson (2006: 70–71).

Three research techniques that crop up again and again in both case study research and surveys are *interviews, questionnaires* and *observation*. While the detail of these techniques is covered in many other texts, it is worthwhile including a brief overview of these techniques here.

2.4.3 Interviews

Interviews can be performed during a number of stages of your project. For example, from the preliminary requirements gathering stages of a software development-type project, to the evaluation of a product you have developed. Interviews are undertaken in either a *structured* or *unstructured* way. Structured interviews involve a series of pre-set questions that you go through with the interviewee. Unstructured (or open) interviews, on the other hand, are less formal and you will ask open-ended questions that allow the interviewee to give extended answers without constraint. In unstructured interviews, you may find that the interviewee is moving away from the agenda you have in mind and you will need to draw them back towards the purpose of the interview. Be aware that unstructured interviews may provide some very interesting data but you may well have to 'dig deeply' through the responses you receive to get to the useful information you require.

You need to put a lot of thought and preparation into your interviews. The interviewee is probably giving up valuable time to help you out so be well prepared and professional in your approach. Before you conduct an interview be clear in your own mind what you hope to achieve from it. If you lack confidence, or are new to interviewing, then a structured interview with specific questions is probably an appropriate way to start. For more experienced interviewers, unstructured interviews can provide lots of useful data.

Berndtsson *et al.* (2008: 61–62) discuss the following points for preparing and conducting interviews:

- **Selecting interviewees.** If you are performing a case study within a company you might not be able to interview the people you really need to. Be aware that people are usually very busy and might not always be available when you need them. Try to be flexible in your approach and consider alternative interviewees who might provide you with the same information (for example, two or three people might cover the area you are primarily interested in).

- **Preparation.** Don't just expect to interview somebody 'off the top of your head'. Have some opening questions to 'get the ball rolling' in an unstructured interview or carefully prepare a set of questions for a structured interview.

- **Questionnaires.** You could prepare a questionnaire and use this as a basis for your interviews. This would ensure consistency when interviewing a number of people, it would provide a useful basis for discussion and it would focus your preparation – forcing you to prepare an appropriate set of questions beforehand. Section 2.4.4 provides more detail on questionnaire design.

- **Have an agenda for the interview.** You will have in your mind an idea of what you hope to achieve from the interview so keep this in mind as the interview progresses and pull the interviewee back on track if they start to move away from the intended topic.

- **Structured replies.** In some cases you might wish to quantify an answer from the interviewee (for example, *On a scale of 1 to 5, what do you feel about the company's approach to staff development?*). This will enable you to perform more objective analyses of the responses – perhaps through some statistical analyses of the results.

- **Note taking.** Consider how you will make notes during the interview. If you have some pre-defined, structured questions, can you simply note the response on your questionnaire? Would it be appropriate to record the interview? Sometimes recording an interview can stifle the openness of the interviewee. You will need to get their permission to do this.

- **Confidentiality.** Not only must you guarantee the interviewee's confidentiality if appropriate, but you may also need to consider whether the information they are providing is confidential to their company too. In this case you may need to arrange some sort of *confidentiality clause* or *disclosure agreement* with the company beforehand. In these cases you will need to consider what happens to the transcript of the interview (whether written or recorded) and also what you will be able to reproduce in your report. You supervisor should be able to help you with this issue.

- **Logistics of the session.** You will need to arrange the interview; the time, location and duration. Be aware that this can take time to organise as people are very busy so leave plenty of time in your project to arrange your interviews.

- **Characterisation.** You might be interviewing several people during the course of your study and they may have different backgrounds (technical, personal, etc.). You should consider how their background might influence their responses and take this into account when reporting your findings. You should also consider how you might preserve an interviewee's anonymity if it might be obvious who gave you a particular response based on their background.

■ **Ethical issues.** Sometimes you may need to arrange ethical clearance for interviews (for example, if you were interviewing children). Most universities will have guidance on this area and you should consult your supervisor for advice.

Berndtsson *et al.* (ibid) go on to point out that a fundamental issue surrounding the interview process is that of *trust*. Interviewees need to be able to trust you and you should not betray the trust they have in you. Without trust your interviewee may not provide you with the depth or breadth of detail you hope to achieve.

2.4.4 Questionnaires

Questionnaires are useful means of obtaining data from a large (possible cross section) number of subjects. Like interviews they can also be undertaken at different stages of your project and can also be used for case studies. Before you undertake a questionnaire, however, you should consider what you hope to achieve from it and whether it is an appropriate technique to use. Be aware that questionnaires are notoriously volatile in terms of replies – most of which achieve only around a 5% response rate.

There are a number of texts devoted to the issues surrounding the development and use of questionnaires (for example, Brace, 2008; Bradburn *et al.*, 2004). We cannot hope to cover all of these issues within this text but the following are guidelines on points you should consider when using questionnaires within your own project. Remember to consult with your supervisor for their advice on this issue.

The target audience

Who are you intending to send your questionnaire to? How will you target them?

Medium

What format will your questionnaire take? Will you send out postal questionnaires? Will you send the questionnaire through email (embedded within the email or as an attachment)? Will you establish the questionnaire as a page (or series of pages) on a web site? Some websites that you can use to set up questionnaires for you include:

■ Survey Monkey: http://www.surveymonkey.com/
■ UCCASS: http://www.bigredspark.com/survey.html
■ Thesis Tools: http://www.thesistools.com/

The advantages of sending out questionnaires via email can be summarised as follows (adapted from Loughborough University, 2008):

■ Quick and free to send out;
■ Large populations can be targeted easily;
■ Respondents can reply relatively easily by returning an email.

Unfortunately, email questionnaires do have some disadvantages too (adapted from Loughborough University, 2008):

■ They may be filtered as spam and easily deleted.

■ If the questionnaire is sent as an attachment it may not be readable or take too long to download.

■ If the questionnaire is embedded in the email it may not appear clearly as formats might change from one system to another.

■ It can be difficult for respondents to reply anonymously which may put them off.

Response rate

How will you persuade your subjects to complete and return the questionnaire? You could offer a prize to a randomly selected respondent to encourage people to complete the questionnaire. You could contact your subjects beforehand (by telephone for example) to get their agreement to respond. This may encourage more people to complete your questionnaire but this is difficult if the target audience is large. Another way of improving your response rate is to offer to send any respondents a summary of the results. For example, if you are evaluating different companies' approaches to software development, they all may be interested in a summary of your findings. Including a covering letter is also a good way of introducing yourself, the purpose of the questionnaire and any benefits the respondent might gain if they complete it. You can also include a reply-paid envelope with the questionnaire – this often persuades people to reply as they feel they are wasting your time and money if they do not.

Layout and size

For paper-based questionnaires the layout is important as it can put people off completing the questionnaire if it appears too long or complex. Try to keep your questionnaire as short and as simple as possible. One way to achieve this is to consider carefully every question you are putting into the questionnaire. Only include those questions that will provide you with something you can use and cut out those questions that will not provide anything useful. In terms of layout, try to keep the questionnaire uncluttered and make sure that the questions are unambiguous. If you have a series of closed, ordinal scale questions (for example, *Rate this on a scale of 1 to 10*), consider how you might lay these out so that the respondent can easily move from one question to the next.

Question types

Consider the type of questions you will include. *Open* questions require extended answers from the respondent (for example, *What do you think about the user interface?*). *Closed* questions provide specific answers to questions that the respondent can select from (for example, *Do you feel the interface was poor, satisfactory or good?*). Respondents are usually quite happy to tick some boxes within a series of closed questions but are more reluctant to complete open questions. Try to mix your use of open and closed questions so the respondent does not become bored ticking boxes or put off by a number of long, open questions. In addition, try to keep the style of questions consistent. For example, don't swap from asking respondents to tick boxes in one question to underlining or circling

Open questions	Closed questions
'Elicit "rich" qualitative data'.	'Elicit quantitative data' – data that can be easy to categorise, measure and quantify.
Can discourage people from answering, as they might be reluctant and unmotivated to provide long answers.	Are easy to respond to and can be answered quickly.
Difficult to analyse as wordy responses can be misinterpreted.	Easier to analyse and quantify.
Allow freedom of expression.	'Can encourage "mindless" replies.' Can stifle responses and not provide options that the respondent wants to give.

Table 2.1 Comparison of open and closed questions

answers in another. The advantages and disadvantages of open and closed questions are shown in Table 2.1 (adapted from Loughborough University, 2008).

For closed questions, consider the type of scale you will use. For example, do you want the respondent to have a 'don't care' or 'average' option? For example, 'rate the software system on a scale of 1 to 5 where 1 is poor, 3 is average, 5 is excellent'. If you made this a 1 to 4 scale there would be no 'average' and the respondent would be forced to select either above average (3 or 4) or below average (1 or 2).

While questions can, on one hand, be classified as open or closed, another way of viewing question types is whether they are *recall* or *thought* questions. Recall questions simply require the respondent to remember a fact, some information, perhaps explaining the way something was tackled, programmed, etc; thought questions require some consideration and perhaps involve opinions, points of view and political interpretations. While respondents might answer recall questions quickly and easily, thought questions may take longer to answer as the respondent weighs up their ideas and interpretations. It might be a good idea to mix recall and thought questions in a questionnaire as the respondent could soon get bogged down with several thought questions following one another.

Blaxter *et al.* (2006: 181) identify seven types of questions that you might use in a questionnaire. They are:

1. Quantity or information. Used to gather specific data that can be quantified or classified (as opposed to qualitative, open-ended questions).

   When did you join the company? _____

   Although this could cause confusion – are we expecting a date (and if so, in what format?) or a time frame (for example, five years ago)? It might be useful to provide an example to show the respondent what we are expecting (for example, October 2005).

2. Classification. Used to categorise responses into two or more groups. The categories have no ordering to them – i.e., one category is no 'better' than the next.

   Are you male or female (please tick)?   Male ☐   Female ☐

When asking people what age group they fall into it is common to group the ages across decadal boundaries. For example, 18–24, 25–34, 35–44, etc. rather than 20–29, 30–39, 40–49, etc. People sometimes feel bad about being classed in an 'upper' age group when they just fall into that group. For example, 30-year-olds do not like to think of themselves as being their thirties and being grouped with 30- to 39-year-olds. By the time they reach the middle of the decadal range they are resigned to the fact that they are in that group (for example, 35-year-olds know they are in their thirties) and are happy to tick that box.

Also make sure that categories are mutually exclusive to avoid confusion. For example, age ranges of 20–25, 25–35, 35–45, etc. would be confusing for those aged 25, 35, 45, etc.

3. List or multiple choice. Provides the respondent with a number of options to choose from (they can select more than one).

What sources of literature have you used for you literature review (please tick all that apply)?

Books ☐   Journal articles ☐   Conference proceedings ☐

Newspapers ☐   Case studies ☐   Company reports ☐

Company documentation ☐   Sales literature ☐

The Internet ☐ Internal reports ☐   Past projects ☐

Other (please specify) _____

4. Scale. Used to rate the respondent's feelings towards something.

How easy do think the software is to install?
Very easy ☐   Easy ☐   Average ☐   Slightly difficult ☐   Difficult ☐

5. Ranking. Used to order a series of options. You should not provide too many options for the respondent to rank (ten is probably an upper limit) as this can make it difficult to complete accurately and honestly.

What did you spend the most time on during your software development? Please rank the following in order from 1 (spent most time on) to 7 (spent least time on).

Requirements capture ☐   Design ☐
Coding ☐   Testing ☐
Documenting software ☐   Debugging ☐
Other (please specify) _____ ☐

6. Complex grid or table. Used to gather similar responses on a range of questions.

Please complete the following table (enter ticks where appropriate) with your views on different aspects of the completed software system.

	Very poor	Below average	Average	Above average	Excellent
Interface					
Installability					
Functionality					
Ease of use					
Robustness					
Accuracy					

7. Open-ended. Used to obtain extended, qualitative answers.

Do you have any further comments you would like to make?

_____

_____

_____

_____

_____

Question order

The order you place your questions in a questionnaire can influence respondents and affect your response rate. Loughborough University (2008) suggests the following principles to follow when deciding on your question order:

- Place the important questions in the first half of the questionnaire. Respondents do not always complete questionnaires so if there are some important questions you would like answered, make sure that these come early on.
- Don't put awkward, difficult or embarrassing questions at the start of the questionnaire. This may put people off completing the questionnaire. This implies that you should put easy, non-threatening questions at the start to draw the respondent in.
- Go from general to specific questions.
- Go from factual to abstract questions.
- Go from closed to open questions.
- Leave questions regarding personal information until the end.

Anonymity

Do you wish the respondent to remain anonymous or do you wish (need) to know who they are? If they are anonymous you may not be able to contact them for clarification or to provide them with a prize for completing the questionnaire. If they are asked to supply their name they may be reluctant to complete the questionnaire. You should always assure respondents of confidentiality and explain how the data you gather will be used.

Respondent details

In addition to their contact details would it be appropriate to ask the respondent information about themselves – for example, their age, professional standing, qualifications, position within the company, etc.? Gather these data only if you are going to do something with them. For example, you may need to know how different levels or experience of employee within a company react to a software system, so knowing their job title and/or when they started working for the company is important.

Draft and redraft

Don't expect to get your questionnaire right at the first attempt. You might want to develop a questionnaire, check it with your supervisor, and send it out to a limited number of respondents to see what feedback you receive. You might then redraft the questionnaire in light of these responses – rephrase questions, restructure the layout, and so on. Flay *et al.* (1983) show how a question might evolve over a period of time into something that provides a response that can be analysed (in this case it took eight attempts to reach the final version of the question):

> First attempt: '*How much time have you been trained here?*'
>
> Eighth attempt: '*I think the amount of training given here is (1) too much; (2) quite a lot; (3) just right; (4) not much; (5) too little.*'

In summary, there are a lot of issues surrounding questionnaire design and deployment. Even with a considerable effort to produce a 'perfect' questionnaire, response rates are usually poor. Be prepared for this and have a contingency plan in place to deal with this when it happens. To conclude this section a few tips on questionnaire design are presented (adapted from Loughborough University, 2008):

- 'Avoid leading questions.' Avoid questions that can lead the respondent to a particular answer – for example; "Wouldn't you agree that…?" or "Is it fair to say that…?"
- 'Be specific.' Try to avoid words that could be interpreted by people in different ways such as *often, locally*, etc.
- 'Avoid jargon.' The respondent may not understand what you mean or have a different interpretation to you.
- 'Avoid double-barrelled questions.' Avoid asking questions that could be difficult to answer, interpreted in different ways or try to elicit two or more answers at a time. For example, "Did you like the system's interface and its functionality?".
- 'Avoid double negatives.' For example, "Do you agree that the system was not designed badly?" would be better phrased as "Do you agree that the system was designed well?".

2.4.5 Observation

Another research technique often used for case studies is *observation*. According to Blaxter *et al.* (2006: 178) observation 'involves the researcher in watching, recording and analysing events of interest'. It can, for example, involve you entering an organisation and observing the workings of that organisation within the area of interest. There are clearly a lot of issues surrounding observational research. The more important points that you should consider include (adapted from Blaxter *et al.*, 2006: 178):

- **Arrangements.** How will you go about arranging an observation? What permission will you need to obtain? Are there any ethical issues that you will need to address (for example, if you were observing children)? When will the observation take place and how long will you be there for? Is there a good time for undertaking the observation when certain events may be happening?

- **Recording the observation.** How will you record the situation or event that you are studying? You might record your observations in real time – by tape recording, videoing or making notes. Alternatively, you may simply observe the situation and record what you remember of that situation later.

- **Participation.** Will you actually get involved in the situation you are studying or will you act as a 'disinterested' observer (Blaxter *et al.*, 2006: 178)? If you are involved in the situation, how involved will you be – will you 'work shadow' or actively participate? Will you need any training or health and safety instruction beforehand? If you are actively involved this may be part of a larger action research method that you are undertaking.

- **The Hawthorne Effect** (Roethlisberger and Dickson, 1939). Between 1924 and 1933 a series of experiments were undertaken at the Hawthorne works of the Western Electric Company, Chicago. These experiments involved the manipulation of various working conditions to investigate their effect on worker productivity – for example, changes to lighting levels, rest breaks, etc. In brief, it seemed that no matter what the investigators did, productivity improved – even when changes appeared intuitively to worsen the workers' conditions (for example, dimming the lights). One of the main conclusions drawn from this study (see Mayo, 1933) was that, despite these detrimental changes, the workers felt valued by being involved in the experiment. Consequently, the workers worked harder because they felt important.

    The main point to draw from this study is that you should be aware of **your** influence on the situation you are observing. What you observe will not be under 'normal' conditions as anyone you look at will be conscious of your presence and may well act differently compared with how they normally behave.

● 2.5 Summary

- Research is defined as 'a considered activity which aims to make an original contribution to knowledge'.
- The research process can be *sequential, generalised, circulatory* or *evolutionary.*
- Research can be classified according to its *field, approach* and *nature.* Approaches to research include *case studies, experiments, surveys* and *action research.*
- Research techniques that are used within the above approaches include *interviews, questionnaires* and *observational* studies.

● 2.6 Further reading

Brace, I. (2008) *Questionnaire design: how to plan, structure and write survey material for effective market research* (2nd Edition), Kogan Page, London.

Bradburn, N.M. Sudman, S. and Wansink, B. (2004) *Asking questions: The definitive guide to questionnaire design*, Jossey Bass, John Wiley, New York.

Czaja, R. and Blair, J. (2005) *Designing surveys: A guide to decisions and procedures* (2nd Edition), SAGE Publications, London.

Gerring, J. (2006) *Case study research principles and practice*, Cambridge University Press, UK.

Groves, R.M. Fowler, F.J. Couper, M.P. Lepkowski, J.M. Singer, E. and Tourangeau, R. (2004) *Survey methodology*, Wiley Blackwell, Oxford, UK.

Yin, R.K. (2008) *Case study research design and methods* (4th Edition), SAGE Publications, London.

● 2.7 Action points

- Try to formulate your own definition of research and ask yourself what research means to you.

- Decide which of the research methods outlined in Section 2.4 is appropriate for your own project.

Setting your project's foundation

CHAPTER 3

Choosing a project and writing a proposal

Aims:

To introduce techniques for choosing an appropriate project, and to discuss the skills needed to write a satisfactory project proposal.

Learning objectives:

When you have completed this chapter, you should be able to:

- Choose an appropriate project.
- Write a project proposal.
- Make effective decisions when choosing your project supervisor.

- This chapter is relevant for both undergraduate and postgraduate projects.

3.1 Introduction

Because the field of computing is extremely diverse, covering a vast range of topic areas from sociological and management issues to highly technical hardware and software developments, it is not always easy to decide on a suitable project for your degree course. The types of projects accepted in different university departments also vary.

Some academic departments may permit students to pursue a highly technical programming project (provided it includes a satisfactory requirements capture, design and implementation), while others require more academic content which emerges from critical evaluation, analyses, and literature surveys. Chapter 1 introduced the general categories for most computing projects: *research-based, development, evaluation, industry-based* and *problem-solving*. This chapter introduces the skills you will need and some tips for choosing an appropriate computing project for your course. It will then discuss ways to present an acceptable proposal for your project and offers advice on choosing a supervisor, if this is possible within your institution.

Note

As you read this chapter, you may wish to read Chapter 5 alongside it. Chapter 5 covers literature searching and literature reviews – activities that can help you understand and contextualise your chosen subject area. Without at least starting a literature search, it may be difficult to define your project or what you hope to achieve.

● 3.2 Choosing a project

Identifying your project can be the most difficult stage of all. Just as an artist ponders over a blank canvas, you must decide on the type of project you would like to pursue over the following six months, twelve months, three years or more. When choosing your project, keep these important principles in mind.

- You must be capable of doing the proposed project in the time available. You must ensure that your project is not overly ambitious and that you have all the relevant skills needed (for example, don't choose a project in an area where you have failed subjects before). However, as part of your project you may want to broaden your knowledge by developing new skills or enhancing existing skills. If so, be sure to allow sufficient time for these tasks.

- Choose a project that interests you. Remember, you will be working on your project for probably six months or more. It is important that you enjoy your work and do not become bored or lose motivation during this time.

- Consider your personal development and choose a project that will assist you in your goals. In recent years, higher education institutions have promoted the concept of personal development planning (PDP) for students. Personal development planning is defined by The Higher Education Academy (2008) as 'a structured and supported process undertaken by an individual to reflect upon their own learning, performance and/or achievement and to plan for their personal, educational and career development'. Through personal development planning, individuals can identify their aspirations regarding personal development and decide (plan) how best to achieve these aims. Your personal development plan may help you identify a project or choose from a number of ideas you might be considering. Projects that support you in reaching your personal goals would take priority over those that do not. When choosing a project, consider your future career aspirations. This may influence your project choice.

■ Your project should have a serious purpose and a clear outcome that will benefit someone. If you undertake a software development project, for example, you should ideally have a **real** client for whom you are developing the system. Many students undertake software development projects for imaginary clients (for example, developing a web site for a make-believe taxi firm, boutique or sports club), but these projects tend to be below average. Armed with advice from their supervisor, students implement what they feel is appropriate (which may be very different from what an actual client would need). Motivation tends to slip as students realise their software will never be used by a real firm but will only sit on a shelf and gather dust after all their hard work.

By securing a real client for your project you will get a much clearer, more relevant set of project objectives. You will also be more motivated, knowing you are working for someone other than yourself (you won't want to let them down). Having a real client will also help with your project's management as you will be expected to produce deliverables to the client by specific dates. Having such short-term goals keeps you motivated and the project on-track.

If you need help obtaining a good client for your project, your supervisor should help you. He or she may already have a client contact you can use. Your supervisor can also provide some official support, for example, writing a letter of introduction for you.

■ Your project has a clear outcome (in terms of deliverables) that focuses your work and direction. Without a clear target, you may lose your focus and motivation as your project progresses.

■ Your project links suitably with your degree course. For example, you would not pursue a highly technical hardware-based development on an information systems course or perform a detailed systems analysis project on an artificial intelligence course.

■ Your project is of sufficient scope and quality to fit the requirements of your course.

■ Your project idea is something that interests you, but not a personal issue about which you may have a subjective view that could cloud your perspective and influence your results.

■ The resources you require for your project are available or can be obtained; for example, software, hardware, a particular client, user or organisation.

3.2.1 Techniques and Information Sources

As you choose a suitable project, take advantage of the various techniques and information sources at your disposal.

Lecturers'/departmental lists

Sometimes this is the only source of acceptable project ideas. These projects may have been proposed by academic staff in your department or in other departments, or they may be small projects requested by local industry.

Industrial projects

If you have spent a year in industry as part of your course (a sandwich placement) or are working part-time, your past or present company may have a project you could undertake. Alternatively, your supervisor, friends or family might have industry contacts that could be a prospective client. However, industrial-based projects could have some inherent problems. Firstly, the company's objectives could differ from yours in terms of the project's deliverables. What might be acceptable to the company may not have sufficient academic rigour for your course requirements. If your supervisor is advising you to take your project in one direction (academically challenging) and the company wants you to take the project in a different direction, it can be difficult to reconcile the differences. Secondly, industry contacts are not always stable or reliable. Sometimes companies go bust, are taken over, departments close down, staff are moved on, people resign or retire. Can you guarantee that your company contact (and, for that matter, the company) will be there throughout your project? If not, will someone else be able to help? Thirdly, access to companies can be difficult. If you are doing a project based at your university this is not a problem, but if you have to travel long distances to meet with the client, will this be feasible? Fourthly, as an outsider working for the company, will you be granted access to all you need for the project – data, files, people? Some companies may be reluctant to allow outsiders (people who are not directly employed by them) to have access to certain information. You might also find it difficult to talk to certain people in the company if you don't work there. You may be asked to sign confidentiality agreements or clauses before the company will provide access to certain people or information. Finally, will you have access to the hardware and software you need to undertake your project? If the company uses particular applications or systems, will you need to access these remotely or can your institution provide appropriate support?

Despite these potential pitfalls, there are a number of advantages to working with an outside company for your project. Your project will have a clear goal and likely a clear set of requirements specified by the client. Working for an external body will provide additional motivation as you will be working for someone other than yourself and have targets to achieve. Finally, you may well have additional support for your project that may not be available otherwise – for example, the company may offer training, you may have access to sophisticated hardware and software and you may benefit from expert industrial knowledge.

Past projects

Usually your department or university library will hold copies of previous projects. These can provide you with working ideas (for example, on how you could develop the work further) and some sense of the scope and amount of work expected. Alternatively, you can use the Internet to search for past projects at other institutions. For example, PhDs are sometimes made available on-line. Past projects may also provide a suitable basis from which to start your own project – picking up from where a previous student left off. If you undertake a development project, you may be developing an existing piece of software further, introducing additional functionality or creating new features to an older system. You need to be aware of the amount of effort required to upgrade existing systems. Quite often existing systems are poorly structured, badly commented and lacking documentation. It can be harder to enhance a piece of software that already exists than to develop a system from scratch. In addition, previous programmers may have used unusual code to create the system and it may take you a long time to deconstruct their software.

Talking with colleagues

Your peers can often provide a different perspective on ideas you might have. They can be helpful in highlighting potential shortcomings of your intended project and may suggest alternatives.

Reading around subject areas

If you read books, journals and articles on a topic that interests you, you can often discover areas that authors have identified as requiring further research and development. As you improve your understanding of the topic area, you may identify a gap that you wish to investigate further. Whatever happens, reading around your intended subject area does no harm and helps you gain a solid understanding of the subject on which you will build your project. Chapter 5 covers literature searching and it may be worth reading that chapter before completing your proposal.

Clustering

You might wish to pursue a project in a particular field but are unsure exactly which aspects of the topic to focus upon. Clustering can help you identify aspects within a topic area that link together and are worthy of further investigation. Clustering is performed in two stages. First, you should list keywords related to your topic area. Second, once you have exhausted all the words and phrases you can think of, you cluster them into related groups and patterns. Doing this can help you identify specific topics that interest you and form the basis of your intended project.

Clustering can be used to develop *Research Territory Maps* (RTMs), *Relevance Trees* and *Spider Diagrams*. An RTM, sometimes called an *affinity diagram,* shows how topics relate to one another within your chosen field or fields of study. RTMs provide you with your own conceptual model of your research area. They represent *your* interpretation of the field – one that you are comfortable with, can clarify and arrange the literature into and can modify as your knowledge of the field grows. These maps can be enhanced with thicker and thinner connecting lines to emphasise the strength of relationships between subjects. Figure 3.1 provides an example of an RTM – in this case, a high-level conceptual map of the field of *software engineering* (remember, this is an interpretation and you may or may not agree with its structure). RTMs will identify specific topics you might wish to focus on within larger subject areas or, for broader studies, inter-related subjects that are dependent and require investigation.

Relevance trees, discussed in more detail by Sharp *et al.* (2002: 36) and Saunders *et al.* (2007: 74–75), are similar to RTMs in that they try to model your field of study. Relevance trees differ from RTMs in their hierarchical structure. While RTMs identify related topics and the links between them, relevance trees break down a particular subject or research question into lower and lower levels of detail, identifying how a subject

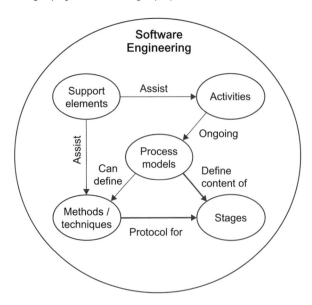

Figure 3.1 A high-level RTM for *software engineering*

is composed or identifying the factors affecting a research question posed. RTMs provide a holistic interpretation of the field of study while relevance trees provide a hierarchy of topics that constitute that field of study. An example of a relevance tree for *artificial intelligence* is shown in Figure 3.2.

Another way of structuring your thoughts and identifying the composition of a subject is through the use of *spider diagrams*. These diagrams are similar to RTMs in that they show how topics within a subject area relate. They are also similar to relevance trees in that they show how topics break down from a central idea, subject or research question. In spider diagrams a central node represents the topic of interest and lines emanating from this node identify how the topic can be organised into its constituent parts. Colours are often used to group ideas and topics. Figure 3.3 provides a spider diagram interpretation of the field of software engineering. This diagram is adapted from the RTM in Figure 3.1.

Remember that relevance trees, RTMs and spider diagrams are structured by **you** to represent your *own* interpretation of your chosen subject area. Other authors may decompose the subject area into an alternative structure or use different terminology for the same things. You must be aware of these differences so that you aren't confused by what appears to be contradictory information, which you gather from your literature search. For example, in Figure 3.2, some authors may subsume *Knowledge representation* within *AI techniques* or might disregard *Philosophical issues* entirely, while others may include other topics not identified here.

Brainstorming

If you are really struggling for a project idea, brainstorming can provide the answer. Brainstorming involves listing all your project ideas on a piece of paper, in any order and as quickly as possible. Write anything down, even if it sounds completely irrational, as

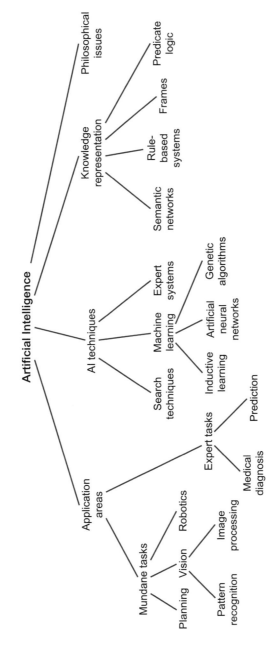

Figure 3.2 Example of a relevance tree for *artificial intelligence*

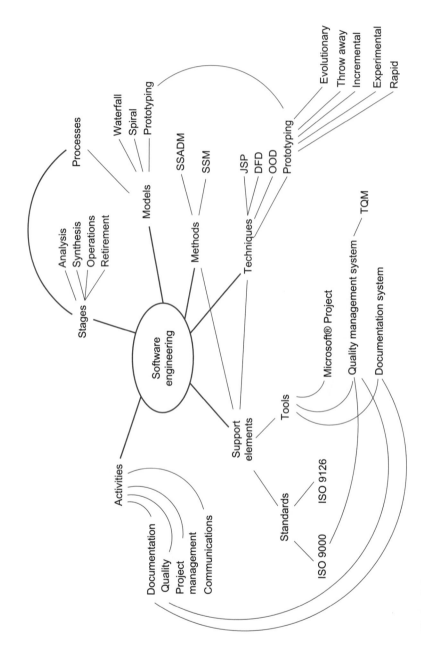

Figure 3.3 Example of a spider diagram for *software engineering*

the process of brainstorming should not be stifled. When you have finally exhausted all your ideas, look at each one in turn and evaluate and assess it in more depth. What may have sounded ridiculous at first may actually lead to a good project idea; perhaps when viewed from a different angle. You might also like to group your thoughts (using clustering) as this may help to clarify in your own mind where your real interests lie. One way to choose between topics is to toss a coin – not to see which way the coin lands but to see how you feel you want the coin to land while it is spinning in the air.

Chapter breakdown

Once you have an idea for your project, it is a good idea to identify how your project will break down into a number of chapters for the final report. If you have difficulty identifying a number of specific chapters for your final report, it may mean you are unclear about the project's detail and don't really understand what it is you hope to achieve. Breaking down your project into chapters will also give you an indication of its scope. If you can identify only two or three chapters, maybe your project is not sufficiently broad. Conversely, if you can identify ten or more chapters you may be trying to do too much.

3.2.2 Additional considerations

After identifying your project, think about these additional considerations:

The 'so what?' test

To ensure that you do not pursue a project that has little value, take the 'so what?' test (Herbert, 1990: 7). Ask yourself, Is the topic meaningful? If you complete the project successfully, will it be of value to anybody? What contribution will it make? Pursuing a meaningless project can lead to poor motivation as your project progresses and you begin to question the point of your work.

Justification

Can you explain your project and justify it (that is, pass the 'so what?' test) in simple terms to the woman or man in the street? If so, you have a good understanding of the subject area and the topic you want to pursue. While your explanation may still be too technical or deep for the average person to understand, feeling that you can explain it in simple terms indicates that the topic is clear to you.

Numerating your understanding

Can you put a number on how much you know about your chosen subject; for example, 80%? If you are able to numerate your understanding about a topic it means that you have, at least, a concept of that field of study and an awareness of its magnitude. If you have no idea what your understanding is, you have no idea of your subject area's depth or breadth and to undertake a project in this area would be very risky.

This principle was initially presented by Lord Kelvin, who stated:

> *When you can measure what you are speaking about and express it in numbers, you know something about it: when you cannot measure it, cannot express it in numbers, your knowledge is of a meagre and unsatisfactory kind. It may be the beginning of knowledge, but you have scarcely in your thought advanced to the stage of science.*

This idea, of being aware of the sum total of your understanding about a specific topic, is sometimes referred to as *metaknowledge*. In some ways, the wiser people become, the more they realise just how little they really know. This is especially true when people place their understanding within the broader context of world knowledge even though their own expertise in a particular subject may be very deep. Figure 2.2 identified this transition of self-awareness in the research as a matrix with four quadrants, from *blissful ignorance*, to *demoralised*, to *confident*, to *complacent*.

Contacts

When you identify the contacts you require for your project, are they available, accessible and willing to help? For example, do you have contacts within a local company who have volunteered to help you with a case study? If not, your project will face problems that need to be dealt with sooner or later.

What do you already know?

Orna and Stevens (1995: 29) suggest that, as you identify your research area, you also think about what relevant information you already know or have access to. This will help you clarify your strengths and, perhaps, form a foundation for your RTM, relevance tree or spider diagram. You might also identify what you want to **learn** by conducting your project. What are your educational objectives? Are there any skills you would like to develop, new programming languages to learn or new techniques to master? If so, include a need for these skills within your project to 'force' yourself to learn them.

Ethical issues

Most institutions have procedures in place to assess, evaluate, monitor and control ethical issues when approving student projects. While these concerns were originally aimed at projects involving medical or sociological studies (for example, drug testing, vulnerable groups and hazardous substances), the codes of practice developed have spilled over into all disciplines. Most projects in computer science and information systems generally do not raise ethical issues. However, if you plan to involve others in your project in any way – conducting a survey, developing a system for a vulnerable group (requiring their interaction and feedback), undertaking action research (working with people), developing a database to store personal data, or working on medical systems – you may well need to obtain ethical clearance for the project from your department, university or some other external agency. Most institutions with have an Ethical Advisory Committee that manages these issues. The areas of concern that usually need addressing when considering ethical issues include:

Data protection

If your project will handle any personal information relating to living people, you need to be aware of the Data Protection Act (DPA) and its restrictions on your project. The DPA, introduced in 1998 in the UK, governs the protection of personal data. These data can include names, addresses, exam grades, medical data, telephone numbers, anniversaries and more. The main principles of the Act that you should be aware of include:

- Data should only be used for the specific purpose for which it was gathered in the first place.
- Individuals have the right to access data held about them.
- Data may not be disclosed to third parties without permission of the individual.
- If personal data are kept, these data must be appropriately protected.
- Personal data should be kept for no longer than necessary.

Recruiting participants

Ethical issues will make you think a little bit more about how to recruit participants for your project (for example, a cross-section of users to give feedback on your system). You will strengthen your study by considering these areas:

- Selection criteria – will this be unbiased and lead to a reasonable cross-section of participants?
- What consent will be required from participants (or their parents/carers/guardians) to take part?
- Will there be any financial incentive or otherwise to take part (which may affect the objectivity of the results)?
- Will participants be able to withdraw at any stage (this should be allowed)? Will any deception be involved? For example, intentionally to evaluate a reaction or unintentionally which might affect the results?

Vulnerable groups

These can include children, pregnant women, people with a mental illness, prisoners, people over 65, people with learning disabilities, etc. Quite obviously these people need some kind of protection and, although you may feel your work will not affect them (for example, just asking their opinions about some software you are developing to meet their needs), ethical clearance will probably still be needed to ensure they are not being exploited in any way. You should also consider whether or not any feedback you receive from such groups will be entirely objective – it could be skewed because of their relationship to you and you should acknowledge and discuss this issue in your final report.

Training

Will you require any training in order to undertake the project (for example, from hardware or software applications to dealing with vulnerable groups)? Will participants require any training? What form will this take and will it raise any issues?

Using these ideas, sources and approaches will assist you in deciding on your project. However, although you may now have an idea for a project that you feel is of suitable quality and scope for your course, you must now 'sell' it to others with a *project proposal.*

● 3.3 Preparing a project proposal

3.3.1 Introduction

It is normal, in most institutions, for you to prepare a proposal for your project so it can be assessed for acceptability. Unless you can present an acceptable proposal, your project will not even start. It can serve as a contract between you, your department and project supervisor – but don't expect it to be used against you if you achieve more than you actually intended to do! In many cases, projects can and do change direction as they proceed; as you become more aware of the topic area and the problem which you are investigating. This is acceptable provided the scope and quality of your project do not become 'watered down' and you are not heading so far away from your initial intentions that the project becomes unrecognisable. If this were the case, you would need to obtain permission for significant changes and possibly have to submit a new proposal.

When preparing your proposal, follow these two golden rules:

1. Follow any guidelines precisely. Most institutions require specific information; for example, project title, project objectives, resource requirements and so forth. Failure to complete these sections may mean your proposal is rejected without even being read, for example, because you failed to get an academic signature or did not complete an essential section properly.

2. Proofread thoroughly and get someone else to check it. Any errors or omissions will appear sloppy and put your commitment and proposed project in a bad light.

There are no universal standards for project proposals, although all proposals should include certain pieces of information. This content emerges from your proposal's *implicit content* and *explicit sections,* which are discussed below.

3.3.2 Implicit content

In general, your proposal should address five principal areas. These may not be identified explicitly in the structure of your proposal, but they should be addressed implicitly within the proposal's content. They are:

1. **Introduction to the subject area.** This will provide the reader with an understanding of the field in which your project lies and an idea of where and how your project fits into this field. This aspect will set your project into an overall *context*

and will show that it is bound within a recognised field – not an idea that you've had that makes no sense and has no recognisable foundation.

2. **Current research in the field.** This will emphasise that your project is not based in a field that is out-of-date and that you are aware of current issues within that field of study. It will also imply that you have done some preliminary research into the topic area and are not approaching your project with little background or motivation.

3. **Identify a gap.** You should be able to identify some aspect of the field that requires further investigation or study. There is no point in repeating the work of others (unless you are evaluating their approaches) and this component emphasises that the field is not exhausted and is worthy of further investigation.

4. **Identify how your work fills the gap.** Having identified a gap in the field, your proposal should show how your project intends to fill this gap, or at least go some way to investigating it further. This will emphasise the *contribution* your project will make.

5. **Identify risks and solutions.** It is also useful in a project proposal to highlight any risks your project might face, and ways you envisage dealing with them. If you do not identify potential risks to your project, your proposal's assessor will not know whether you have considered the risks. If they feel you have not accounted for potential risks to your project, your proposal may not be accepted, as they may not appreciate that you have potential contingency plans in place.

3.3.3 Explicit sections

Detailed below are the most common sections that project proposals should include. If you receive no guidance as to the content of your project proposal, include, at the very least, the first three of the following sections in your document.

Title

This should be clear and concise. Try to avoid using acronyms if possible. Examples of clear and concise titles include:

- 'Evaluation of soft systems methods as analysis tools in small software houses';
- 'Artificial neural networks for software development cost estimation';
- 'Development of process models for building graphical software tools'.

Aims and objectives

Aims identify at the highest level what it is you hope to achieve with your project – what you intend to achieve overall. An aim is a broad statement of intent that identifies your project's purpose. Objectives, on the other hand, identify specific, measurable achievements that build towards the ultimate aim of your project. They are more precise than aims as they are 'quantitative and qualitative measures by which completion of the project will be judged' (Turner, 1993: 108). They represent major components of your project that direct your work activity (Weiss and Wysocki, 1992: 13).

Identifying aims and objectives clarifies, both for you and the reader, what you specifically hope to achieve with your project. You will use your aims and objectives to assess your project at the end. For example, did you really achieve all that you set out to do? Because of this, aims and objectives should be clear and unambiguous. Chapter 4 discusses aims and objectives further.

Examples of aims and objectives are:

Aim:

■ Evaluate artificial intelligence techniques for modelling weather patterns.

Objectives:

■ Identify and evaluate existing weather pattern modelling techniques.
■ Identify artificial intelligence approaches suitable for modelling weather patterns.
■ Design and develop at least three artificial intelligent systems for modelling weather patterns.
■ Compare and contrast the developed systems with one another and existing approaches to modelling weather patterns.

Expected outcomes/deliverables

This section of your proposal will identify precisely what you intend to submit at the end of the project. It may well identify a written report that covers particular points and makes certain recommendations. A chapter breakdown may be included where appropriate. It can describe programs and user documentation and it might include models and algorithms that will be developed to address specific problems. You might also be delivering a functional specification for a piece of software, a prototype, or a test plan.

These three headings represent the minimum set of sections your project proposal should include. In addition, consider including the following:

Keywords

Keywords are used to identify the topic areas your project draws on. People use keywords to see at a glance what subjects your project relates to which might not be clear from your project's title alone. Libraries and databases use keywords to help classify material. You might be limited on the number of keywords you can use; for example, four or five. Remember, keywords are not necessarily single words but can be simple phrases as well; for example, artificial intelligence or software engineering.

Introduction/background/overview

This section provides an overview of your project and introduces the background work to it. In this section you might wish to include reasons why you feel you are a suitable candidate for performing the project (why you feel you can do it, what skills are required and how you fulfil these requirements), why the topic interests you specifically, and why you chose the project in the first place. This section might also include an introduction to the industry or organisation being investigated or evaluated. Overall, this section will set the scene for the project.

Related research

This section identifies other work, publications and research related to your topic. It will demonstrate that your project does not exist in an academic vacuum but relates to other research topics and fields of current interest. Related research can also help demonstrate your understanding of your topic area, showing the reader that you are aware of what is currently happening in the field and are conversant with other topics that impinge upon it.

Type of project

You might wish to identify the type of project you are undertaking, for example, *research-based, development, evaluation,* etc. However, make sure these terms are recognised and provide more detail if appropriate.

Research questions and hypotheses

 Your project proposal may also include the research question you intend to investigate and, hopefully, answer to some extent within your project. Computing projects do not necessarily set out to answer particular questions, but for some projects (particularly research degree projects) a statement of your research question is essential. Examples of research questions are:

- Does the size of an organisation affect its commitment to software quality standards?
- What is the relationship, if any, between software maintainability and coding structure standards?
- Is there an optimum solution to the prediction of software development costs?
- How do large organisations maintain quality standards in the development of internal software?

While research questions on their own are 'open-ended opportunities to satisfy one's curiosity' (Rudestam and Newton, 2005: 74), they are often linked closely with one or more hypotheses. A hypothesis is 'a tentative proposition which is subject to verification through subsequent investigation' (Verma and Beard, 1981: 184 cited by Bell, 2007: 32). Although you do not have to define hypotheses alongside a research question, they do present potential 'answers' to the question(s) you have posed and provide definitive statements that will focus your research. For example, suppose your project intended to answer the fourth research question posed above. One of the following hypotheses might be investigated based on that research question:

Hypothesis #1: Large organisations invariably employ recognised standards to maintain internal software quality.

Hypothesis #2: Large organisations generally have quality departments which oversee the implementation of procedures that ensure the quality of internal software.

It is also worth mentioning the importance of maintaining research *symmetry* with respect to research questions and hypotheses. Research symmetry implies that your 'results will be of similar value whatever you find out' (Gill and Johnson, 2002 cited by Saunders et al, 2007: 20). With this in mind, it is important to realise the implications of the hypotheses you have stated. If they are true you must ask yourself 'so what – was that really worth proving?' Thus, each hypothesis you state should have a similar value if proved.

Methods

This section describes the research and project methods you will use in performing your project. This section should not identify methods that you might be investigating as part of your project, but those methods you are actually using. It might include development methods that you are using as part of a systems development (for example, SSADM); survey methods for a case study evaluation and evaluation methods for comparing two or more systems. Research methods would include those introduced in Chapter 2, such as *action research, case study, survey* and *experiment.*

Resource requirements

You might need to identify any resource requirements for your project, such as hardware, software and access to particular computers. If you have access to particular resources, this fact should be pointed out in this section. Quite clearly, if the resources for your project are not available in your department, or are too expensive to obtain, your project will be unacceptable. However, if you know you need a particular piece of software or hardware, you must find out its cost and include this information within this section. A proposal that omits this information may be rejected if the assessor does not know how inexpensive or available the item is and might assume it is beyond your project's budget.

Note, if you are relying on an external source (a company, for example) for computer access, hardware, software, case studies and the like, it will be your responsibility to ensure these are available and to bear any risk if the resources fail. While your department will accept responsibility if something goes wrong with your project because their own software or hardware fails, they will not be responsible for external sources of support that you have arranged.

Within this section or under a separate heading, you might include a list of the literature you will need to perform your project – for example, specific journals, company reports, books, etc. If these materials are unavailable, realistically speaking, your project may be impracticable and you may need to change its focus. Access to particular companies for performing case studies could also be identified here. Without this access your project might flounder, so it is important to show you have contacts that can be utilised.

Project plan

It is very useful to present a project plan as part of your proposal. This emphasises that the project is 'doable' in the time allowed; it shows that you have some idea of the work involved and you have a clear pathway to follow in order to complete that work. The best way to present a project plan is by using a visual representation such as a *Gantt chart*. These figures are described in Chapter 4. While the presentation of a Gantt chart is important, for the purposes of your project proposal, limit your chart to a single page. A multi-page project plan is difficult to read and, for a proposal, only a general overview is required.

3.3.4 Reviewing your proposal

The second golden rule for preparing a project proposal states that you should proof-read your complete proposal thoroughly.

Check your proposal for spelling mistakes, omissions and grammatical errors. Have you included all the sections you were supposed to and have you completed them in sufficient depth? Is the proposal well presented (typed rather than hand-written, for example)? Do the sections flow logically?

The following are two examples of final-year project proposals for a student on a taught bachelor's degree. Both proposals represent the same project and have been kept short for clarity.

Example

Title:
Software migration.

Project type:

Aims and objectives:
- Migrate a series of software applications from a mainframe to a client/server systam within a local company.

Outcomes and deliverables:
- Connectivity to the mainframe for approx 1000 PCs;
- Full integration into a client server environment;
- Education of users;
- Coding and testing completed.

Research methodology:
PRINCE II.

Hardware and software requirements:
All available at local comnpany.

This proposal is quite poor. Its *Title* is rather vague and only represents the type of project that is being proposed. The section identifying *Project type* has been left blank and the *Aims and objectives* represent a basic, technical, industry-type project with no academic content or justification. Expected *Outcomes and deliverables* emphasise this point and merely identify the technical outcomes of the project. The *Research methodology* section identifies the method that will be evaluated, rather than the research methods that will be employed (PRINCE II is a project management method that is used to manage large projects). The proposal also includes a number of spelling mistakes and abbreviations. Overall, this project lacks any academic quality or rigour and is poorly presented.

Let's look at this project proposal from a new angle:

Example

Title:
Project management issues of software migration.

Project type:
Evaluation project, industry based.

Aims and objectives:
Aim: To evaluate the use of the PRINCE II method as a means of managing the migration of software from a mainframe to a client server system.
Objectives: An evaluation of tools and methods to assist the technical aspects of the migration and organisational management aspects.
Evaluation of similar companies performing migration for comparative purposes.
The migration of a series of applications at a local company (to which access has been obtained) will be used as a vehicle for critically evaluating the PRINCE II method in particular.

Outcomes and deliverables:
A report detailing the following:
– an explanation of the perceived benefits of such a migration;
– an analysis of the difficulties experienced;
– a critical evaluation of the PRINCE II methodology and its application;
– an outline methodology for future migration projects;
– a discussion and evaluation of alternative tools and methods for software migration.

Research methodology:
Case study, action research.

Hardware and software requirements:
All available at a local company.

This proposal is a far better representation of an academic project than the preceding one. Although the project is based on the same software migration, it identifies, far more clearly, the academic side of the project and the critical evaluation required by such projects. All sections are now completed correctly; for example, *Research methodology* identifies those methods actually employed and *Project type* has now been identified. The proposal reads well and has been checked for errors and omissions.

● 3.4 Choosing your supervisor

Academic departments have different ways of assigning project supervisors to students. There are only a finite number of projects a supervisor can effectively supervise and you may find you are allocated someone who knows little about your field (although this **must not** happen at research degree level). If you are lucky enough to be able to choose your own project supervisor, there are a number of considerations you should contemplate when making your choice. Sharp *et al.* (2002: 31) identify five questions that students should ask of potential supervisors:

1. 'What are their records in terms of student completions?'
2. 'What are their views on the management of student research – and, in particular, the supervisor's role in it?'
3. 'How eminent are they in their specialisms?'
4. 'In addition to being knowledgeable about their subjects, have they high competence in research methodology?'
5. 'How accessible are they likely to be?'

The fifth point noted here can relate not only to a supervisor's general availability but to their approachability as well. It is all very well being able to see your supervisor regularly, but if you do not trust or get along with your supervisor, this time is wasted.

While research degree students will require a supervisor to be an expert in their subject area, this is less important for taught degree students. At the taught degree level a supervisor's role may be more managerial and pastoral than technical – for example, helping you with project plans, checking you are achieving your milestones and assisting you with any project-related problems. At the taught degree level, your supervisor, although not an expert in your chosen field, can still be a good supervisor and may well have sufficient technical understanding to assist you when necessary. You should also be able to approach other members of academic staff in your department (or other departments) for technical assistance. However, if there is no one in your department who is knowledgeable in your chosen field, your project is probably not appropriate anyway. Chapter 7 looks in more detail at the student/supervisor relationship and discusses how to effectively manage the time you spend with your supervisor.

● 3.5 Summary

- Choosing the right project is probably the most important stage of any project.
- A number of techniques have been presented that you can use to assist you with choosing a suitable project.
- When preparing a proposal there are two golden rules; follow any guidelines precisely and proofread it thoroughly.
- A project proposal should include, at least implicitly: *background, related research, identification of a gap, how your project fills that gap* and *risks and contingency plans*.

- Project proposals should include, at the very least, the sections *project title, aims and objectives* and *expected outcomes/deliverables.*
- Questions have been presented that you should ask yourself before you choose your project supervisor (if this is possible within your own institution).

● 3.6 Exercise

1. Can you think of any ways to improve the 'corrected' version of the proposal in Section 3.3.4?

● 3.7 Action points

- Try to build an RTM, relevance tree and/or spider diagram for your own computing project.
- Put together a proposal for your own project using the ideas and skills you have learnt in this chapter.

● Solutions to selected exercises

1. The following are areas in which this proposal is lacking and could be improved still further (did you spot these shortfalls and did you identify any others?).

    Objective 1 – other than Prince II, no other methods or tools are explicitly identified in the proposal although they are alluded to.

    Objective 2 – there is no reference to the companies needed for this contrasting evaluation or any indication of how the data might be obtained for this part of the study.

    Outcome 3 – the report is going to comment on the effectiveness of Prince II in migration projects only. This is not clear from Outcome 3.

    There is no project plan so it is difficult to see how long the migration will take and how long the research component of the project will take.

    No risks or contingency plans are identified – for example, what if something goes wrong with the migration and the project is significantly delayed?

CHAPTER

4

Project planning and risk management

Aims:

To introduce techniques and approaches to project planning and risk management.

Learning objectives:

When you have completed this chapter, you should be able to:

- Understand the five elements of projects that need to be managed.
- Describe the typical stages of an academic project from a project management perspective.
- Define a project in terms of aims and objectives.
- Discuss the activities performed during the initial planning stage of a project.
- Understand the use of project management techniques for project planning.
- Manage risk in your project effectively using a defined risk management process.

- This chapter is relevant for both undergraduate and postgraduate projects.

● 4.1 Introduction

4.1.1 Overview

Before tackling the actual work you need to complete your project, it is important to have some idea of how you are going to undertake that work. Without an appropriate project plan in place you will have little direction, you will lose sight of where your project is going and you will not complete your project on time. In this chapter we will look at some techniques you can use to plan how you will tackle your project. With a reasonable project plan in place it will enable you to manage your time more effectively, decide on priorities for your project at different stages and give you clear direction and motivation. We will also look at risk management, which will enable you to identify, manage and control any potential risks to your project. We will begin by discussing a generic interpretation of the project process before using this framework to introduce a number of project management techniques.

4.1.2 The project process

Figure 4.1 provides a generic view of the project process and introduces the five elements inherent in all projects – *time, resources, cost, scope* and *quality*. This view can be applied to any project to a greater or lesser extent – from large industrial projects right down to small, one-person projects like your own. The diagram shows that all projects consume *time, resources* and *money* (a budget or cost) in order to produce a particular product which has its own *scope* and *quality*. This product can be something tangible like a bridge, a report or a software system; or it could be something intangible like a change in working practices, restructuring a department, improving company profits and so on (although these projects would undoubtedly have some tangible documentation associated with them).

In the case of your own project, Figure 4.1 shows that this will take a certain amount of time to complete and it will require the use of certain resources – primarily **you,** but probably other resources too – for example, your supervisor, a client/user, computer hardware, books and software. You should be aware that you will need 'access' to these resources as your project progresses and be confident that they will be available as and when you need them.

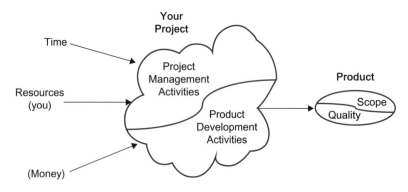

Figure 4.1 A generic overview of the project process

Although commercial projects have budgets associated with them, it is unlikely that you will have any real budget to manage. Some institutions do provide small budgets for student projects (for example, to purchase hardware, software, books or perhaps travel to visit clients) but normally it will be your supervisor or client who will be responsible for this issue.

Figure 4.1 goes on to show how these 'inputs' are used to produce the project's product. The project itself consists of two main activities – *project management activities* (the focus of this chapter) and *product development activities*. Project management activities are concerned with planning how you will undertake your project, controlling your project as it is progressing, checking your progress, meeting milestones, monitoring deliverables and managing risk. Product development activities are involved with the actual project work itself; for example, developing a program, writing reports, literature searching, meeting clients, quantitative research, qualitative research and seeing your supervisor – in other words, everything you need to do to complete your particular project successfully. Generally speaking, project management activities should take no more than around **10%** of your overall effort on the project. Many students do not stick to this principle and spend many hours planning and re-planning the minutiae of their project, rather than getting on with the real task in hand. Their projects might be well planned and controlled but they leave themselves insufficient time to pursue a worthy project.

You should be aware that the 10% effort you put into your project's management is not distributed evenly throughout the life span of the project. You will spend a lot of project management effort towards the start of your project planning how you will perform it, and less effort, as the project continues, actually controlling it.

The final stage of the project process in Figure 4.1 shows the outcome from the project – the project's product – i.e., the artefact that is finally assessed. This will probably be a report of some kind, a thesis or dissertation, a presentation, perhaps a fully documented computer program and an associated user guide and demonstration, a new model or algorithm, a literature survey, a case study, etc. There are two aspects to this 'product' – it will have a certain *scope* (what it covers, what it does – i.e., what it achieves) and a certain level of *quality* (how well it does it). These are two aspects of your project over which you have control. You can, for example, reduce the scope of your product in order to improve its quality. Alternatively, you may want to cover more aspects in your report, or include more functionality in your program at the possible expense of quality. This is a difficult trade-off to make and is discussed in more detail in Chapter 7.

4.1.3 The project's stages

From a project management perspective, all projects progress through **five** main stages during their lifetime; from the time the project is established as an initial idea to the time the project is finally completed. These stages apply to all kinds of projects; from your own academic computing project to large industrial projects spanning several years. At this level of detail specific activities that might be unique within academic computing projects are not of interest. We are interested in the broader stages in which project activities are performed. Each of these stages requires managing in one way or another and there are different considerations you will have to make as your project progresses through them. The five main stages are:

1. *Definition*
2. *Planning*
3. *Initiation*
4. *Control*
5. *Closure.*

Project definition and *project planning* collectively relate to your project's ***inauguration***. Project inauguration refers to the activities you perform before you actually start work on the main body of the project itself (the product development activities). Project definition is the preliminary stage of this process and includes the activities presented in Chapter 3; deciding on your project and getting it approved by submitting an acceptable proposal. In addition, this stage also includes establishing a more detailed project definition in order to prepare the ground for project planning. Project planning is the stage in which you decide how you will fulfil your aims by deciding how to approach the work you need to perform. Project definition and project planning are the focus of the project management activities within this chapter. Note that you will also use these preliminary stages to plan how you will manage the risks associated with your project. Section 4.4 introduces the risk management process that runs in parallel and complements the project management stages.

The following three stages of the process represent the project management activities you perform as you undertake the product development activities of your project – i.e., actually 'doing' your project and working on developing the project's product. *Initiation* represents the activities that you perform to start the main content of your project. It involves arranging yourself into some kind of routine and can include the initial work you perform on your literature survey. If you are working on a group project you will have to assign tasks to, and organise, other members of your project team. You will arrange to meet with your project supervisor and lay down some ground rules and routines for the work ahead. This is discussed in more detail in Section 7.1.2.

Once you have organised yourself and your project is underway you will need to *control* it as it is progressing. Project control is covered in detail in Chapter 7. The last stage of any project is *closure*. In your computing project this will represent the completion of your project, writing up your report, perhaps preparing for a final presentation or viva voce examination, completing any programs and associated documentation and finally handing everything in. How you complete your project by performing these activities is the subject of Chapters 8 and 9.

● 4.2 Project definition

4.2.1 Overview

The purpose of project definition is to clearly specify what it is you hope to achieve with your project. As mentioned above, this stage initially includes deciding on your project and putting together a proposal (covered in Chapter 3). In many ways your project definition and your initial project proposal are closely linked. Both should be written at the start of your project and, while your proposal aims to get your project accepted, your definition will help to clarify what it is you are really setting out to achieve.

Your project definition must identify the *aims* and *objectives* of your intended work. Chapter 3 briefly introduced the difference between aims and objectives for the purposes of producing a project proposal. In this section these ideas are extended so that your project can be defined clearly in these terms. Defining your project in this way is important for a number of reasons;

- If you have difficulty defining your project in terms of aims and objectives then you will have difficulty deciding on the work you ought to be doing and what your focus will be. It might also mean that your understanding of the subject area is lacking and you need to do some additional preliminary research in the topic area or, more drastically, choose an alternative project.

- It gives you a clear target for which to aim. This provides a continual reference point against which you can assess your progress.

- It provides you with a means of evaluating your success at the end. For example, did you achieve all that you intended to do or more?

4.2.2 Defining your aims

Your project should be defined at two levels. At the top level you define your project's aim or *goal*. All projects have one major aim that they hope to achieve and your computing project is no exception. If you are ever in any doubt over what work you ought to be doing or which direction you ought to be taking, you can refer to your project's aim to guide you. Examples of typical aims for computing projects are:

- to evaluate the effectiveness of requirements capture techniques in small software development companies in India;
- to develop and evaluate a user interface for statistical software packages;
- to design a methodology for GUI development of technical courseware material;
- to investigate and produce an evaluation of fourth generation languages for database development.

Each of these aims provides you with an understanding of that project's main purpose. They identify the area of investigation and the focus of the intended work. In order to achieve these aims each project will have a set of *objectives;* smaller sub-goals that are significant steps towards achieving the project's aim.

4.2.3 Setting objectives

As Chapter 3 specified, objectives identify significant measurable achievements you hope to make that build towards the ultimate aim of your project. Having identified and defined your project's aim you should continue to define your project in terms of its objectives. For a project expected to last approximately one year, you wouldn't expect to identify more than twelve objectives for your project. If your project has more objectives than this it may be that you are attempting to do too much or that you are breaking your project down into too much detail.

Take, as an example, a computing project that is going to evaluate artificial neural networks for predicting stock market indices (not an easy task!). You might identify the following aims and objectives for this project.

Project's Aim:

■ Develop and evaluate an Artificial Neural Network to predict stock market indices.

Project's Objectives:

1. Complete a literature search and literature review of existing stock market prediction techniques.
2. Develop a suitable artificial neural network model.
3. Identify and collect suitable data for analyses and evaluation.
4. Evaluate the model using appropriate statistical techniques.
5. Complete final report.

Note how the objectives build towards the ultimate aim of the project. They also appear in approximately chronological order – in other words, they identify the order in which you would expect to tackle the work. Notice, also, how you could further break down these objectives. For example, objective 2 would need you to investigate, evaluate and identify a suitable tool and topology before you could develop a suitable neural network. Objective 4 may require you to investigate and learn how to use some suitable statistical techniques or statistical software packages. However, breaking objectives down into progressively lower and lower levels of detail serves little purpose other than to cloud your vision of your ultimate goal. This will become clear in the following sections, which discuss how to break down the actual work you will need to do to complete your project using *work breakdown structures*.

4.2.4 SMART objectives

The objectives identified above still require further refinement. This is achieved through the application of the SMART technique. There are a number of definitions of the SMART acronym, the most applicable to student projects being:

■ **S**pecific
■ **M**easurable
■ **A**ppropriate
■ **R**ealistic
■ **T**ime-Related.

For each of the objectives you identify in your project you should apply these criteria to ensure that those objectives are clearly defined. For example, take Objective 1 from our example project:

1. Complete a literature search and literature review of existing stock market prediction techniques.

Applying the SMART criteria:

- Is this *specific*? Does this provide us with enough idea of what we should be doing? (Yes)
- Is it *measurable*? How can we measure progress on this objective? How will we know when the objective is completed? How much literature must we access in order to conclude that the literature search is complete? (Probably not)
- Is it *appropriate*? Is it an appropriate objective to have, bearing in mind the long term goal of our project? (Yes)
- Is it *realistic*? In the time we have available can we realistically expect to complete this task? (Probably – although until we start this task we won't know how much work we will need to do on it)
- Is it *time-related*? Have we identified how long the task will take and when we expect to complete it by? (We don't know yet but we will attempt to pin this down during project planning)

According to SMART, the problems we have with this objective at the moment are that it is not clearly measurable and we don't know how long it will take. Because of the nature of this objective we may well have to accept this as it stands. It is difficult to know how long a literature search will take as the search usually 'snowballs' as it continues. Our best approach will be to allocate a specific amount of time to this objective and draw a line underneath it at that point – on the understanding that we have done the best we can in the time available. However, until we complete our project planning, discussed in the following section, we don't know how long to allocate for this objective so we shall leave it open-ended for now.

● 4.3 Project planning

Although you are now clear about what you intend to achieve with your project, what you must now do is identify the work you need to do in order to fulfil these aims. Project planning assists you by identifying the work you need to perform, clarifying the order in which you should tackle the work, and revealing how long you need to do it. It is at this point that you may realise that your project is either overly complex or of insufficient depth for the requirements of your course. You may then decide to redefine your project (expanding or reducing its scope) before re-planning your work once more.

Project planning is performed through a series of six steps that utilise a number of project management techniques:

1. *Work breakdown*
2. *Time estimates*

3. *Milestone identification*
4. *Activity sequencing*
5. *Scheduling*
6. *Re-planning.*

Three techniques that are suitable for these stages are *Work Breakdown Structures, Activity Networks* and *Gantt charts.* Each of these techniques will be looked at in turn as the six steps of project planning are discussed.

4.3.1 Step 1 – Work Breakdown

Work breakdown structures (WBSs) are used to break your project down into lower and lower levels of detail to reveal exactly what work you will need to do to complete your project. You should begin a WBS by breaking your project down into its main objectives that you identified during your project's definition. You might only be able to break your project down into two or three main areas of work or you might be able to identify several broad areas of activity.

Figure 4.2 provides an example of a WBS for the Artificial Neural Network (ANN) stock market project introduced earlier. Five main objectives have been identified that need to be performed to complete this project. Notice how these tasks represent the five objectives identified earlier.

You should continue to develop your WBS by breaking your objectives down into lower and lower levels of detail. You may well find that some activities can be broken down further than others. For example, in Figure 4.2 the WBS has identified that the *Literature survey* will actually require the completion of a *Literature search* and a *Literature review* (although in Chapter 5 you will see that the literature survey process is much more complicated than this). To develop the ANN it will first involve

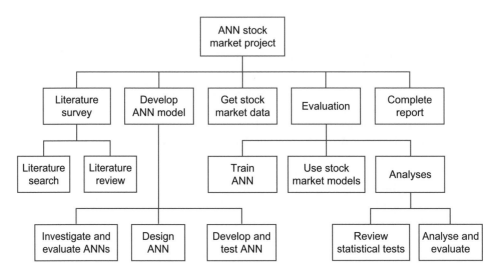

Figure 4.2 An example of a work breakdown structure

investigating and evaluating ANN topologies and tools (*Investigate and evaluate ANNs*) before designing the ANN (*Design ANN*) and then developing and testing it (*Develop and test ANN*).

Evaluation will involve three activities; training the ANN developed (*Train ANN*), using the market models evaluated from the literature review (*Use stock market models*) and performing an *Analyses* of the two approaches. Notice how *Analyses* has been broken down into another level of detail – showing that it requires a review of appropriate statistical tests and tools (*Review statistical tests*) before analysing and evaluating the results (*Analyse and evaluate*).

As you break down your project in this way you should ensure that tasks at all levels are separate from one another and an activity in one part of the structure is not repeated or revealed within another area of work. If this happens you may be duplicating effort on your project unnecessarily or your WBS may be incorrect.

You can continue to break these activities down further but you must stop somewhere; otherwise you could be identifying work which might take five minutes to complete! A general rule of thumb is that you should continue to break your project down into activities that take no less than around 5% of your project's total effort. For example, there is little point in identifying activities that will take you less than a week to complete in a six month project. If you do this you may spend more time adjusting and controlling your plans as your project progresses than actually doing any work (remember, only 10% of your time should be spent on project management activities). There are always unforeseen events in projects and activities will invariably take longer than you expect. Planning at too fine a detail is unwise as things will certainly happen to affect minutely planned activities before your project has finished.

4.3.2 Step 2 – Time estimates

When a project's aims and objectives are identified it provides little indication of exactly how long the project will take to complete. You would hope that your project is of a suitable scope to keep you busy during the allotted time and is of sufficient depth for you to obtain a good grade. However, it is not until you break the project down using a WBS that you really begin to see just how much work is involved.

Now that the project is broken down into a number of tasks it is much easier to estimate how long the project will take. It is far harder, for example, to predict how long it will take to complete the project's *Evaluation* than it is to predict the effort needed for individual tasks that make up that activity; *Train a neural network, Use stock market models* and perform the *Analyses*. You may, however, feel that these lower level tasks are still not explicit enough and there is nothing to stop you breaking them down further within reason. This is just what was done with the *Analyses* activity in the example.

Focussing now on the lowest level of the WBS it is possible to make reasonably accurate predictions of the effort needed to perform these activities and consequently the project as a whole. For example, using the WBS in Figure 4.2, the following time estimates in Table 4.1 can be made for the **lowest** level tasks:

By working backwards from our overall project duration we have also been able to allocate an appropriate amount of effort to our *literature search* and *literature review*. This goes some way to satisfying the SMART criteria applied to our preliminary project objective in the previous section.

Activity	Estimated Duration
Literature search	8 weeks
Literature review	4 weeks
Investigate and evaluate ANNs	4 weeks
Design ANN	4 weeks
Develop and test ANN	2 weeks
Get stock market data	1 week
Train ANN	1 week
Use stock market models	2 weeks
Review statistical tests	2 weeks
Analyse and evaluate	4 weeks
Complete report	8 weeks
Total Effort	40 weeks
	(approximately 10 months)

Table 4.1 Time estimates for example stock market ANN project

You should be reasonably happy with this estimate of the total project effort as it is much more accurate than you could have achieved working from the project's title alone. You might now realise that, perhaps, you have aimed to do too much in the time available (you might have only six months to complete the project) and need to reduce what you intend to achieve. Alternatively you might decide to allocate yourself less time to complete particular activities if you feel your estimates for these tasks were conservative.

4.3.3 Step 3 – Identify milestones

Milestones are significant steps towards the completion of a project. They help you to appreciate your progress by providing you with intermediate reference points. This enables you to assess, at the earliest opportunity, how you are progressing against your planned schedule. Because you know these milestones are leading you towards the ultimate goal of your project you can use these as intermediate goals at which to aim. Figure 4.3 provides a simple illustration of this point. In this figure the milestones are providing mini targets that you can use to focus your work in the short term.

To identify milestones you should focus on your project's work breakdown structure and identify any key stages that appear to be significant breakthroughs in your project's

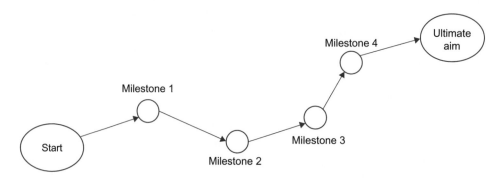

Figure 4.3 Milestones leading to the project's ultimate aim

progress. It is best to do this at the top level of the WBS and use some (if not all) of your project's objectives as milestones. These milestones then identify areas of work that, when completed, indicate you have achieved a significant step along the way. The number of milestones that you will identify for your project will vary depending on the project's size. For a year-long project, six or seven milestones should be more than adequate as these would represent, on average, the completion of approximately two months' work. Milestones can also be associated with the production of various reports, documents or sub-systems – for example an interim deliverable or a project proposal, etc. One milestone you must always identify is the project's completion.

For simplicity only two milestones will be identified in the example project we are looking at; the completion of the literature survey (milestone 1; M1) and the completion of the project as a whole (milestone 2; M2). M1 shows that a significant step has been made in establishing the project's foundation. You would expect to achieve this milestone within the first 12 weeks. M2 is the end of the project and clearly represents a significant event in the work! How these milestones are symbolised in the project plan is discussed in the following sections.

4.3.4 Step 4 – Activity sequencing

You now have an understanding of the work you need to perform in the project and the effort required to complete the individual tasks involved. An *activity network* can now be used to identify the order in which you should perform that work. Activity networks were first developed towards the end of the 1950s and are sometimes referred to as PERT networks, CPM or network diagrams. Two forms of activity network were developed at that time – Activity-on-the-arrow networks and activity-on-the-node networks. We will look at the simplest form of these diagrams in which activities are represented by rectangles or *nodes* – the activity-on-the-node network.

Activity-on-the-node diagrams represent the tasks you are performing in your project as nodes connected by arrows. The arrows show the order in which activities must be performed. For example, in Figure 4.4, Task A can start at any time as it does not rely on any other task completing. Task A would therefore start at the beginning of the project. Task B cannot start until Task A has finished and Task D can only start after **both** tasks B and C have completed successfully. Task C is similar to Task B in that it cannot start until Task A has ended.

If this representation is applied to the example stock market project introduced earlier it results in the activity-on-the-node representation shown in Figure 4.5. In this example the completion of the project's report has been identified as an activity that is

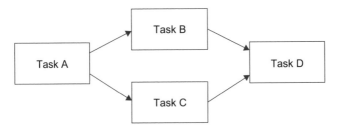

Figure 4.4 An example of a simple activity-on-the-node diagram

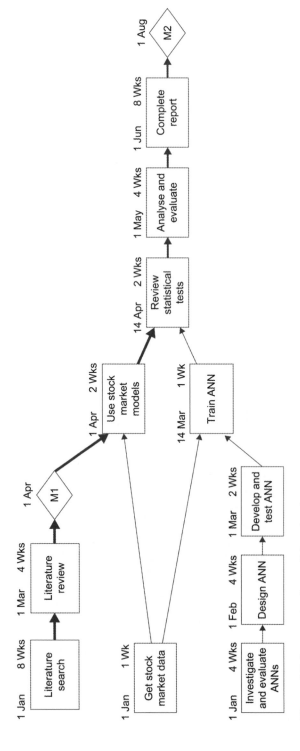

Figure 4.5 An example of an activity network

performed during the last eight weeks of the project. In reality, however, you would probably be working on your project's report throughout the lifetime of your project and the activity identified here really represents the final drawing together of the report; checking and completing your references, writing your abstract and contents listing, proofreading and spell-checking.

There are three additional markings to Figure 4.5 that are not shown in the example of Figure 4.4, which have yet to be explained. The first point to note is that the milestones identified earlier have been included as diamonds called M1 and M2; M1 being the completed literature survey and M2 representing the completed project. Notice how these have been placed in the relevant positions on the diagram and represent the completion of the significant step they are identifying.

The second point to note is that dates and durations have been added to each task node. Each activity now has two figures – the start date of the activity, shown at the top left of each node, and the duration of the activity (in weeks), shown on the top right. These durations are taken from the time estimates made earlier in Table 4.1. It is up to you what time 'granularity' you use for your project (hours, days, weeks, months or even years) but, in a student project of this size, weeks or months are suitable.

For simplicity it will be assumed that a month consists of exactly four weeks and there are no breaks in the project for holidays! However, in reality holidays, sickness, revision, field trips and the like can often impede your progress and these events should be considered when forming project plans.

The date, which is noted at the top left-hand corner of each activity, represents the time at which that activity can start. For activities that can start straight away (i.e., they do not need any other activities to have completed beforehand) this is simply the start date of the project. In the example, three activities can start straight away – *Literature search, Get stock market data* and *Investigate and evaluate ANNs*. All these activities have the same start time – 1 January – which represents the start date of the project overall (this start date has been chosen for simplicity).

To calculate the start times of subsequent activities it is necessary to look at the tasks leading into them. For example, in this simple case, *Literature review* can begin as soon as the *Literature search* has completed. As the *Literature search* takes eight weeks to complete (approximately two months) the *Literature review* can begin from 1 March onwards. The first milestone (M1 – complete literature survey) occurs when this review is completed and consequently, as the review takes four weeks to complete (approximately one month), M1 will (should) occur on 1 April. Notice how M1 has no duration associated with it because it does not represent any work but simply an event in time.

Calculating the start time for activities with more than one task leading into them is not quite so straightforward. When two or more tasks lead into another, that task can only start when **all** its preceding tasks have completed. For example, in Figure 4.5 notice that *Train ANN* starts on 14 March – this is when you would expect *Develop and test ANN* to complete, **not** when *Get stock market data* has completed (which is due to finish on 7 January). Remember that subsequent activities can only begin when **all** preceding activities leading into them have completed.

Continuing with the calculation of start times for each activity in the project, the final milestone, M2 (completed project), is reached. Thus, it is possible to conclude that the project should be completed by 1 August. However, this may be optimistic, as it does not account for any delays or problems that might occur.

The final additional marking to this network diagram is the *critical path* which still requires explanation. This path is the longest route through the project network and is represented in Figure 4.5 by the bolder arrowed lines. It identifies the activities in the project that must not be delayed, as to do so will delay the project overall. For example, if *Complete report* were to take twelve weeks instead of eight, the project would finish on 1 September – four weeks later than before. This is because *Complete report* lies on the critical path and any delay to this activity will therefore affect the project overall.

To identify the critical path you work backwards through the network diagram from the project's final milestone. Begin, therefore, at M2 and look to see which task(s) leading to this milestone is causing it to occur on 1 August. There is only one activity in this case leading into M2, *Complete report,* so this task is on the critical path. Looking next at *Complete report* we see, once again, that only one task leads into it – *Analyse and evaluate.* Consequently, *Analyse and evaluate* must also be on the critical path.

You continue to work your way backwards through the network, along the critical path, until you either reach the project's start or an activity that has two or more activities leading into it. In the latter case, *Review statistical tests* is the first activity in this situation. However, just as before, you look back through the network to see which activity(ies) is (are) forcing *Review statistical tests* to start on 14 April and see that, in this case, it is *Use stock market models* **not** *Train ANN. Use stock market models* is also, therefore, on the critical path. Continue in this way, working backwards through the network, until you reach the start of the project – in this case ending up at the *Literature search.* The critical path is thus identified by the bolder arrowed lines linking each of these critical activities together.

There is no reason why you cannot have more than one critical path in your project network. In some cases, two or more activities may force a subsequent task to start on a particular date. In these cases, proceed as before, following all critical paths back to the start of the project or to a point where they rejoin. The activity network is now complete.

This representation has made several assumptions. The first is that you can perform several tasks simultaneously. This often happens in computing projects where you might, for example, be performing aspects of your literature search and literature review alongside an initial systems analysis or program design. This also allows you to avoid becoming bored with one activity or another because you can switch between them as your project progresses. However, although identifying several simultaneous tasks may be satisfactory for group projects, where several members of the project team can work on tasks separately, for individual projects this can cause a problem. To identify instances when you are expecting to work on too many activities simultaneously and to see how you can deal with this problem, you must use a *Gantt chart,* which is introduced in the following section.

The second assumption made is that once activities are completed, they are finished with and your project moves on. In reality, however, many activities are ongoing throughout the lifetime of your project, for example, the literature survey and report writing. However, emphasis on these ongoing activities changes as the project progresses. There are also situations where activities are repeated and you find yourself performing a loop – for example, the literature search and literature review, which are part of the repetitive literature survey process discussed in Chapter 5. An example of loops occurring within software development projects is when an evolutionary prototyping approach is used. This approach is discussed in detail in Chapter 6.

These situations cannot be planned explicitly using ordinary activity network diagrams and, although there are networking techniques that can be used to identify repetition and loops, they are not widely available. Consequently, project planning tends to identify distinct activities that occur either in parallel or in sequence and limits activity network plans to these representations.

4.3.5 Step 5 – Scheduling

Gantt charts are similar to activity networks in that they attempt to represent a project in diagrammatical form. However, unlike activity networks, they do not show the relationships between tasks, but they do explicitly show the durations of activities and identify instances when tasks are performed simultaneously.

Just like activity-on-the-node networks, Gantt charts represent a project's activities as rectangles or nodes, and milestones by diamonds. In this case, however, the size (length) of an activity's node represents the duration of that activity. For example, in Figure 4.6 a Gantt chart has been put together for the example stock market ANN project. The scale running along the bottom of this chart represents the dates during which the project is performed. Notice how each activity in this chart is represented by a rectangle, which is as long as the activity's estimated duration. For example, the *Literature search* lasts for two months starting at the beginning of the project. It is therefore drawn up until 1 March. The *Literature review* follows on from the *Literature search* and lasts for one month – again shown by the length of the task box – finishing by 1 April. Milestone 1 (M1) is shown at the appropriate point at the end of this task.

It is important to keep an eye on the activity network when drawing a Gantt chart to ensure that activities are performed in the correct sequence and activities do not start in the Gantt chart before all their preceding tasks have completed. Some Gantt charts allow you to include the arrowed connections between activities like those in the activity network. However, trying to include all this information on one diagram does mean it is very messy and difficult to follow. It is therefore best to use both these techniques simultaneously – each one complementing the other.

In Figure 4.6 notice how activities that do not fall on the critical path of the activity network have shaded extensions to them. These shaded areas represent an activity's *slack* or *float* time. Remember that activities on the critical path cannot be delayed without delaying the project overall. This implies that activities which don't lie on the critical path can be delayed to some extent without affecting the project. The extent to which an activity can be delayed without affecting the project is called its *slack* or *float*.

To identify slack time in your project, you need to focus on activities that do not lie on the critical path. Work your way backwards through your project (starting at the project's completion milestone as before) until you meet one of these activities. In the example, looking at the activity network in Figure 4.5, the first activity encountered like this, working back through the network, is *Train ANN*. *Train ANN* leads into *Review statistical tests* (which *is* on the critical path). As long as *Train ANN* is not delayed for so long that it starts to delay *Review statistical tests*, the project will not be affected. Thus, *Train ANN* could be delayed so that it finishes no later than the start of *Review statistical tests* (i.e., 14 April). This delay represents the slack time of *Train ANN* and is shown as the shaded area in Figure 4.6. In this case the delay can be up to three weeks before the impact is felt on the project overall.

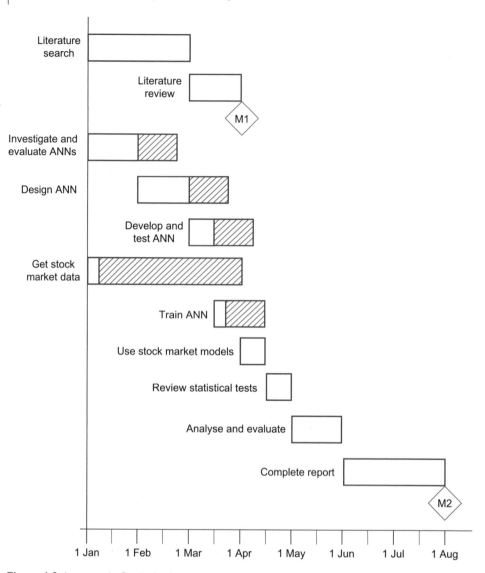

Figure 4.6 An example Gantt chart

Working backwards from *Train ANN* we will now look at *Develop and test ANN*. Because this task leads directly into *Train ANN*, this activity may also be delayed by three weeks without affecting the project overall. This is because we know that delaying *Develop and test ANN* by three weeks will only delay *Train ANN* by three weeks, which is fine as *Train ANN* has three weeks of slack. The same argument is applied to *Design ANN* and *Investigate and evaluate ANNs*. Consequently, these activities have the same float applied to them as *Train ANN* (i.e., three weeks).

Get stock market data is the only other activity not lying on the critical path that still needs considering. This activity must complete before *Use stock market models* and *Train ANN* can begin. As *Use stock market models* is on the critical path, we must ensure that

Get stock market data finishes no later than the critical start time of *Use stock market models*. Thus, *Get stock market data* can be delayed so that it finishes no later than 1 April (the start of *Use stock market models*). Notice, if it was, that it would also delay *Train ANN* by two weeks. This is acceptable because *Train ANN* is not on the critical path (it has three weeks of slack) and so delaying this task by two weeks will not impact on the project. Be careful in these situations however, to ensure that if a task is allocated slack that this will not impinge on other non-critical tasks to such an extent that they become critical and delay the project overall.

Notice that some of the slack we have identified on tasks relies on subsequent activities with slack being delayed (for example, *Get stock market data* running into *Train ANN*), while other activities with slack do not rely on subsequent non-critical tasks moving (for example, *Train ANN*). This implies that there are different kinds of slack that can be identified in Gantt charts. In fact, there are four kinds of slack one could identify in a project plan – *free* slack, *independent* slack, *interfering* slack and *total* slack. However, for the purposes of a student project, you do not need to go into this level of detail on the Gantt chart. What we have identified in this case is simply *total* slack, which is sufficient for projects of this nature. The total slack for a task represents the amount of time that task can be delayed by, assuming all other tasks with slack are able to be delayed to accommodate it where necessary. The Gantt chart is now complete.

What this chart now highlights is that there are times when you need to perform more than one activity at a time. For example, looking at the first week of the project in January you will see how you should be working on the *Literature search, Investigate and evaluate ANNs* and *Get stock market data* all at the same time. For group projects this is not a problem as these tasks can be assigned among team members. However, for individual projects, this might well be unacceptable and something needs to be done about it.

One solution might be to use the float time on various activities. For example, *Get stock market data* could be delayed for a few weeks without affecting the project overall and it would reduce the number of activities that needed to be performed during the first week of the project. However, this is only putting off the inevitable. At some stage in the project, *Get stock market data* will have to be tackled and it will inevitably clash with some other work at that time. The problem lies in the fact that ten months' worth of work (40 weeks) is being attempted within seven months (1 January to 1 August) with only one person available. This is impossible unless you are able to do more than one activity at a time. If you cannot, you must accept that your project will take ten months to complete and you should adjust your Gantt chart accordingly.

Project management software packages are well suited to these kinds of problems – known as *scheduling*. They attempt to schedule out people's (resources') time on projects in order to achieve a balanced allocation of work over a project's life span.

In this case, a popular project management package called Microsoft Project has been used. Figure 4.7 shows a print-out of a Gantt chart from this package for the example ANN stock market project. Notice how similar this is to the representation shown in Figure 4.6. Microsoft Project was then used to re-plan the project on the understanding that only one person was available to do the work. Microsoft Project rescheduled the plan to that shown in Figure 4.8. Notice how the project is now scheduled to last for ten months, finishing at the end of October, and only one activity is being performed at any one time. However, this is not necessarily an ideal solution as, for example, there now

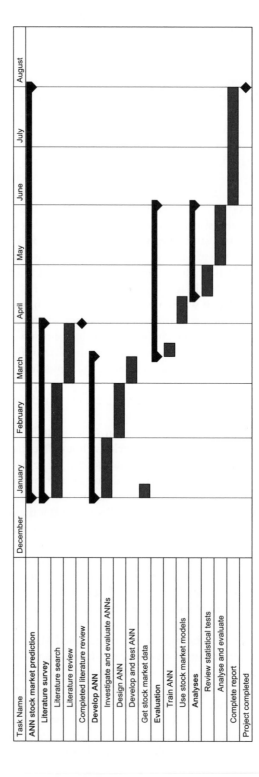

Figure 4.7 Gantt chart using Microsoft Project

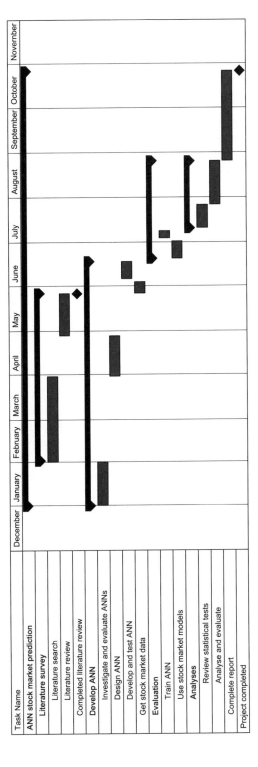

Figure 4.8 Scheduled Gantt chart of example project

appears to be quite a delay between performing the *Literature search* and writing the *Literature review* – two activities that, in reality, are closely intertwined. With this in mind, you should always pay close attention to scheduling adjustments that are made by project management software tools.

4.3.6 Step 6 – Re-planning

Now that you have completed all your plans, you may realise you are trying to do too much in the time available. Re-planning simply means that you go back through your plans, adjusting and rescheduling them accordingly. Project management software tools are particularly useful for making these changes and assessing the impact of your adjustments. However, try not to spend too long on this stage by getting drawn into the usability of these tools and end up using them for their own sake. You may find yourself re-planning and rescheduling at minute levels of detail rather than getting on with the 'real' work of your project (remember, the 'real' work should take around 90% of your effort).

Note, also, that plans you have produced should not be cast in stone. For instance, in the example project, you may find that after completing your investigation of ANNs you decide that it might be more appropriate to use an off-the-shelf package rather than develop your own ANN model. This will clearly lead to some reworking of the plan and may release some time later in the project for you to concentrate on other activities.

4.3.7 Rolling wave planning

A technique that can help you when your project is not all that clear is *rolling wave planning*. Rolling wave planning means that you do not construct a detailed plan at the project's inception but a *skeleton plan,* which only identifies the key stages of your project. Your project planning is thus performed 'on the fly' as your project progresses. You make decisions as to where you are actually heading and what work you will have to perform in the subsequent stage of your project, as you complete the previous stages. Thus, your planning detail ebbs and flows (like a rolling wave) as your project progresses and you make decisions on where to go and what to do next.

As a skeleton plan is relatively broad it can be suitable for many projects. Although it is of little use if you don't have *any* idea of what you want to do, it can help you to identify universal milestones that you must adhere to – for example, complete a literature survey, hand in your final report, etc. – whatever these turn out to be. Figure 4.9 provides an example of a typical rolling wave skeleton plan – in this case a software development-type project that lasts for about six months. Although this plan does not provide explicit detail about what this project is really about, it does identify the significant tasks that need to be completed and by when.

4.3.8 Project Initiation Document

The project initiation document (PID) is a document that draws together many of the sections discussed above in one place, representing a definitive overview of the project – its purpose, objectives, outline, plan, risks, etc. It can form a contract in terms of defining what the project will achieve. PIDs come in various shapes and sizes with different content

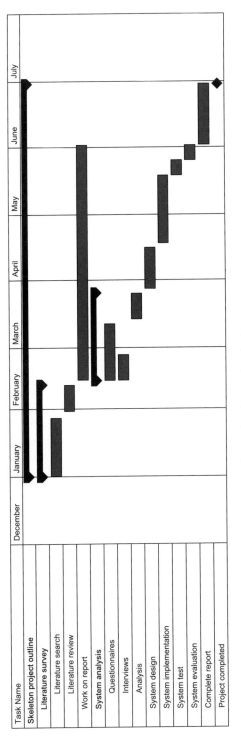

Figure 4.9 Example rolling wave skeleton plan for a software development project

requirements. Many companies have their own definitions of what a PID should contain. It is always a good idea to put together a PID at the start of your project. The components used in the project proposal (see Section 3.3) can form the basis of your PID, namely:

- Title
- Aim and objectives
- Expected outcomes/deliverables
- Introduction/background/overview
- Project type
- Related research
- Research question/hypothesis
- Methods
- Resource requirements
- Project plan.

These may need some updating once your project is accepted as you may have made some progress and made some changes since the proposal was put together. In addition it would be worthwhile including the following three sections in the PID:

1. **Risks.** Include a list of critical risk factors and means of dealing with these risks should they occur. How might you reduce their impact or limit their chances of occurring in the first place? Risk management is covered in the following section and this will give you some ideas of what to include in the PID.

2. **Organisation.** If you are undertaking a group project it would be worthwhile outlining how your team will be organised; who is the team leader, secretary, spokesperson; how often the team will be meeting; communication arrangements (email addresses, web site, etc.); configuration management, etc.

3. **Milestones.** Now that your project plan is completed you can identify the major milestones within the PID. These milestones should include both project specific ones (i.e., any deliverables you are producing) and generic, course related ones (for example, deadlines for interim reports, final reports, presentations, etc.).

You might to keep you PID in a project folder so that you can refer to it easily as your project progresses. Sections such as the project plan and risk plan may need to be readily available and accessible. The idea of establishing a project folder is covered in Section 7.1.2 when project initiation is discussed.

● 4.4 Risk management

4.4.1 Introduction

Risk management is a process that is inexorably linked to project management; it runs in parallel with project management and follows a very similar process. Just as project management involves the development of a project plan and control of the project using that plan as the project progresses, risk management involves the identification of risks at the project's outset and the control of those risks as the project unfolds. As you undertake the stages of project management you will also be incorporating the activities of the risk management process. In this section we introduce a risk management process that you can use to manage and control risks within your own project. The four main stages of this risk management process are:

1. *Identify risks*
2. *Assess impact of risks*
3. *Alleviate critical risks*
4. *Control risks.*

4.4.2 Identify risks

As you are putting together your project plan, you should also be identifying any *sources* of risk to your project. These risks can be individual events (*event-driven risks – acute*) that might have an impact on your project (for example, your supervisor leaving, your hard disk crashing, etc.) or they may be longer term risks that evolve over time (*evolving risks – chronic*) before eventually coming to a head (for example, underestimating the time it will take you to develop part of your system, deteriorating relationship with your client, etc.).

Whether the risks to your project are *event-driven* or *evolving*, they can be further classified as either *technical* or *non-technical* risks. Technical risks refer to any risks that are associated with the hardware or software you might be using. For example, will there be problems interfacing the components of the software and hardware system you are developing? How well do you know the programming language and platform you are going to work with? Is your project dependent on the development of an algorithm that may be difficult, if not impossible, to develop? Is the specification for the system clear? Are the requirements likely to change? Is the project beyond your technical ability? What are the chances of your hard disk crashing and you losing all your data?

Non-technical risks are all other risks associated with your project. These can include such things as losing your client, your user or your supervisor; illness; over-running your time estimates; discovering work during your literature search that already covers (in depth) what you intended to do; etc.

As well as identifying potential risks to your project it is also useful to identify risk *triggers* (sometimes called risk *symptoms*) at this stage too. Risk triggers are events or things that happen during the course of your project (not necessarily 'bad' things) that might give an indication that something is wrong or that one of the risks you have identified is increasingly likely to occur. They are useful in that they give you warning, ahead of time, that something will happen and you can be better prepared to deal with it when it does. For example, missing preliminary milestones in your project is a good indication that your project is going to over-run; struggling with a straight-forward implementation of a component in a new programming language will probably mean you will encounter severe implementation difficulties later on; having difficulty in arranging a meeting with your client early on may be a good indicator that s/he may be difficult to contact and meet later when you are desperate for feedback towards the end of your project.

All projects encounter problems to some extent, so don't be disheartened if some of the risks you identify during this stage of the risk management process occur. The point of risk management is to ensure you are in a position to deal with these risks if they do occur and you are not facing them ill-prepared.

4.4.3 Assess impact of risks

Having identified the risks associated with your project in the first stage of the risk management process, you should then calculate their *impact*. The impact of any risk on your project is given by the following equation:

Risk impact = likelihood × consequence   (4.1)

Thus, although a risk may be highly likely to occur, if its consequences are low its impact will also be low. Similarly, if a risk has severe consequences for your project but its chances of happening are very low, its impact is also calculated as low. The risks you need to worry about are those that are highly likely to occur and have significant consequences to your project if they do.

Example

Turner (1993: 242) provides an interesting illustration of how the risk impact equation works in practice. If we consider the likelihood of a severe earthquake (say, greater than Force 7 on the Richter scale) occurring in the British Isles, we would probably conclude that the chances of this occurring are small. We then consider the consequences of this risk on two different kinds of building – a car park and a nuclear power station. In the case of a car park the consequences of a severe earthquake are quite small – a few cars may get damaged and (unfortunately) a small number of people may be injured or killed if it collapsed. As the consequences of the risk are relatively low (unless it is your car that gets crushed!) and the likelihood is low, the overall impact of this risk is also deemed to be low. Thus, in the British Isles, car parks are not constructed to be 'earthquake-proof'.

In the case of the nuclear power station however, the consequences of a major earthquake could be catastrophic – hundreds of thousands of people could be killed. In this case, while the likelihood of the earthquake is the same as for the car park, the consequences are much higher – leading to an overall risk impact that is deemed very high. Thus, nuclear power stations within the British Isles are constructed to withstand such events.

Turner (1993: 256) goes on to provide a quantitative measure for assessing the risks to your project. A risk's likelihood is classed according to a three-point scale – Low/Medium/High. Similarly, a risk's consequence is measured on a five-point scale – Very Low/Low/Medium/High/Very High. Turner assigns numbers to these measures as shown in Tables 4.2 and 4.3.

By assessing each of the risks to your project according to these scales, you can determine a risk's impact as a value between 1 and 15 based on Equation 4.1 (1 × 1 being the

Risk Likelihood	Score
Low	1
Medium	2
High	3

Table 4.2 Risk likelihood scores

Risk Consequence	Score
Very Low	1
Low	2
Medium	3
High	4
Very High	5

Table 4.3 Risk consequence scores

lowest score and 3×5 being the highest possible score). For example, suppose we feel that there is a small chance that we may lose our client during the course of our project (s/he may have told us in a preliminary meeting that their department may be restructured during the next six months – risk likelihood is *medium;* 2), yet the consequences of this are quite severe (how would we assess our final system? We might feel the consequences are therefore *high;* 4). The overall risk impact of this risk is $2 \times 4 = 8$.

Although this (dimensionless) number doesn't really mean anything as it stands, it does provide us with a *relative* measure that we can use to compare all the risks we identify in our project. We can then rank the risks to our project according to this measure and begin to focus on the 'critical' ones.

Depending on how many risks you identify you can choose to categorise *critical risks* in one of two ways; either the 80/20 rule or by impact factor with *RAG grading*. The 80/20 rule works on the theory that approximately 20% of your risks will cause approximately 80% of your problems. You should therefore focus on these critical risks and be confident of addressing 80% of the problems your project is likely to face.

In reality, your risk list may not partition easily into a 80/20 split, or there may be another natural break point where three or four risks appear significantly 'riskier' than others. You may therefore decide to focus on critical risks by impact factor alone – for example, those that have an impact factor greater than nine. One approach you can use here is *RAG grading*. RAG stands for Red, Amber, and Green and is used to classify risks according to their impact factor. Those with an impact factor of 1 to 5 are classified as green risks; those with an impact factor of 6 to 10 are amber risks; those with an impact factor greater than 10 are red risks. It is the red risks (critical risks) that you need to focus your attention on. Although not critical, you should keep a wary eye on amber risks, and green risks can generally be ignored.

Whichever approach you use, you will end up with a short list of critical risks that you are going to do something about. How you deal with these critical risks is discussed in the following section.

4.4.4 Alleviate critical risks

There are three ways that you can deal with the critical risks you have identified in your project: *avoidance, deflection* (sometimes called *transfer*) and *contingency*. Avoidance means reducing the chances that the risk will occur at all. Deflection means passing the risk onto someone or something else. Contingency means accepting that the risk is going to occur and putting something in place to deal with it when it does.

Example

Pym and Wideman (1987) provide a neat analogy that contrasts these approaches. Take the situation in which someone is about to be shot at. They can avoid this risk by moving quickly to somewhere safe (avoidance). They can deflect this risk by putting something (a shield) or someone between themselves and the assassin (deflection). Or, they can assume they are going to be hit by some bullets and ring the ambulance service in advance (contingency). You may like to think which of these approaches to dealing with this risk *you* prefer!

The nature of the risks within your own project will influence which of these approaches are suitable. Although your supervisor should be able to give you advice in this area, the following examples may provide you with some ideas you could adopt in your own project.

■ **Contingency.** If you feel there is a chance some tasks may over-run in your project it might be an idea to build some contingency into your project plan at the start. You could, for example, aim to complete your project four weeks ahead of its submission date – giving you four weeks of flexible time (float) that can be used if unexpected delays occur. Alternatively, you might like to add 10% to each of the time estimates you have made to cover any possible delays.

■ **Deflection.** You might be able to get someone else to do part of the work for you in an area where you are weak (although you would have to acknowledge this clearly in your report). For example, you might be undertaking a research-based project focussing on the impact of a particular software technology in an organisation. The project may require the development of a software system (and your programming skills may be weak) but this is not the main focus of your work. It might, therefore, be possible, to get someone else to develop that software system for you while you remain focussed on the important evaluation component of the project. This is certainly something that would need approval from your institution or supervisor to ensure that the integrity of your own work was not compromised.

■ **Avoidance.** If there is a risk that you will not be able to develop a program because you are considering using a new programming language, perhaps you could resort to using a language with which you are familiar.

■ **Avoidance.** If your software system requires the development of an algorithm to solve a problem and you are unsure whether you can do this or not, you might be able to use an existing algorithm instead (but make sure this does not reduce the potential marks you can achieve for your work).

■ **Contingency** and **Avoidance.** Is there a possibility that your computer might crash and you might lose all your work? Contingency planning would involve arranging an alternative machine you could use if such a problem occurred. Avoidance would involve making sufficient back-ups of your work to ensure that your work would not be lost if this happened.

4.4.5 Controlling risks

You have now identified all the risks in your project, focussed on the critical ones and decided what you will do about them. This is not the end of the process; you cannot just sit back and relax. While risk management can make you aware of the risks involved and put things in place to deal with those risks, it does not take away the risks to your project entirely. The last stage of the risk management process is concerned with planning your risk strategy approach, monitoring risks as your project progresses and dealing with those risks if they occur. In Chapter 7, when we look at controlling your project as it is progressing, we will examine some specific problems your project might face in more detail (and ways to deal with those risks). This section is concerned with the process of controlling the risks rather than the risks themselves.

The first task you must undertake as part of this stage is to decide how you will manage the risks you have identified. This is not in terms of how you will *deal* with those critical risks, as this was covered in the previous section. This task involves deciding how you will go about controlling risks in your project and making sure you have the right resources available to deal with the risks – in other words, what is your *strategy* going to be towards risk management in your project?

One strategy you can adopt is to identify specific *checkpoints* in your project's progress, when you will re-visit your critical risk list and adjust it according to your latest understanding. However, be aware that triggers or risk events can still occur outside these checkpoints and should be dealt with accordingly. You may decide to hold check-points at the end of every week, fortnight or month. Alternatively, you may decide to hold check points at the end of particular stages of your project – for example, after the literature search is completed, after the design is completed and so on. Another alternative would be to arrange checkpoints during meetings with your supervisor – s/he may wish to know how your project risks are changing.

Part of the process involves checking for those risk *triggers* you identified during risk identification. Another part involves invoking your contingency plans when risks occur, while another part requires you to constantly monitor and update your critical risk list. Risks are not stationary; they will evolve over time. Some risks will become more 'risky' (their impact will increase), while others will become less so. As your project progresses some risks may be 'promoted' to your critical list, whilst others may be 'demoted' from it. Risks can therefore move from green to amber to red risks and vice versa in the RAG grading scheme.

● 4.5 Summary

- Project planning consists of two stages; defining what it is you want to achieve and planning how you will achieve this. Project definition involves identifying your project's aims and objectives.

- Planning itself consists of six steps; identifying the tasks involved using *Work Breakdown Structures;* estimating the duration of these tasks; identifying critical stages in your project called *milestones;* identifying the order in which activities should be performed using *activity networks;* scheduling your time so that you are not trying to do more than you can physically achieve using *Gantt charts;* and re-planning your project to fit the time available.

■ Project management software packages, such as Microsoft Project, can be used to assist you with planning and managing your project. While you can put together your own Gantt charts and activity networks by hand, such as those shown in Figures 4.5 and 4.6, project management software tools can automate this process for you. However, these packages do take time to learn and you can often find yourself spending more time planning and 'tweaking' your project with these packages than actually doing any real work. Remember – you should only spend around 10% of your time at most on project management.

■ Risk management is performed in parallel with project management and involves the following four stages: *risk identification, risk quantification, risk alleviation* and *risk control.*

4.6 Further reading

Barker, S. and Cole, R. (2007) *Brilliant project management: What the best project managers know, say, do,* Prentice Hall, Englewood Cliffs, USA.
Levine, H.A. (2002) *Practical project management: tips, tactics and tools,* John Wiley, New York.
Lock, D. (2007) *Project management* (9th Edition), Gower, Aldershot, UK.

4.7 Exercises

1. Try to identify objectives for the example projects listed in Section 4.2.2.
2. Apply the SMART criteria to the remaining objectives in the example in Section 4.2.3.
3. Try to state whether the technical and non-technical risks identified in Section 4.4.2 are *event-driven* or *evolving* risks.
4. What are the risks associated with the ANN stock market project? Can you identify any triggers in this project?

4.8 Action points

■ Identify aims and objectives for your own computing project.
■ Apply the SMART criteria to your own project's objectives.
■ Follow the six steps of planning to complete your project's plan.
■ Apply the four stages of the risk management process to your own project. What are the three main risks to your project and what do you intend to do about them?

CHAPTER 5

Literature searching and literature reviews

Aims:

To introduce the skills needed to undertake literature surveys.

Learning objectives:

When you have completed this chapter, you should be able to:

■ Understand the process of literature surveys.

■ Define and conduct a literature search.

■ Manage information obtained during a literature search.

■ Understand how to conduct critical evaluation.

■ Write a literature review.

■ This chapter is particularly relevant for research degree projects.

■ The chapter is also appropriate for taught degree projects –
especially those that are research-based.

■ This chapter provides useful material for all taught degree projects.

● 5.1 Introduction

In virtually all computing projects (especially at research degree level), you are assessed on what you submit at the end, be it a written report, a working program, a specification, detailed system designs, test plans or whatever. However, it is often your initial investigative work that can make the difference between a good project and a borderline fail; even for practically-based programming projects in which the development of a piece of software is the main component. The initial foundation for your project is a *literature survey*. This survey has two main components; a *literature search* and a *literature review*. The literature search represents the mechanics of looking for, sorting, managing and digesting the available research material. The literature review represents your written understanding, critical evaluation, conceptualisation and presentation of the material you have obtained. A skill related closely to both of these components is *referencing*. How to reference material correctly will be discussed in Chapter 8.

A literature survey acts as an introduction to your project and serves a number of purposes:

■ It justifies your project – i.e., it shows that your project is worth doing; the area that you are investigating is recognised and meaningful. At research degree level you will also be identifying that your project is not merely repeating the work of others, but has a contribution to make, perhaps by identifying a current gap in the literature of your field of study which you intend to fill.

■ It sets your project within context by discussing and critically evaluating past and current research in your area. Through this *contextualisation* you will identify how your project fits within and contributes to wider issues. This will depend on the level (undergraduate or postgraduate) of project you are undertaking.

■ It provides other researchers with a starting point from which they can understand how your project evolved and to identify what literature is relevant to your project in order that they can continue where you left off.

5.1.1 Justification

The importance of a literature survey within academic projects cannot be over-emphasised. For example, Figure 5.1 helps to illustrate a literature survey's contribution within the context of a computing project by analogy to building a block of

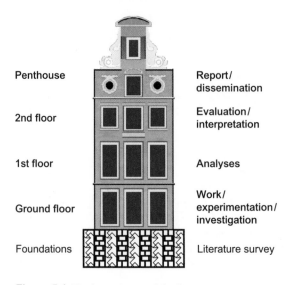

Figure 5.1 The importance of the literature survey

flats. Although people might come from far and wide to visit your luxury penthouse on the top floor (i.e., they are interested in reading your *project report*), this penthouse (report) will be unstable, of poor quality and limited in its academic worth if it doesn't rest on firm foundations (the literature survey). Sometimes students start their projects at the ground floor; tackling what they feel is the main content of their project without justifying it or identifying its context within the wider issues. This can often prove disastrous because investigations are narrow, conclusions are weak, influences of other relevant issues are ignored, and you may just be repeating the work of others.

5.1.2 Context

It is very important for any academic project to justify its content by identifying how it fits into a broader context. Figure 5.2 shows two potential student projects; one at taught degree level and one at research degree (PhD) level (contributing to world knowledge). This is an alternative viewpoint to that shown in Figure 2.1, which aimed to show your own understanding within world knowledge. Figure 5.2 represents a somewhat simplified interpretation of world thinking, knowledge, understanding, theories and philosophies (and a taught degree project probably represents a lot less than the 10% of all world thinking as indicated in this diagram!). Advances to current understanding, through research discoveries and inventions, are shown as expansions to this domain by the dashed lines. Conversely, contractions in world understanding might also occur as historical skills are forgotten. However, although Duell (Commissioner of the U.S. Office of Patents) stated in 1899 that 'Everything

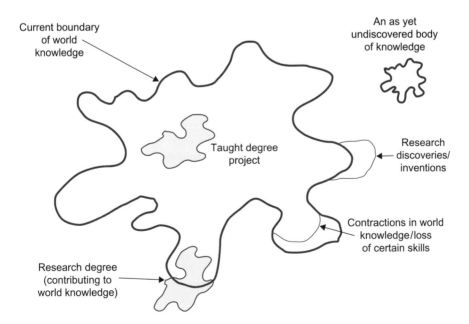

Figure 5.2 Projects within their wider context

that can be invented has been invented', on the whole, world knowledge continues to expand as new discoveries are made.

Figure 5.2 also recognises that the world is by no means at the limits of understanding and there are (possibly) an infinite number of discoveries and inventions yet to be made. This is highlighted by the isolated region towards the top right of the diagram. This knowledge domain may seem ridiculous and fanciful at the moment, based on current philosophies and understandings, but it might, in future, become an area of accepted theory and knowledge. For example, 500 years ago people thought the earth was flat. The understanding that the earth was round and revolved around the sun appeared a ridiculous notion at that time and would have appeared as the disjoint region shown in Figure 5.2. World knowledge has now expanded to accept this understanding/belief within its boundaries. In addition, as world knowledge expands, not only do we find out things we did not know but we also find out how little we know about certain subjects and perhaps identify a whole new set of questions that need to be asked and answered.

Some interesting examples where world understanding has changed over time are highlighted by the following two quotes:

> *'Computers of the future may weigh no more than 1.5 tons.'*
> (*Popular Mechanics* magazine, 1949)

> *'I think there is a world market for maybe five computers.'*
> (Thomas Watson, IBM Chairman, 1943)

5.1.3 Research degrees versus taught degree projects

If you are pursuing a PhD or an MPhil, your project should be at the boundaries of world understanding in your particular field of study (see Figure 5.2). Completing a PhD must enhance world knowledge. In other words, you would be expected to make a *contribution* to world knowledge and consequently expand its boundaries. An MPhil, on the other hand, would not necessarily make a major contribution to knowledge, but it would be involved with an investigation into potential developments to world knowledge and be concerned with work at the boundaries.

At taught degree level, however, this would not be expected. At this level you would be required to understand how your project fits into its wider context and have some appreciation of developments in that area. Examiners at taught degree level are interested in your own ideas, interpretations, theories and concepts of the particular field of study. They are not expecting a major contribution to knowledge from your project at this level.

Figure 5.3 focuses more on the context of an individual taught degree project. This figure shows how a project can draw on information from a number of different topic areas (in this case, two). This project's main focus is the overlap between these two subjects, although it does concentrate a little more on field B than field A. The project does not ignore issues from these two fields on their own, but uses material from them to identify the broader context in which the project lies. An example would be a project that looked at the application of artificial intelligence methods to predicting breast cancer rates in patients.

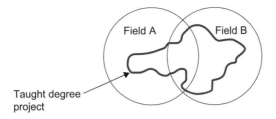

Figure 5.3 A taught degree project in context within two subject areas

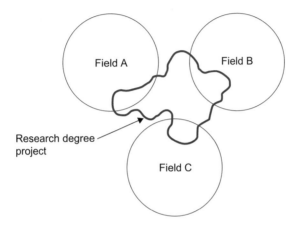

Figure 5.4 A research degree that draws together three previously unrelated subject areas

Figure 5.4 shows a potential PhD project along similar lines. This time the project might draw on three currently unrelated fields and contributes to knowledge by filling the gap between these fields. In both these cases the projects have been identified within their wider contexts and the reader has an understanding of how the projects draw together and focus on particular subject areas.

5.1.4 A starting point

Your literature survey also enables other people interested in your work to see the grounds from which your project developed. A thorough literature survey will provide other researchers with a starting point for their studies and provide anyone wishing to develop your project work further with a comprehensive literature base.

● 5.2 The literature survey process

In Chapter 4, when project planning was discussed, the literature survey was split into two distinct, concurrent stages of *search* and *review*. For planning purposes it might well be acceptable to define the literature survey in this simplistic way to aid clarity. Although these two components represent the bulk of the work involved in performing

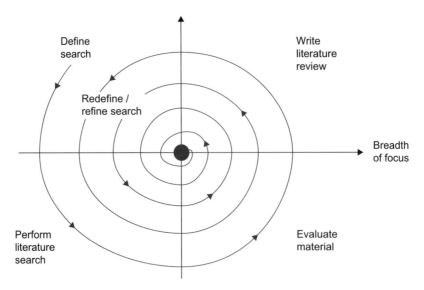

Figure 5.5 The literature survey process

a literature survey, there is more to a survey than just this. Figure 5.5 provides a far more accurate representation of this process. In this figure the angular axis represents time and the radial axis represents your subject focus.

The starting point for your literature survey is the *definition* of your literature search – starting in the top left hand quadrant of Figure 5.5. This definition begins to identify the boundaries of your literature search and the topics you are interested in and provides a starting point from which to focus on appropriate research material. This definition might be as simple as your subjective understanding of your project area and might lead you to popular texts in your field. However, you may be more focused and limit your search definition to key authors, specific journals and/or particular research articles. Alternatively, you might want to use a conceptual model such as a *relevance tree, spider diagram* or *research territory map* introduced in Chapter 3, whereby the relationships between topics within your project are identified. These conceptual maps will help you to identify the starting point for your literature search.

Continuing around the spiral of Figure 5.5; having decided broadly (or specifically) what you are interested in searching for, you can then begin to perform your *literature search* (this stage and the following two stages are discussed in more detail in separate sections later). Your literature search will provide you with material that requires your *critical evaluation*. This critical evaluation will provide you with a firm understanding of your chosen subject area and will form the basis of the next stage of the process – your *literature review*. Note that these stages are not independent – you will not visit your university's library, gather all the references you need, return to your office, read and evaluate them and complete your literature review. You will perform some of these tasks in parallel. For example, you may be evaluating some articles while you wait for others ordered through inter-library loans. You might read part of an article or a book relating to a topic you are currently focusing on and tackle the rest of the article or book at a later date. You might use only part of a book to provide you with insight into one aspect of your project or you might use one article you have obtained to direct you quickly to other papers on a subject.

Having completed one cycle of the literature survey process you will find that you are really just beginning. You may have uncovered more questions and misunderstandings than you started with. You may feel other issues you had not considered appear to be influencing your project and justify further investigation. You may feel that you have been too broad with your initial aims and decide to focus on one particular aspect that interests you. Alternatively, you may feel that you were too focused on a particular issue and need to broaden your search. Whatever the case, you will find that you are moving back into the cycle once again by refining and redefining your search for material. Once again, you may define your search explicitly or maintain a subjective understanding of material in which you are interested. The cycle thus proceeds as you continue to search and evaluate the literature, focusing ever more closely on information relevant to your project.

The 'spiralling in' effect apparent in Figure 5.5 represents your increased focus on the particular *topic* of interest. This is not to say that your search draws in consistently over time as indicated in Figure 5.5. There are times when your search may broaden but the focus on material relevant to your project will always improve. Thus, from a broad starting point, which might include books, journals, documentation, news reports and the like, you will find yourself drawn more and more towards specific articles relating directly to your project. Your literature review is therefore seen to 'evolve' over a period of time as you become more confident with the subject material and your conceptual understanding of the topic area increases.

This iterative process highlights the fact that the literature review is not something that you can write as a one-off having read everything you can get your hands on. It must develop over time. Although you will have to stop work on your literature survey at some point and move onto the main content of your project, you may well find that you are making changes to your literature review right up to the end. This will be inevitable as you should continue to gather and evaluate material throughout the lifetime of your project to keep your understanding of the field fresh and up-to-date.

Berndtsson *et al.* (2008: 59) discuss the idea of *completeness* with respect to a literature review. They highlight the point that it is difficult to know when to stop – how do you know when you have collected sufficient material? While it is probably impossible to read every single artefact that has been published in your area, Berndtsson *et al.* point out that 'by undertaking a systematic process, which can be conveyed to the reader, the validity of the resulting study will be enhanced'. They go on to state that the reader (examiner) should understand why certain material has been covered and why certain material has been omitted.

● 5.3 Literature searching

5.3.1 Introduction

A literature search is a '*systematic* gathering of *published* information relating to a subject' (University of Derby, 1995). There are two important terms italicised within this statement that require further explanation. The first is *systematic*. A literature search should not be performed in an *ad hoc* manner, but should be approached in a structured and professional way. Reading everything you come across will eventually become boring and will certainly be a waste of time. It is important to focus your literature search on those articles, books and so on that are relevant. Of course, when you first begin your literature search you won't know which material is relevant and which is extraneous. However, as you continue to cycle through the literature survey process, your focus will improve as your boundaries draw in towards your specific topic of interest. You should, therefore, identify your boundaries and know when to stop. Although this can be difficult at the start of your project, you should try to limit your search as much as possible. Knowing when to stop can also be hard as you will still have a lot of unanswered questions you may wish to solve before moving on to the main part of your project. However, remember that you will never actually stop literature searching as you might still be gathering/understanding material in parallel with the rest of your work to the conclusion of your project.

The second significant term within the definition is *published*. This implies that the material which you trace should be *recognised*. In other words, the material is not merely somebody's opinion you happened across through a conversation in a corridor, or a block of un-refereed text downloaded from the Internet. Recognised works are those that have been suitably *refereed* before publication. In other words, they have been assessed for their academic worth by other 'experts' in the field and accepted as significant artefacts that contribute to that field. Using only material from sources on the Internet (such as Wikipedia) will undermine the legitimacy of your project. While such sources can provide useful background information and overviews, you should try to extend your literature search to peer reviewed sources.

Bearing these two points in mind, there are two golden rules you should remember when performing a literature search:

■ Allow plenty of time – it can, and probably will, take a long time. Therefore, you should start as soon as possible, avoid procrastinating (see Chapter 7) and steer clear of material unrelated to your chosen topic.

■ Ensure that you make note of the full reference of any material you obtain. This will save a significant amount of time at the end of your project because you won't waste time trying to remember precise details of articles you have read but have since lost or returned to your local library. It is also important to avoid plagiarising the work of others (plagiarism is covered in Section 8.5). The full reference will also be needed if you wish to apply for inter-library loans.

It is also worth noting that you should not be overwhelmed by the vast array of literature you might find on your topic. You need to be selective and focus in on precisely those articles and books that are specifically relevant to your work. If, however, you find several books and numerous articles that cover your specific subject area in detail, then it might mean that your subject aim is still too broad and you should focus even more.

When you are assessing whether a book is worth reading you should begin (obviously) with the title, move on to the contents listing, and scan the index for keywords that are important to you. Is the author well recognised in her/his field, is the book up-to-date, is it the latest edition? When you are thinking of reading or obtaining an article, again, begin with the title and ask yourself if it is up-to-date or might it have been overtaken by other publications by now? Read the abstract and keywords, look at the list of references at the back (are key works cited? Are there useful references you can use?). Move on to reading the introduction and the summary/conclusions. Assess its level; is it highly technical, readable, is it a review paper, an introductory paper, a discussion paper? Only if you are satisfied that books and articles address all your needs should you read them from cover to cover. In many cases, a select number of chapters in a book may be useful to you and only some sections of an article may be relevant.

Not only will your search require you to obtain literature on your chosen subject but it might also involve you searching for, identifying, and obtaining suitable software for your project. For example, if your project is aiming to evaluate different software tools in different organisational environments you will need to ensure you have traced suitable, up-to-date tools for this evaluation. While software you obtain will not be used to justify and contextualise your project in a literature review, it may well be crucial for you to complete your project successfully. It is important, therefore, that you begin to search for and obtain this software as soon as possible and you may well find yourself pursuing this at the same time as your literature survey.

The points made above and the rules which you should follow provide you with a broad, subjective understanding of the nature of a literature search. In addition to these points you will need to understand the mechanics of the search. There are two aspects to this: understanding the format in which the information can be found and tracing this information. These two aspects are now discussed in turn.

5.3.2 Format of information

Literature is presented in a number of different formats. Some forms are more accessible than others and some are recognised as being more 'academically' valuable and worthy (see the points made on *recognised* works earlier). The following list is a summary of the forms of material you might come across during your literature search. The list is by no means exhaustive and for more details on these and other sources you should refer to texts such as Blaxter *et al.* (2006), Dochartaigh (2007) and Saunders *et al.* (2007).

Books   Books will probably prove to be the starting point for your literature survey. They will provide you with a good grounding and a good overview of your chosen topic area. However, remember that they may be out-dated and out of line with current thinking in your field. Books are also written for different audiences; some being more technical than others. You should ensure that any books you acquire provide sufficient detail for your needs. Generally speaking, books **are** refereed and do provide a suitable basis for a literature survey.

Journals   Journals contain (normally refereed) articles discussing up-to-date issues in their field. You may find it daunting at first to read journal articles as they (should) represent the current limits and developments in your subject area. You may, therefore, find it easier to build a solid understanding in your chosen subject using books before attempting to investigate the latest developments and theories from journal articles.

Journal articles will also tend to be quite specific – focusing on developments in detailed areas of a particular topic. You may find that only part of an article is suited to your needs.

As you continue your literature survey you should find yourself using journal articles more and more as your understanding of your subject becomes deeper. Indeed, when you complete your literature review you should find that the majority of references you make are to journal articles which represent the latest thinking in your field.

Conference proceedings

Conference proceedings contain articles and papers that have been presented at national and international conferences. The quality of articles in conference proceedings varies widely – some conferences are not refereed while others bring together the latest findings from internationally renowned experts in particular fields. Sometimes conference proceedings may contain more up-to-date ideas than you can find in journal articles and sometimes they present preliminary results from research that has yet to mature.

CDs and DVDs

Increasingly these days material is being presented on CDs and DVDs. CDs and DVDs generally present information from other sources in a more easily accessible format. For example, CDs and DVDs contain varying types of information from book-type material and conference proceedings to journal articles.

Company reports

Company reports and documentation can provide valuable information for case studies. However, care must be taken with these kinds of material as they might be subjectively biased in favour of the company and may contain information that you cannot use as the company does not wish it to be made public.

Theses

Theses are the published reports/dissertations of PhDs and MPhils. They represent the work of a research degree and provide a contribution in their particular field. Not only will they provide you with ideas on current thinking in a particular area but they will also provide a useful source of relevant references and, if you are a research degree student, an idea of the scope and requirements of a research degree. Having said that, theses are sometimes difficult to obtain – probably being lodged only at the awarding institution – although they can be obtained through inter-library loans or sometimes downloaded from the Internet.

Manuals

Within technical computing projects, manuals may prove to be a valuable source of information. For example, it might be impossible for you to perform your project without having access to the relevant technical manual. However, remember that they are just manuals; they are not refereed academic articles providing insight into current thinking in your field. You should treat manuals just as they are and not use them as foundations for academic discussion within your report.

Software

Any software that you require for your project, such as software tools, libraries and reusable components, should be obtained as soon as possible. You would not want to be halfway through your project and find that the software you needed was no longer available or too expensive. You may have identified some relevant software when you completed your project proposal (see Resource requirements in Section 3.3.3) but it is important that you obtain this as soon as you can. Sources you can use to trace relevant software include the Internet (using keyword searches and company web sites), local companies (who may well be using suitable software tools) and professional organisations. Professional organisations (such as the IEEE, the Project Management Institute and so on) often have *special interest groups* in particular areas and they can be contacted for help and information. This might include software reviews on tools used in their particular field of study and databases of companies supplying relevant software.

The Internet   The Internet is a valuable source of information but it must be treated with caution. You can spend hours 'surfing' the Internet wasting time, without finding anything of value. In addition, material that you do trace might well be unqualified, un-refereed opinion that has no recognised grounding within your particular field of study. Data are also 'unstable' being updated and modified regularly. While this can be a good thing in that material is always up-to-date, it can mean that the information disappears quickly as well. Having said that, the Internet can prove to be a useful search tool for accessing academically sound material, company information and software. You can often find articles published elsewhere that are difficult to obtain through normal sources – for example, through digital library resources. Make sure if you do use any material from the Internet that you note the full web address of the material for referencing purposes.

Some points that you should consider when evaluating the quality of material on the Internet include (some of these points are adapted from Ohio State University Library, 2008):

- What is the purpose of the site – is it to provide information or to sell a product?
- When was the site updated? How up-to-date is the material on the site? Is it still relevant?
- Is the site part of (or related to) an official organisation (a professional body, government department or academic institute or research group)? For example, the IEEE, the Project Management Institute, British Computer Society, etc.?
- Are there any copyright issues associated with the material? Will you be able to use the material without breaching copyright?
- Is there an author for the material? Is the author qualified to provide the information? Are they presenting opinions rather than facts? Are they biased?
- Is the site recognised from other sources? Is it a recognised body? Are there other links to the site and is it reviewed anywhere?
- Is the material biased? 'Does the author have a "vested interest" in the topic' or an axe to grind?

For more detail on how to use the Internet wisely for research purposes, refer to Dochartaigh (2007) and Munger and Campbell (2006), who have written entire books devoted to this topic.

In addition to the above media, you may also find material in forms such as video/DVD and microfiche. Treat these sources with the respect they deserve. For example, a refereed journal presented on microfiche is as valuable as a refereed journal on paper. An introductory DVD on your subject area may provide you with as good grounding in your topic as an introductory textbook.

Other sources of information that should be treated with more caution include letters and memos, newspaper articles, computing magazines, company sales literature and television programmes. Newspapers, television programmes and computing magazines may provide popular material but their depth may be somewhat limited. However, computing magazines often discuss up-to-date technical issues and provide topical quotes from key orators for use in your report. Letters, memos and company sales literature will provide limited material and they are likely to be quite biased.

5.3.3 Tracing the information

You now know the format in which literature is presented, but how do you actually trace these sources of information? The best place to start any literature search is in your own institution's library. You should also make good use of the librarians who know the most efficient ways to trace particular sources of information within your institution. Detailed below are some examples of material you can use to trace literature on your subject. The list is by no means exhaustive and you should consult your own library staff for other search material they might have.

Internet   Although you should be careful when using the Internet to access literature for your project, the Internet *is* a valuable tool for tracing articles and information. The Internet in this context refers to the use of web browsers (such as Microsoft Internet Explorer) to access web sites. It is useful to employ some form of *search engine* when looking for particular items on the Internet. Three such engines can be accessed at:

- http://www.google.com/
- http://www.yahoo.cm/
- http://www.lycos.com/

Wikipedia (http://www.wikipedia.org/) is a useful starting point for tracing general information about a subject and identifying references. However, like most Internet sites, Wikipedia is not academically refereed and you should use the information you obtain there with caution. Having said this, for a general overview of a subject or as an introduction to a new area, it is a valuable tool.

Through the Internet you will also be able to access *mailing lists* and *news groups*. Mailing lists are provided by *list servers* and are established to deal with particular subjects or special interest groups. By submitting your email address and subject interest(s) to a list server you will be added to their mailing list. You will then receive mailings from people on your particular subject of interest. This works by people submitting comments, questions, discussion points, etc. to the list server, which are then forwarded to everyone on the mailing list. The messages that are forwarded are either moderated (checked by a human before hand) or un-moderated (all messages are forwarded).

One such list server is JISCmail provided by Janet (UK). To find out more about this service and the subject areas that are available, you can access the JISCmail web site at: http://www.jiscmail.ac.uk/.

News groups are similar to bulletin boards or notice boards. They cover an enormous range of topics from specific academic subject areas to general interest 'chat' groups. The most common way to access news groups is through your own web browser. Your Internet Service Provider (ISP) or university computer services department will be able to advise you on what groups are available locally and how this facility is supported.

The following links provide some useful resources and sources of information on the Internet for those undertaking research in computer science and information science. These sources were compiled in October 2008 so be aware that new sites may now be available and some may have moved.

Intute (http://www.intute.ac.uk/sciences/). Intute is a free service that provides access to information in engineering, mathematics and computing. According to the Intute web site it provides 'access to the very best Web resources for education and research'.

ISI Web of Knowledge (http://wos.mimas.ac.uk/). A database for UK education that covers engineering and science publications (both journals and conferences). It indexes over 57,000 journals across 164 scientific disciplines. It provides a full search facility and ability to download abstracts but you (or your institution) must subscribe to this service.

Research Navigator (http://www.researchnavigator.com/). This site is maintained by Pearson and provides a useful starting point for students undertaking research in a number of disciplines. It provides access to the *New York Times* archive and EBSCO's ContentSelect, which provides access to lots of computing journals.

Berndtsson *et al.* (2008) identify a number of other useful Internet resources. Some bibliographies they identify include:

ACM Association of Computing Machinery (http://www.acm.org). Contains a digital library of all material published by the ACM and a guide to computing literature.

The Collection of Computer Science Bibliographies (http://liinwww.ira.uka.de/bibliography/). According to the site this 'is a collection of bibliographies of scientific literature in computer science from various sources, covering most aspects of computer science. The bibliographies are updated weekly from their original locations such that you'll always find the most recent versions here. The collection currently contains more than 2 million references (mostly to journal articles, conference papers and technical reports)'.

IEEE Computer Society (http://www.computer.org). The IEEE's online bibliographic database, where you can search for journal articles and conference proceedings. Note that you will have to pay for most of the articles you want to download from this site.

Lecture Notes in Computer Science (www.springer.de/comp/lncs). Springer's online database containing literature from this series of publications.

DBLP bibliography (http://dblp.uni-trier.de). According to the site 'The DBLP server provides bibliographic information on major computer science journals and proceedings'. It was originally focused on database systems and logic programming (hence the acronym) but it has since expanded to other areas of computer science.

HCI Bibliography (http://www.hcibib.org). Dedicated to Human Computer Interaction research. The site is maintained in Canada.

IngentaConnect (http://www.ingentaconnect.com/). 'IngentaConnect offers one of the most comprehensive collections of academic and professional research articles online – some 20 million articles from 30,000 publications, including 10,000 online'.

Neuron AI directory (http://www.neuron.co.uk/). Provides links to academic and commercial publications and those primarily within the field of artificial intelligence (expert systems, neural networks, fuzzy logic, etc.).

Intute (2008) also provide a comprehensive list of Internet resources for computing. You can download a booklet that details these resources from http://www.intute.ac.uk/sciences/booklets/. The booklet is split into sections covering (amongst others) *Journals and Magazines, Programming and Software, Organisations and Societies, Subject Gateways, Learning and Teaching* and *Other Interesting Sites* (publishers for example). Amongst the sites they reference are:

Free on-line dictionary of computing (http://foldoc.org/). Based at Imperial College London, it does what it says.

IBM Systems Journal (http://www.research.ibm.com/journal/sj/). Provides access to papers published within this journal.

Journal of Digital Information (http://jodi.tamu.edu/). A free service that allows you to download papers on 'the management, presentation and uses of information in digital environments'.

OPAC Most institutions have an OPAC (Online Public Access Circulation) that you can use to perform searches for material held in your library. OPAC provides an efficient way of performing searches (be it an author's name, title, keywords and so on). Your library will invariably have one of these systems and you should learn how to use it.

You can also access OPACs at other institutions via the Internet. For example, over 50 UK institutions OPACs can be accessed via: http://copac.ac.uk/copac/, which is a merged online catalogue.

British National Bibliography This provides a list of all British books published and deposited at the British Library each year. It is available in printed format and as a CD-ROM.

Global Books in Print	A CD-ROM containing information on all books recently published in America, UK, Continental Europe, Africa, Asia, etc.
ASLIB	An index of PhD theses completed in the UK each year. It provides abstracts and is arranged in subject order. It is available on line at: http://www.hull.ac.uk/lib/infoskills/aslib.html.
Current Research in Britain	A catalogue that presents, in institution order, research activity that is ongoing within UK universities. Computing research is covered within the physical sciences volumes and it is published annually.

5.3.4 Inter-library loans

Although the search material detailed above can provide you with a comprehensive list of material that will support your project, there is no guarantee that you can download the material you need from the Internet or that your local library will stock the items you require. This is when you need to make use of the inter-library loans system. Your institution will be able to obtain material for you from other institutions using this system. However, the system has three potential drawbacks:

■ It is expensive and often taught degree students will have to pay for this service.

■ It can take time before you receive an article you have ordered – possibly too long in some cases.

■ You can be severely limited on the duration for which you can keep the material (for example, one or two weeks when you may want a book for two or three months).

Having said this, the system is well worth using if you require pertinent articles and books for your project that are not available locally.

5.3.5 Some tips for performing a literature search

We finish this section with a few tips on undertaking a literature search:

■ Note interesting quotes and their **full** reference as you go along. This will be invaluable later when you write your report and try to trace your references.

■ Use review articles and books to help your search.

■ Reference correctly from the start (covered in Chapter 8).

■ Know when to stop – or at least when to move on to the next stage of your project. You will know this from your project plan and the research boundaries, which you have set yourself.

■ Have a system to organise and catalogue the material you read. The following section provides a discussion on how to manage your information effectively.

■ Read recognised leaders and original theorists in your field.

■ Start with a broad search before you focus; don't jump straight into the most complicated recent article on your subject. You may be put off by its apparent complexity.

● 5.4 Managing information

Collecting a large number of articles and books relating to your subject is all very well but, depending on the size of your project and the breadth and depth of your literature search, you may soon find yourself swamped under paperwork and books. Some people manage to work well under these conditions, able to put their hands on a particular piece of paper under a pile of 'debris' on their desk. For the rest of us it makes sense to have some means of managing and controlling the literature and information gathered to avoid losing sight of important articles or losing references that are needed later. This section briefly introduces some tips and ideas to help you manage the articles, books and references you obtain from your literature search. For a more detailed discussion on managing research material you can read Orna and Stevens (2009), a book devoted to 'Managing information for research'.

The best way to begin managing your research is by using the conceptual model you have created of your subject area (using your RTM, relevance tree or spider diagram). Use this model to identify the topics in which you are interested and how these topics link together. You can use this model to arrange articles and books that you obtain into some sort of order. Some articles may cover broad issues while others may draw together two or three important topics. Arrange photocopied articles and your own notes into plastic wallets or folders suitably labelled. In this way you will quickly and easily be able to draw together relevant information as you tackle different parts of your project.

Another important strategy to follow is to set up an index system of some sort that includes information on every article and book that you read. You should use a computer to do this as the information is readily available in a format which you can use (paste) in your final report and it can be updated easily. You can use a word processor to record details of your references – such as title, keywords (for quick searching for similar topics), brief overview, useful quotes, etc. Alternatively, there are software packages available that manage references for you – for example, Reference Manager (refer to http://www.refman.com/ for more details).

Also, try to record references in the correct format from the start – this will enable you to use them directly when you complete your project later on. It is also a good idea to note the primary reference of each article you obtain – i.e., how did you discover that article in the first place – was it referred to by another article you read or did you just come across it by chance as you searched the Internet or the library shelves?

When you are reading articles highlight key phrases, sentences and paragraphs by underlining or using a highlighter pen. You may set up a system whereby you use a green pen to highlight useful quotes, orange to highlight explanations to key topics, pink to highlight new ideas or contributions, and blue to highlight contradictions or arguments with your way of thinking. In books you can use Post-it-type notes to quickly identify important pages and also to make brief notes on the book at key points.

Another useful idea is to make brief notes on the front page of articles and within the papers themselves. This might provide explanation to yourself of what the author is trying to say or to note another reference you feel is related to this particular point (be it supporting or contradicting the argument). You might like to provide your own brief summary of the paper at the start as well. This will save you having to reread the entire paper six months later when you have forgotten what it was all about and you are trying to incorporate it into your report.

These ideas will not provide you with a comprehensive information management system. This is something only you can develop based on your own way of working and your own feelings and ideas. However, the approaches discussed above will provide you with a useful basis as they cover the key skills used by researchers to manage information.

● 5.5 Critical evaluation

You have gathered some articles and books together, have read them to some extent and have an idea of what each one is about and what the author is trying to say. How do you critically evaluate them?

Normally when people hear or read the word 'criticise' they think of it in a negative sense; that is, finding fault with the object in question. However, to critically evaluate an article means far more than looking for faults – this is certainly not the aim of critical evaluation.

When you read an article or a book, consider the following points. This is not to say that you should apply these points as a 'tick list' but you should be thinking about these ideas implicitly as you read the article. You should also try to think how the article could contribute to your own work.

- What kind of article is it – a review paper, an evaluative paper, a theory paper, a practical paper, a case study, etc.?

- What can you gain from the article – ideas, techniques, useful quotes?

- Is the author well recognised in his/her field? Is the author an authority in this area?

- What contribution is the article making? What kind of contribution is it? Can it make a contribution to your own project? If so, how?

- How does the article fit within its context? How does the article fit into and support the context of your project? How important is the article in its field and your own? Does the paper classify and summarise its field in a clearer or more logical way than has been done before? How does it fit into your conceptual understanding of the field?

- Do conclusions follow logically from the work that has been presented? Are the arguments logical? Do they follow one another? Are they supported or contradicted by the work of others? Are alternative conclusions consistent with the discussion?

- Can you differentiate fact from unsubstantiated opinion? If there are opinions in the article do you agree with them? Are these opinions supported by logical arguments or other authors?

- What do you feel about what has been written? Do you agree with statements that are made? Are there any counter-arguments?

- Does the article contradict other viewpoints or support the status quo? How does the article relate to other literature in the field?

- What references does it use? Are these appropriate, relevant and up-to-date? Which references can you use? Is the article referenced by other authors?

- Are there limits to what the author is suggesting? Is his/her argument applicable only in certain cases?

- Can you use the results from the article in your own work? How do these results contribute and fit into their field and your own?

Rudestam and Newton (2007: 67–68) suggest some additional points which should be considered when reading and critically evaluating articles. They break their points down into five key areas: *Conceptualization, Theoretical Framework and Hypotheses, Research Design, Results and Discussion* and *Summary*. Those which supplement the points made above and are applicable for computing projects can be summarised as:

- What is the major problem or issue being investigated?
- How clearly are the major concepts defined/explained?
- Is there a clear research question/hypothesis that can be, and is, tested?
- What type of research design/methodology is employed? Is it suitable and reliable?
- Have algorithms and statistical techniques been used appropriately? Can you apply them in your own work? What are the limitations of these techniques?
- Is the choice of measures, sample sizes and data appropriate? Have extraneous factors/variables been considered?
- Can generalisations be made from these results? What are the limitations of these generalisations?
- Are the implications of the results discussed?
- What is your overall assessment of the study – in terms of its adequacy for explaining the research problem and the contribution it is making?

Taking all of these points into consideration, you will see that critical awareness of your chosen subject means a lot more than just understanding it and being able to regurgitate parts of it. Reading and understanding what you have read is really only the first part of the process. You should be aware of its boundaries, its limitations, contradictions, developing areas and dead ends. The main point of critical evaluation is that you **think** about what you are reading. This *critical reading* is defined by Blaxter *et al.* (2006: 117) using a number of points, some of which are listed below. They define a critical reading as one that:

- 'goes beyond mere description by offering opinions, and making a personal response, to what has been written';
- 'relates different writings to each other';
- 'does not take what is written at face value';
- 'views research writing as a contested terrain, within which alternative views and positions may be taken up'.

Using these pointers as you read and interpret the material that you obtain will ensure that you develop a deeper (not superficial) understanding of your subject area. You will be developing the depth of knowledge that will be expected on your degree course.

● 5.6 Writing literature reviews

You are now critically aware of your subject area and the literature in your chosen field. How do you present your understanding of your field and set the foundation for your project using the literature you have obtained as a literature review?

As a starting point for discussion, Gall *et al.* (2002, cited by Saunders *et al.*, 2007: 57–58) identify the purpose of a literature review as, amongst other things:

- to refine your research question and objectives;
- to highlight research possibilities that have either been explicitly identified by other authors or have possibly been overlooked in the past;
- to avoid repeating the work of others;
- to identify research methods and strategies that may be usefully applied in your own research.

Building on these points a literature review should provide 'a coherent argument that leads to the description of a proposed study' (Rudestam and Newton, 2007: 63). This is achieved with reference to past and current literature in your field(s) and will involve a discussion of current omissions and any biases you might have identified (Saunders *et al.*, *loc. cit.*). You will have great difficulty achieving these aims if you merely read and digest a number of articles and books related to your project. It is through your critical evaluation (discussed in the previous section) and critical understanding of the relevant literature that your literature review will develop.

Figures 5.6 and 5.7 help to illustrate how a literature review should be presented. Figure 5.6 shows a particular research field that a student wishes to discuss as part of their literature review. The world's understanding of this field is covered by numerous books, articles, papers, documents, knowledge in people's minds, etc. The 'furniture sales catalogue' approach (Haywood and Wragg, 1982) would explain this field in a literature review by discussing each article (source of information) in turn as a separate paragraph or section – for example:

Book A: Covers...,

Book B: Discusses...,

Paper A: Introduces...,

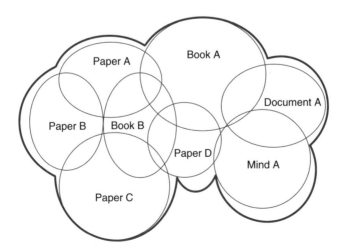

Figure 5.6 A research field made up of a number of articles, books, documents, etc.

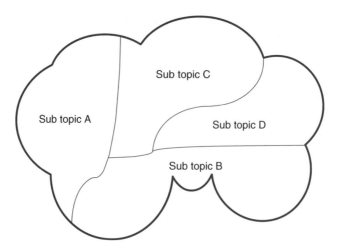

Figure 5.7 How the research field shown in Figure 5.6 might be structured and presented in a literature review

Person A: Thinks . . . ,

and so on.

A better way of presenting this material is to view the field as a series of inter-related subtopics (your own interpretation and understanding of that field and how it is made up). Figure 5.7, as an example, shows how the field in Figure 5.6 might be interpreted. The field can now be discussed in a literature review from this alternative perspective **using** references where appropriate to support the arguments made and explain the topics covered.

You will not be able to write a literature review without reference to other material in the field. References should, therefore, be used to support your arguments **where appropriate**. They should not be used to pad out your report and 'prove' that you have read (or, at least, have obtained) a number of key texts.

There are no specific, infallible rules you can apply to write the perfect literature review. It is something that improves with practice and something that you can get a feel for by reading examples within the varied literature you will come across. However, at a 'mechanistic' level within project reports, Saunders et al (2007: 61) identify three common ways for presenting literature reviews:

1. as a single chapter;
2. as a series of chapters;
3. subsumed within the report as various issues are tackled.

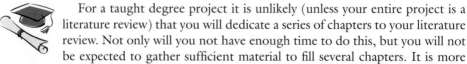

For a taught degree project it is unlikely (unless your entire project is a literature review) that you will dedicate a series of chapters to your literature review. Not only will you not have enough time to do this, but you will not be expected to gather sufficient material to fill several chapters. It is more common that your report will contain an introductory chapter dedicated to a literature review or that you will subsume your review within each chapter of your report where you discuss different elements of your project. Quite clearly the approach you adopt is up to you and is something about which your supervisor should advise you.

When writing your literature review remember what it is not:

- It is not a report that lists all the papers and books you have read whether they are relevant or not. You must be selective about that to which you refer.

- It must not dedicate a page or paragraph to each article in turn merely reporting on their content. Haywood and Wragg (1982: 2) refer to this as 'the furniture sales catalogue, in which everything merits a one-paragraph entry no matter how skilfully it has been conducted' (see Figure 5.6).

Perhaps the best way to explain the presentation of a literature review is through a small example. The following example represents a short introduction to an academic paper. Quite clearly academic papers of only two or three thousand words are much shorter than an entire project report. However, the example shows how the scene is set for the rest of the paper and its context is justified with respect to other literature in the field.

Example – An artificial neural network approach to rainfall-runoff modelling

The United Nations General Assembly declared the 1990s the International Decade for Natural Disaster Reduction with the specific intent to disseminate existing and new information related to measures for the assessment, prediction, prevention and mitigation of natural disasters (WMO, 1992). A prominent element within this programme has been the development of operational flood forecasting systems. These systems have evolved through advances in mathematical modelling (Wood and O'Connell, 1985; O'Connell, 1991; Lamberti and Pilati, 1996), the installation of telemetry and field monitoring equipment at critical sites in drainage networks (Alexander, 1991), through satellite and radar sensing of extreme rainfalls (Collier, 1991), and through the coupling of precipitation and runoff models (Georgakakos and Foufoula-Georgiou, 1991; Franchini *et al.*, 1996). However, in practice, successful real-time flood forecasting often depends on the efficient integration of all these separate activities (Douglas and Dobson, 1987). Under the auspices of the World Meteorological Organisation (1992) a series of projects were implemented to compare the characteristics and performance of various operational models and their updating procedures. A major conclusion of the most recent intercomparison exercise was the need for robust simulation models in order to achieve consistently better results for longer lead times even when accompanied by an efficient updating procedure.

The attractiveness of Artificial Neural Networks (ANNs) to flood forecasting is threefold. First, ANNs can represent any arbitrary non-linear function given sufficient complexity of the trained network. Second, ANNs can find relationships between different input samples and, if necessary, can group samples in analogous fashion to cluster analysis. Finally, and perhaps most importantly, ANNs are able to generalise a relationship from small subsets of data while remaining relatively robust in the presence of noisy or missing inputs, and can adapt or learn in response to changing environments. However, despite these potential

Example (*continued*)

advantages, ANNs have found rather limited application in hydrology and related disciplines. For example, French *et al.* (1992) used a neural network to forecast rainfall intensity fields in space and time, while Raman and Sunilkumar (1995) used an ANN to synthesise reservoir inflow series for two sites in the Bharathapuzha basin, S. India.

The use of artificial neural networks for flood forecasting is an area which has yet to be fully explored. Up until now the majority of work in this area has been mainly theoretical; concentrating on neural network performance with artificially generated rainfall-runoff data; for example Minns and Hall (1996). However, these theoretical approaches tend to overlook the difficulty in converting and applying actual data to artificial neural network topologies. Hall and Minns (1993) go some way to address this criticism by applying neural networks to a small urban catchment area. However, their discussion is limited to the performance of a neural network on a small number of events.

This paper goes one stage further by discussing how artificial neural networks may be developed and used on 'real' hydrological data. It discusses the problems that need to be addressed when applying neural networks to rainfall-runoff modelling and demonstrates the effectiveness of artificial neural networks in this particular domain. By applying a neural network to flood simulation in two UK catchments, the prospects for the use of ANNs in real-time flood forecasting are evaluated. Finally, suggestions are made concerning necessary refinements to the existing ANN prior to transfer to operational use.

(Reproduced in part from Dawson and Wilby, 1998)

Notice how this introduction/literature review begins by justifying the content of the paper with reference to a WMO report. It continues by showing how the subject area has evolved over the years. Literature reviews often employ this kind of approach – focusing in on the topic of concern through a chronological discussion of literature in the field. This approach generally leads to a natural focus on the topic of concern. The review then moves on to explain a little bit more about the area of study, setting the scene for the reader, before focussing more precisely and discussing some recent developments in research within the field. The literature review concludes by highlighting current limitations in the field, once again justifying the relevance and importance of the paper by showing how it aims to fill these gaps.

In summary, your literature review forms the **foundation** of your project. Remember, literature reviews evolve over a period of time (they cannot be written as one-offs, after you have read a few articles on your chosen subject) and although you will not split your literature review into specific sections your review should implicitly cover the following four points:

1. Arrange relevant literature in the field.

2. Critically evaluate past and current research in the field.

3. Identify your project within a wider context.

4. Justify the existence of your project by identifying a gap in the field and showing how your project will fill that gap (particularly important at research degree level).

● 5.7 Summary

- A literature survey will help to place your project within a wider context and justify its presence within a particular field (or fields) of study.

- Your literature survey consists of two main components: the literature search (supported by an ability to manage the information you gather) and the literature review (which requires a critical understanding of material that you obtain). These components are performed repetitively over a period of time and (probably) in parallel with one another.

- Although you will eventually need to move on to the main investigation/development part of your project, your literature survey will continue to be performed throughout the lifetime of your project to some extent, as you refine and consolidate the information you gather ensuring that your project remains up-to-date.

● 5.8 Further reading

Blaxter, L. Hughes, C. and Tight, M. (2006) *How to research* (3rd Edition), Open University Press, Maidenhead, UK.

Dochartaigh, N.O. (2007) *Internet research skills: How to do your literature search and find research information online* (2nd Edition), SAGE Publications, London.

Intute (2008) *The best web resources for education and research,* <http://www.intute.ac.uk/>, (10 October, 2008).

Munger, D. and Campbell, S. (2006) *What every student should know about researching online,* Longman, Harlow, UK.

Orna, E. and Stevens, G. (2009) *Managing information for research,* Open University Press, Buckingham, UK.

Rudestam, K.E. and Newton, R.R. (2007) *Surviving your dissertation* (3rd Edition), SAGE Publications, London.

Saunders, M. Lewis, P. and Thornhill, A. (2007) *Research methods for business students* (4th Edition), Prentice Hall, Essex, UK.

● 5.9 Action points

- Consider how you will undertake your own literature review. Try to identify the boundaries for your search.

- Put in place an information management system that will enable you to manage the literature you obtain effectively.

- Speak to your supervisor and library staff about sources of information for your project. Search the Internet for relevant material.

Conducting your project

Software development

Aims:

To introduce different approaches for developing software systems, testing those systems and ensuring software quality.

Learning objectives:

When you have completed this chapter, you should be able to:

- Understand what is meant by a software development process and describe a number of different development processes.
- Choose an appropriate process for your own project.
- Evaluate your chosen process.
- Understand the differences between bottom-up and top-down development.
- Understand the differences between verification, validation and testing and apply these techniques to your own project.
- Discuss what is meant by software quality and be aware of different quality standards.

- Relevant primarily to taught degree projects – specifically those that involve software development.
- Background for research degree projects – providing they require the development of a software system.

● 6.1 Introduction

6.1.1 Overview

As this book is aimed at Computer Science/Information Systems/Software Engineering students, it is possible that your project will involve the development of a software system of some kind. At one extreme, your course may require you to undertake a software development as the fundamental component of the project; at the other extreme you may just decide to develop a small program to evaluate some ideas in a more research-oriented project. For example, for an MPhil or PhD you may need to develop a program as a 'vehicle' for testing out a new theory, but the program itself will not be examined – so it will not have to be perfect or fully documented. Whatever the case, the sections within this chapter will be useful. They will provide you with a grounding in the approaches you can use to develop software systems, and means of evaluating those systems when they are complete. If your project does not involve the development of any software, you can skip this chapter.

Note that the term *process* model and *life cycle* model are two terms that are used interchangeably in this text. While some might view processes from the perspective of improvement, life cycle is sometimes used to refer to a more generic overview of a software system's development. This distinction is not made here and the terms are used interchangeably to assist presentation.

One area that this chapter does not cover is the use of development methods (of which there are tens, if not hundreds, in existence). Development methods are used in different stages of software development and provide a set of rules and techniques for undertaking different tasks in the software development process. Examples include SSADM (Structured Systems Analysis and Design Method – used in analysis and design), UML (Unified Modelling Language; a modelling notation for object oriented design), DFDs (Data Flow Diagrams) and Soft Systems (used to elicit requirements in complex environments). Methods can be used within the overall development process model you are using and it is these process models that are discussed in this chapter.

If you are using a particular method as part of your project you may not need to follow the method in depth and undertake all of its prescribed stages. Methods are normally tailored for the development of large software systems and, therefore, many parts of the method may be inappropriate or excessive for your own work. Your supervisor should be able to advise you on the use of appropriate methods for your own project.

6.1.2 The past

When software systems were first developed in the mid twentieth century they were done so in a rather *ad hoc* manner without any reference to a defined development process. It was soon realised that this undisciplined approach led to systems that were poorly constructed and difficult to manage and control. Some form of development process was required that could assist software developers in producing more structured code in a more manageable way. According to Knott and Dawson (1999: 20), the advantages of structuring software development into a defined process model are that:

- it divides a large problem down into easy-to-understand tasks at each stage;
- it sharpens focus;
- it supports planning and control – improves time estimates;
- it provides progress visibility;
- it provides structure;
- it leads to better coding and documentation.

The same is true for student software development projects. By following a recognised process in the development of your software, you will reap the benefits outlined above. This chapter, therefore, introduces some common development approaches that you can use (and perhaps adapt) for your own project.

6.2 The software development life cycle (SDLC)

6.2.1 Introduction

The SDLC represents a generic model for software development and consists of a number of stages. These stages, shown in Figure 6.1, are: *requirements capture, design, build, test* and *implement*. All software developments follow this generic model in one way or another and yours will do the same.

Requirements capture represents all activities that are performed to elicit the requirements from the user and the documents that are produced during this stage. *Design* represents the design of the software based on the requirements. *Build* is the coding/ development of the software system. *Test* is the testing of this code and *Implement* is the eventual installation/acceptance of the software system in its target environment (this can also include evaluation of the system with respect to the user's initial requirements).

In practice there is often some overlap and iteration between these stages. For example, if you develop a prototype (discussed in more detail in Section 6.6) you will be performing some *requirements capture*, some *design* and some *building* work simultaneously. You will then perhaps return to the *requirements* stage to redefine these in light of feedback from the prototype and repeat the *design* and *build* stages again. *Build* and *test* usually overlap significantly. For example, you might write some code (a module, object or function) and test it; you might then write some more code and test it; you might then integrate these two components and test this combined sub-system, and so on.

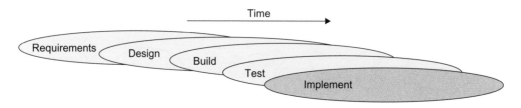

Figure 6.1 The software development life cycle

By understanding how large commercial software systems are developed it will help you in the development of software within your own project. The following sections discuss in more detail each of the stages of the generic SDLC.

6.2.2 Requirements capture

Requirements capture is quite often the hardest stage of the SDLC to perform well and, subsequently, get right. Numerous methods and techniques can be employed to capture a user's requirements for a system and whole texts are devoted to this issue (for example, see Maciaszek, 2007; Robertson and Robertson, 2006). The outcome from this stage of the process is a series of documents that clearly define what the software system is required to do (but **not** how it should do it – that is the purpose of *design*). These documents should be produced in the following order:

1. Requirements definition
2. Requirements specification
3. Functional specification

You would probably not produce all these documents separately as part of your own project but may be required to produce a single *requirements report* or *system specification* that encompasses the essence of each of these. Some institutions, for example, require students to produce a formal requirements report that must be approved (perhaps by an examining committee) before the student is allowed to continue with their project.

Figure 6.2 shows the conventional process of requirements capture (we will discuss the Time/Problem ovals later). Stages in ovals can, theoretically, be represented unambiguously. Stages in 'clouds' cannot be clearly specified and represent qualitative understanding or subjective documentation that contain ambiguities, contradictions or unclear statements.

In Figure 6.2 we begin on the left-hand side with a problem that needs resolving. While the user's understanding of this problem is subjective (they may not fully understand the problem or all its corresponding issues), the problem itself is, in reality, unambiguous. Unfortunately, the user is our only link to this problem – they are the 'experts' in this area. As their understanding of the problem is not perfect (notice the *user understanding* 'cloud' in Figure 6.2) we will be developing a system on incomplete or ambiguous knowledge. The analyst attempts, with the user, to define the problem and produce a preliminary definition of the user's requirements – what they require of the system. This stage of the process results in a *Requirements Definition* that is written in the user's terms – usually in natural language (i.e., English). Because this document

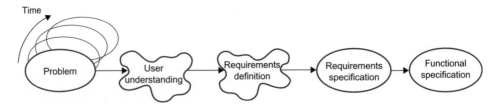

Figure 6.2 The conventional stages of requirements capture

is written with the user and is based on their incomplete understanding of the problem it is likely to contain contradictions and ambiguities and hence it is also represented by a cloud in Figure 6.2. It is also possible, even with a single user, that the requirements definition can contain conflicting requirements even at this stage.

The analyst must then take this document and rewrite it unambiguously to produce a *Requirements Specification*. This is a much more formal, structured document that is not open to interpretation – hence the oval in Figure 6.2. It forms a basis for a contract between the client and software developers and, consequently, it is important that it is properly and professionally produced. It states what the user is expecting the system to do.

Having identified the requirements for the system with the requirements specification it is now the job of the analyst to specify **one** system that will satisfy these requirements – the *Functional Specification*. This document usually contains an introduction, a rationale for the system, project objectives, *functional* requirements and *non-functional* requirements. Functional requirements state what the system is required to do and the data and user-interface requirements. Non-functional requirements refer to various constraints, standards, limitations (costs, delivery dates, configuration, language, resources, etc.), performance requirements, verification requirements (that ensure conformance with the system specification) and validation criteria (which form a basis for system testing after the system has been written and tested). You should be clear in your own mind as to the difference between functional and non-functional requirements as this will help you to understand how your project has fulfilled these requirements when it is complete. The functional specification should be an unambiguous document that states exactly what the system will do.

6.2.3 Design

Having decided what the system is supposed to do during requirements capture, it is now time to decide exactly how the system will achieve this. This is the purpose of design. Design works on a number of levels and a number of issues. For example, systems can be designed as a series of modules (or objects) that are gradually brought together to produce a fully working system. Design can include flowcharts and pseudo-code that plan how certain functions within the program will operate. Object-oriented design techniques (for example, UML) can be used to build systems from a series of objects. Design can also encompass interface issues – human computer interaction (HCI), screen layouts, navigation between screens, and story boards. Design might include database design – for example, structuring data tables using *Normalisation* techniques or *Entity Relationship* modelling. You should consult with your supervisor over the most appropriate design techniques to use for your project.

6.2.4 Build

Build simply represents the coding and construction (bringing together the individual modules or objects) of the software system. How this is achieved depends largely on the programming language(s) used, the design methods used and any coding standards and quality standards you might be following.

6.2.5 Test

This is the final testing of the system as it is brought together into a working whole. Testing is discussed in more detail in Section 6.12.

6.2.6 Implementation

The final stage of the SDLC is implementation. This represents the final hand-over of the system to the user. It can include acceptance testing by the user, it will invariably involve training, it might involve a formal handover, the setting up of data files, implementing new work procedures, documentation and so on. In this stage of the process *change management* is particularly important. This can also include overcoming resistance to change and data migration issues, etc.

Having introduced a generic model showing the broad stages through which all software systems develop, we will now look more closely at specific models you can use and adapt for your own project.

● 6.3 The earliest 'model': build-and-fix

As we saw earlier, in the pioneering days of software development there was no recognised process for developing software. Programmers merely attempted to grasp an understanding of the problem as best they could and 'cobbled together' some code to address this problem. The *build-and-fix* or *code-and-fix* 'model' represents this early approach to the development of software. It is not a formal model as such, but a representation of a simple approach to *hacking* code together. There is no formal requirements capture in the process and no formal design. Programmers would first write some code, run the code and then correct any bugs in the software (see Figure 6.3). In this case there is no formal breakdown of the process into stages. The model merely iterates until the software becomes unworkable and is eventually retired and/or replaced. Turner (1993: 470) identified a number of issues with this 'model':

- After several fixes the software becomes difficult to maintain as it becomes poorly structured.
- It often does not match the user's requirements – it is rejected or requires extensive redevelopment.

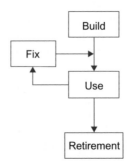

Figure 6.3 The build-and-fix 'model'

- It can be costly to maintain because of its poor structure and lack of definable output that can be tested.

Although the build-and-fix approach is still used today by many programmers working on small and personal systems, you should not be using it for your project. You should, instead, look to one of the more defined and recognised processes outlined in the following sections.

6.4 The stage-wise and classical waterfall models (conventional models)

Because of the problems encountered with the unstructured approach of the build-and-fix model, several more detailed models were devised. The earliest of these models was the *stage-wise* model from which the *classical waterfall* model developed.

The stage-wise model was developed in 1956 by Benington in an attempt to provide an engineering process to the development of software. It represents a unidirectional, sequential process – once a stage has been completed, the results of that stage become a fixed baseline from which the following stages develop – there is no revision. While this appears to be rather rigid and naïve, the development of a defined process at that time was a significant breakthrough in software engineering.

It was soon recognised, however, that the sequential nature of the stage-wise model was causing problems and some form of reworking was required in order to allow a user's needs to be addressed more effectively. For this reason the *classical waterfall* model was developed – shown in Figure 6.4. The *classical waterfall* model differed

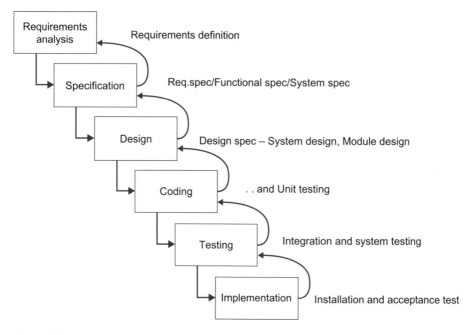

Figure 6.4 The classical waterfall model

from the stage-wise model in that it allowed some limited iteration between stages – shown as 'splashing back' in Figure 6.4.

Figure 6.2 highlights one of the main problems with the conventional waterfall-type approaches. As we move through the stages of the process the problem we are trying to solve is not static and moves on (shown by the shifting problem ovals with respect to time in Figure 6.2). Thus, by the time we complete our analysis, design and building of the software system, the program we present to our user no longer solves the problem they currently have – i.e., the software is already obsolete. Another problem is that the user's understanding of the problem is unclear and there are ambiguities in the subsequent requirements specification. We cannot then guarantee that the system we design and develop is matching the user's needs at all. The conventional approach to software development is, therefore, only really appropriate for projects that are:

- short (say six months to one year maximum – a typical student project length) so that the problem does not have time to evolve; and
- understood clearly – so that the initial requirements are captured accurately and subsequent specifications and designs are very close matches with what is actually needed.

You should, therefore, only use this approach for your own project if you are confident that you fully understand the requirements of the system or they have already been provided to you in an unambiguous way by the client. In most cases we cannot guarantee to fully understand the needs of our user – in which case one of the following approaches is perhaps more suitable for you to follow.

● 6.5 The incremental model

Rather than delivering your software to your client towards the end of your project in one 'big bang' as the conventional models do, it might be better to deliver the system to them as a series of intermediate working sub-systems over a period of time. Thus, you add more functionality to the software at each release of the system. This means that you need to get an overall software structure (*kernel*) in place as part of the first release of your system. The other parts of the system are then brought on-line and released to the user as the system is developed. Thus, each release to the user provides added functionality to the existing system. In a project lasting around six months you would not really expect to have more than three releases.

Figure 6.5 (adapted from Ould, 1999) illustrates the incremental model – in this case there are three incremental releases for the system. Notice that the requirements for the system are gathered in the usual way at the start of this process. You then design and prepare the first release of the system. This includes a kernel for your program and the first component of functionality that will be useful to the client. The second phase of the process involves designing the second increment of the system and developing and implementing this within the existing system. This process continues until all the increments have been completed and the system is fully working.

Figure 6.5 also highlights two other aspects of the incremental approach. The first point to note is that the design stages of the later increments are not as detailed as the design stage of the first incremental release. This is because the first increment of

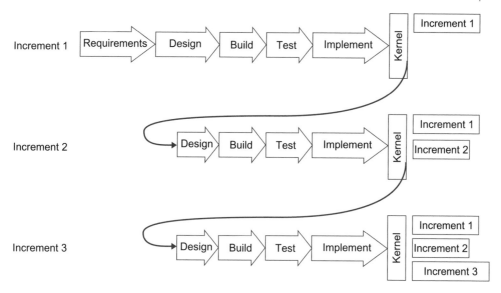

Figure 6.5 The incremental model
Source: Adapted from Ould (1999).

the system must also include the design of the all important system kernel (structure). Subsequent releases just need to focus on the individual increments and hence the design stage of these increments is reduced. The second important point to notice is that the increments are not all the same size – some will add more functionality to the system than others, and some will be harder to produce than others. Consequently, the design, build, test and implement stages of each increment may not be the same size.

When planning to undertake an incremental development it is important to have an outline plan in place for the entire system at the start. You cannot just plan the easiest parts of the system, develop and release these to the user, and worry about the more complex aspects of the system later. It may be that later, as you tackle the harder parts of the development, you discover a fundamental flaw with your ideas that require you to rework significant parts of your program. This would mean that earlier, easier work that you did on your project would be wasted. You must ensure that you have a good understanding of how the overall system will operate before beginning work on the intermediate releases.

When deciding which increment to complete next in a development it is useful to draw up a table of *value to cost ratios*. Value represents, on a 1-to-10 scale, the usefulness this increment will add to your system; 10 being extremely useful (if not essential), while 1 represents perhaps 'nice to have' features that will be good to include in the system if time allows. Cost is also measured on a 1-to-10 scale and can be measured in terms of the time it will take you to develop that feature. For example, some functionality that you estimate will take 15 weeks to design, program and test may be assigned a cost value of 10, whereas a simple piece of functionality that may only take a day's programming may be assigned a cost value of 1.

While these estimates of values and costs are subjective, they do provide you with a relative measure of the importance and effort required for adding certain aspects of functionality to your system. By dividing the value of the increment by its estimated cost (the value to cost ratio) you can determine the added value that increment will provide to your system and draw up a priority list – identifying the order in which the increments should be tackled. Note that estimated costs and values do not remain static as the project progresses and after each increment is released it is worth revisiting your cost and value estimates to determine if any changes need to be made. For example, having developed part of the system in one release your understanding of the coding involved may have improved and you might wish to revise down some other developments costs (particularly if you can reuse some code). Conversely, having completed an increment, you might realise that your cost estimates were too low and revise up the remaining estimates accordingly. Having provided the user with another release they might have new ideas or change their mind on what aspects of the system are important to them. This may result in you having to readjust your value estimates and change your prioritise accordingly. The second example below provides an outline of how value to cost ratios might work in practice.

Example 1 – Two increments

Suppose you were developing a system for a user that logged and statistically analysed calls to a help desk. You might release this system to the user in two increments during the course of your project. The first release would provide the overall structure for the system and would allow the user to log calls to the help desk. The second release would provide the added functionality of the statistical analysis of the logged calls (for example, identifying peak periods, common problems, regular callers, etc.). Thus, by providing the user with a partially working system early, it allows them to become familiar with the system's operation before the added complexities of the analysis component are brought online. The first release would also enable them to start gathering data into the system earlier – data that would otherwise have been lost had they waited for a fully working system later on. This also means that you can check that the right information is being gathered by the system for subsequent analysis by the second release.

Example 2 – Multiple increments

Table 6.1 provides an example of a value/cost table for a student project that aimed to develop a simple web site to support a local, amateur football club. The club wanted to keep members and potential members informed of various aspects of the club including: match fixtures; results; important dates (presentation evenings, etc.); duty rotas (who was responsible for cutting the grass, assisting the referee on match days, etc.); contact details for the club committee and other officials; photograph

Example 2 (*continued*)

album (players, trips, matches, etc.); information about the club (joining fees, training days, etc.); and a feedback/discussion section. After interviewing the client the student was able to prioritise each of these requirements according to their value on a 1-to-10 scale. For example, having an attractive home page was identified as the most important feature of the site and was assigned a 'value' value of 10. Having a photographs section was deemed least important and this was assigned as 'value' value of 4. The student then estimated how long each of these requirements would take to develop and produced a cost scale. In this case the student estimated that setting up a discussion forum on the web site would take the most effort (needing to develop a database in the background to store comments and link threads together) and consequently assigned this an effort score of 8. Conversely, setting up a page with contact details for club officials would be relatively easy and this was assigned an effort score of 4. The resulting Value-Cost table is shown in Table 6.1.

Once the student calculated the value-to-cost ratios, she was able to prioritise the order of the development shown in the last column of the table. The student worked on the home/main page first, getting an overall structure in place and showing this to the client. With a few minor changes and suggestions from the client, the student then went on to design and develop the club information page and so on. By prioritising the release of the system in this way, the student ensured that only those additions valuable to the site were implemented in order. It reduces the chances of 'gold plating' (adding features to a system that cost a lot of effort for very little reward) unless time allows. If the student ran out of time on the project they would at least have added a number of useful features to the system. Any features not included may be identified as future work/enhancements.

Functional Increment	Value	Cost	V/C Ratio	Priority
Home/main page	10	5	2.0	1
Match fixtures page	8	6	1.3	4=
Results page	6	6	1.0	7
Diary/dates page	7	6	1.2	6
Duty rota page	8	6	1.3	4=
Comments/feedback page	5	8	0.6	8
Committee contact details	6	4	1.5	3
Photographs	4	8	0.5	8
Club information page	8	5	1.6	2

Table 6.1 A value/cost ratio table for an amateur football club web site development

Advantages

- The user gets something early so that they can get an idea of the system's capabilities and an idea of what you are able to produce in the longer term for them. Thus, the user/client can provide early feedback if something isn't right or improvements can be made. This is particularly useful if the system requirements were not entirely clear at the project's outset.

- By delivering something early it gives you a sense of achievement and the user/client a clear understanding that progress is being made.

- It can help you plan and manage your project more effectively. By breaking the project down into a number of deliverables, you will be able to plan, reasonably accurately, how long each deliverable should take to develop. In addition, when you are controlling your project, any slippage in meeting a deliverable will provide an early warning that your project may be falling behind schedule and you will be able to do something about it.

- The user does not need to learn how to use the entire system in one go. They can be introduced to the system over a period of time, becoming confident with its functionality before later releases add to its complexity.

Disadvantages

- It might be difficult to break your program down into a series of sub-systems that are worth delivering to the client/user as separate units. For example, you don't want to end up providing a large number of small deliverables to the user that appear to provide little improvement over earlier releases. This wastes your time and can lead the user to think that you are making little progress and wasting their time too.

- Although it is advantageous to meet your user/client regularly, additional contact with them can encourage them to identify *too* many improvements. They may identify more changes than you have time to implement and the changes they request may take your project in a direction that is inconsistent with the requirements of your course.

● 6.6 Prototyping

6.6.1 Introduction

The *conventional* and *incremental* models that have been introduced can be used in projects where the problem is well defined, the requirements can be clearly elicited and defined, and the technical feasibility of a solution is understood. However, in many projects it is often difficult to pin down exactly what is required from a software system at the start of the project and/or we may not have a clear understanding of the technical issues surrounding that system. This is often the case in student projects where they are working with a supervisor or client for the first time, perhaps in a new field or in a developing research area. In these cases it is useful to produce a prototype in order to:

1. explore the requirements of the system with the user – *requirements capture,* and/or
2. explore the technical feasibility of a system – *experimental prototyping.*

1. Requirements capture

During requirements capture, a prototype is used to pin down and refine a user's requirements for the system. It can also be used during design to test the user interface – assessing how well the user can use and navigate around the system. According to Knott and Dawson (1999: 42), 'Prototyping provides an effective method for generating feedback about what is good and what is bad about an idea and it is often the only really effective method for doing this'.

2. Experimental prototyping

Experimental prototyping is used when one is unsure about the technical solution to a problem. For example, if you are developing a new algorithm, working in an emerging field, working on a new hardware platform, or using a new application or programming language, it is often useful to produce an experimental prototype to assess the feasibility of your proposed solution. You might discover, for example, that you will need to re-design your proposed solution because it is inefficient and runs too slowly, or you might discover that your assumptions about the system were incorrect and an alternative strategy needs to be undertaken. Alternatively you may discover you don't have the technical ability to use the programming language or the hardware platform or software application you are intending to employ.

There are two things you can do with a prototype once you have developed it. You can throw it away and start the development of the system from scratch (*throw-away prototyping*), or you can develop (evolve) the prototype into the final system (*evolutionary prototyping*). These two approaches to prototyping are discussed in the following sections.

6.6.2 Throw-away prototyping

There are a number of approaches you can use to develop a throw-away prototype, depending on what you want to achieve, explore with the user or experiment with. The following are some ideas you might want to use in developing your own throw-away prototype.

■ The prototype need not be developed on the same hardware platform as the final system. For example, you could mock-up some sample screen designs using a word-processor or drawing package. If you were going to develop a system for a Pocket PC or a mobile telephone, you might develop a mock-up using an emulator on a PC first.

■ You might develop a prototype in a different programming language. For example, if you wanted to develop an experimental prototype to evaluate a new algorithm you might test out that algorithm by developing it quickly in C first. You might then throw this code away before re-coding the final system with a graphical user interface in Visual C++™. Alternatively, you could develop a user interface for a multimedia product using a web-page editor.

Knott and Dawson (1999) discuss the following techniques for [throw-away] prototyping:

■ You could simplify the system by partitioning the program such that a prototype could be built for part of that system. For example, you could prototype the graphical user interface first, leaving the underlying functionality until later.

- Use a reduced database. You could quickly generate a test database for a system to provide an idea of how that system operates on particular data sets.

- You can develop a much simpler version of the program that has simplified data handling and error checking – sacrificing quality and reliability. As the prototype is merely intended to show the user what will happen when the right or wrong input is used, it need only handle one example of each for demonstration purposes.

- You could use a modified version of another program or another system to illustrate your ideas. For example, if there is a commercial product that has some components that you wish to incorporate into your own system, you could demonstrate this to your user and check what aspects of functionality they require (and the type of interface they prefer).

Advantages

Throw-away prototyping has a number of advantages over conventional approaches. Knott and Dawson (1999) note the following:

- Something tangible is produced quickly which keeps you and your user happy.

- The tangible nature of the system helps the user to clarify their ideas and refine their requirements.

- Misunderstandings, errors and omissions in the requirements can be sorted out.

- It improves communication with the user. It is easier to look at a working model than a document.

- The prototype can test the feasibility and usefulness of the product.

- Alternatives can be compared using different prototypes.

Disadvantages (things to be aware of)

- The throw-away prototype might look messy and unsophisticated and contain bugs. This might give a bad impression to the user.

- The user might think your prototype is really good and may want you to develop it into the final system, even though you had intended to throw it away. As a consequence you will end up building your final system on perhaps poorly structured code.

- If you develop the throw-away prototype on a different system or in a different programming language you may not spot a technical issue that will be difficult/impossible to overcome on the target system.

It can take a lot of effort and commitment to develop something that you are eventually going to discard. For this reason students often prefer to use an *evolutionary prototyping* approach to develop their systems. This approach is discussed in the following section.

6.6.3 Evolutionary prototyping

The evolutionary prototyping approach differs from the throw-away approach in that the prototype is not discarded but developed (it evolves) into the final product. At first glance it might appear similar to the build-and-fix approach – something is built, assessed and modified until the final system is released. However, the evolutionary approach is

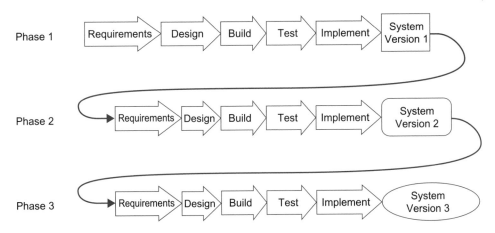

Figure 6.6 The evolutionary prototyping model
Source: Adapted from Ould (1999).

much more defined than the build-and-fix approach. An initial specification for the system must be investigated and produced, and the process must follow a planned series of releases (evolutions). You are also aware from the start that your program is going to evolve so it must be designed and structured logically from the outset with suitable comments, variables, data structures and so on. This will ensure that changes can be incorporated 'gracefully' and you are not left with masses of 'spaghetti code' that you have to unravel to make simple modifications.

Figure 6.6 (adapted from Ould, 1999) illustrates the evolutionary process – in this case showing three releases of a system. Notice that you complete a preliminary requirements capture for the system and pursue the remaining stages of the conventional process in order to develop the first prototype (System Version 1). This works in much the same way as a reduced version of a conventional waterfall-type approach. Following feedback on what is right, wrong or missing and could be improved or changed from the user on this prototype, you can then go back and readdress/adjust the requirements before developing (evolving) the second deliverable of the system (System Version 2). In this way the system is seen to evolve from an embryonic core into the final system. You might decide to focus each deliverable on different aspects of the system, investigating each component in turn, in a similar fashion to the incremental approach. However, in this case you are explicitly looking to change the requirements and design of the system based on user feedback. The requirements and design stages in Figure 6.6 are not as big (as detailed) in phases 2 and 3 of the process compared with phase 1 as the bulk of this work has been done during that first phase. Also, the system is getting larger as it evolves in phases 2 and 3 and its functionality increases. Note that the evolutionary approach is sometimes referred to as *iterative development*.

The advantages and disadvantages of the evolutionary prototyping approach are similar to those of the throw-away prototyping approach. However, in the evolutionary model you do not lose code you may have spent a lot of effort developing. Contrary to the throw-away approach you must be careful to produce well structured and commented code that can be evolved into the final system. This means that your first prototype must be well thought out and cannot be a 'quick and dirty' throw-away artefact.

● 6.7 Agile methods

The term *agile methods* was adopted in 2001 by a group of eminent software engineers at a meeting in Utah, USA. It refers to approaches to software development that reduce risk by delivering software systems in short bursts or releases. In contrast to 'heavy weight' development approaches, such as the Waterfall Model (in which the delivery of a working system can take many months, if not years to be released), the concept behind agile methods is to release working systems to the user in a matter of weeks. Although each iteration might not release a fully working system to the user at the end of each cycle, the aim is still to have an available release at the end of each iteration. The evolutionary prototyping approach and incremental model introduced in the previous sections are, from a process point of view, agile methods.

The other main characteristics of agile methods that differentiate them from older, more conventional models include: their emphasis on smaller development teams (which are invariable working together in open plan offices); and face-to-face communication with the users who are quite often based in the same working environment as the developers.

Agile methods are well suited to projects that have unclear or rapidly changing requirements; the project team is fairly small but highly competent and can be trusted; and close interaction with the user must be possible.

A number of key principles were established by the founding group – referred to as the *agile manifesto* (see http://www.agilemanifesto.org). These principles include:

■ satisfying the customer through early and continuous delivery of valuable software;
■ welcoming changing requirements;
■ short iterative timescale of weeks;
■ close working relationship between developers and users;
■ face-to-face conversations rather than detailed documentation;
■ working software is the measure of progress;
■ teams are self-organizing;
■ teams reflect on how they might improve themselves regularly.

Because of the reduced amount of documentation agile methods produce, they have come in for some criticism. However, for smaller projects (student projects, for example) the principles can lead to the development of software that goes a long way to meeting the users' requirements.

● 6.8 Extreme programming (XP)

Extreme programming is a software development approach that encompasses many of the ideals of agile methods. It was introduced in the 1990s in an attempt to improve the way in which software is developed. It is designed for teams of between two and 12 members, so it is ideally suited for student projects. For more information on this method you should refer to the Extreme Programming web site at: http://www.extremeprogramming.org/.

Extreme programming is an approach that is well suited to projects in which the requirements are likely to change. The approach actively encourages the users to be involved with the development process and anticipates the positive influence they will have on requirements capture. It emphasizes teamwork and, in the case of student projects, encourages the users, supervisor(s) and the project team to work together towards a common goal of developing quality software. According to Wells (2006), extreme programming 'improves a software project in four essential ways; communication, simplicity, feedback and courage'. One of its principles is to deliver the software early, obtain feedback on the system and implement any required changes. In some ways the approach is similar to that of *evolutionary prototyping* although there is much more guidance on how the team should work together and how testing should be pre-planned than is provided by the evolutionary model.

Although the detail of this approach's methodology is beyond the scope of this book, some if its guiding principles are worth remembering; involve the user in the project, pre-plan testing before coding, deliver the system early and ensure strong communication between all stakeholders.

● 6.9 Configuration management

One thing that you must be careful to control when pursuing an evolutionary or incremental approach, or in a team project when a number of people are working on different parts of the system simultaneously, is the system's *configuration*. Configuration management is used to control the different versions of a system that are produced as the system develops. It is closely related to *version control* and *revision control*. In large industrial projects configuration management is an important activity and typically involves four stages:

1. **Configuration identification:** identifying the attributes that define the item you are hoping to control – what makes it as it is – and setting this as a baseline.

2. **Change control:** managing and approving changes to the item and adjusting the baseline.

3. **Status accounting:** recording the configuration baselines.

4. **Configuration audits:** ensuring that changes to configuration do what they state they will do and the system continues to satisfy the requirements (it does not drift).

For student projects a comprehensive configuration management system is unnecessary. However, as you develop and release new versions of the system you must make sure that you keep track of these versions; what changes have been made, who has made these changes, who has received them, where they are saved/backed-up to, etc. If something goes wrong with a 'release' it is useful to be able to go back to the previous version to try to determine what has gone wrong. Make sure that you date stamp each version of the program that you produce (no matter how small the change that is made) – perhaps by including the date on a splash screen or main menu. You might also consider updating the version number too (particularly for major changes). This will allow you to keep track of the latest version of your system and, as you make frequent back-ups, which back-up is the most up-to-date. Also, for team projects, keep a note of which team members are working on which parts of the system and consider these questions – will these parts integrate seamlessly? Do you need to define certain coding standards that everyone must adhere to? What are the likely effects of one part of the system on another when they are merged?

If configuration management is going to be an important part of your project it may be worth considering using a software tool to support this. An example of such a tool is TortoiseSVN (see http://tortoisesvn.tigris.org), which is free. Running under Windows, TortoiseSVN is a version control system that works with any development tool. It can also be used for document control so can be useful when trying to piece together a final report when working on a group project and each team member is working on a different part of the report.

● 6.10 Which approaches should I use?

6.10.1 Which development approach should I use?

In the majority of projects that I supervise, the students tend to follow an evolutionary prototyping approach for their software developments. For a six-month project starting in October, I usually recommend that students provide their client with (and get feedback on) a prototype before Christmas (i.e., within two to three months of the start). This allows them to consider any revisions, modifications and changes to their system over the Christmas break. In these cases, the students usually end up providing no more than two evolutionary prototypes to their clients before the final deliverable is released. However, some projects do follow a conventional model while others use incremental or throw-away prototyping approaches. So which is best to use?

The following provides some guidance on which model is suitable in which circumstances. You should discuss these options with your supervisor and choose what is right for you. You may, as part of your project report, be expected to justify and evaluate the process model you used, so make sure you choose an appropriate one. (Some of the following advice was adapted from LevelA Software [2005].)

Conventional waterfall-type model

This is well-suited to projects that have a low risk in areas such as the user interface and performance, but a high risk in terms of schedule and control. It is useful in projects where the requirements are understood clearly by all involved and are unlikely to change during the course of the project. An example would be a specification provided by your supervisor that requires implementation.

Incremental development

This is appropriate for systems in which the requirements are generally clear and the system can be partitioned into a series of intermediate deliverables. It is preferable to the conventional approach in that it provides some user involvement and it can also be 'terminated' at any time yet still leave the user with a partially working system.

However, if the user is difficult to contact and you can only arrange one or two meetings with them, the conventional waterfall-type model may have to be used.

Throw-away prototyping model

This is useful for 'proof of concept' situations, exploring technical uncertainties, or in situations where requirements and user's needs are unclear or poorly specified.

Evolutionary prototyping model

This is useful in projects that have a high risk in terms of the user interface design and uncertainties in user requirements. It is perhaps more appropriate than a throw-away prototype in situations where the programming language and target system are well-understood by the student.

Hughes and Cotterell (2006: 89) provide the following rules-of-thumb in selecting process models (adapted):

- If uncertainty is high then use an evolutionary approach or throw-away prototyping approach.
- If complexity is high but uncertainty is low then use the incremental approach.
- If uncertainty and complexity are both low then use the conventional waterfall-type model.
- If the schedule is tight then use a conventional or incremental approach.

Davis *et al.* (1988) provide a useful technique for comparing development models – the *Functionality-Time graph*. Discussion of this technique is beyond the scope of this book. However, it does provide a useful means of comparing models by showing how they provide functionality to the user and how systems meet the user's needs as time progresses – from the time the project is started to the retirement of the system.

6.10.2 Which programming language should I use?

Unfortunately, there is no simple answer to this question since the choice of which programming language to use in your project depends, not only on the application you are developing, but on a number of other issues too. Students are often concerned that their choice of programming language will have a significant impact on the marks they can obtain for their project. However, providing they use a language that is 'suitable', and this suitability can be **justified** within their report, this should only improve the marks they obtain. For students on software engineering and computer science-type courses, a question sometimes asked is whether good marks can be obtained if an 'easy' language is used (a fourth generation language, for example) instead of one more technically challenging. In these cases it is still advisable to use the programming language that is best suited to the task in hand. There is no point in making the software development more difficult than it needs to be just to 'show off' your technical programming skills. It would be far better to produce a fully working system using a more appropriate language in less time, thereby allowing you to develop other academic aspects of your project in more depth.

The choice of programming languages available these days is quite breathtaking. Languages have evolved from first and second generation languages such as Assembler; through third generation languages such as Pascal, C, C++ and Fortran; to fourth generation languages such as Visual Studio and Delphi. Not only can you view languages from this 'generational' point of view, but you could also class languages according to whether they are *object oriented* or *procedural* in nature. Object oriented languages, such as Java and C++, encourage code reuse, while procedural programming languages are perhaps well suited to the implementation of sequenced algorithms.

Deciding on which language to use is primarily based around who the client/user of the system will be and the platform on which the system will be based. For example, if you are developing a simple application for your own use (to test out an idea or process some data, say) you may decide to 'knock something together' quickly in your preferred language. However, if you are developing a system for a client or a number of users, you will need to consider more deeply the language you will use. While your supervisor should provide you with some guidance in this area, it is worth considering the following list of factors that you should take into account when making your decision:

■ What languages do I already know – how good am I at programming using those languages?

■ Are there any languages I would like to learn as part of my project?

■ What language(s) does my supervisor use – will I need a lot of technical support from him/her?

■ What languages are supported by my department or others within my institution? If I develop a system using a language that is not supported by my own department, will I be penalised if things go wrong? If things do go wrong with a language that is supported by my department, and my project goes badly as a result, who will be responsible?

■ If I need to get technical help or support, is it readily available (for example, either locally or via the Internet)?

■ Are there any language requirements imposed on my project by the client/user?

■ What languages are supported by the client/user?

■ How much does the nature of the system I am developing affect the choice of language?

If there is no single language that emerges as an obvious choice for your project (for example, as specified by the client in the requirements) it would be worth considering the languages available to you as part of your literature review. A systematic approach to language selection might include a *comparison table*. This table allows you to evaluate the alternatives on offer and grade them according to appropriate criteria such as *maintainability, support, HCI capability, database connectivity* and so on. An example of such a table is presented in Table 6.2 in which four languages are assessed. In this table the *weighting* relates to the importance of each criterion for this particular project on a scale of 1 to 5 (1 being the least important). For example, in this particular project the interface requirements are a particularly important and so *HCI capability* (Human Computer Interaction) is given a weighting of 5; the importance of learning a new language (*learning*) is felt to be of little importance in this case so this has been given a weighting score of 1. For your own project you may weight these criteria differently and may well choose other criteria that are appropriate. The values that are

		Language			
Criteria	Weighting	A	B	C	D
Maintainability	2	3	4	3	4
Support	4	4	5	4	4
HCI capability	5	5	3	5	3
Database connectivity	4	4	3	3	3
Simplicity	4	3	4	3	5
Learning	1	4	5	2	2
Score	–	79	76	73	73

Table 6.2 Example comparison table evaluating overall suitability of programming languages for a project

then awarded to each language are subjective estimates of how each language meets the criteria specified (again on a scale of 1 to 5). For example, in this case it is felt that language A has an average rating for *maintainability* and is thus assigned a value of 3 in the table. The overall scores for each language are then calculated by multiplying each language's criterion score by the associated weighting, and summing them. This score provides us with a *relative* measure that we can use to compare each language. In this example, language A has the highest overall score and we may, therefore, justify choosing this language for our project based on this comparison. Be aware, however, that by reducing the comparison of programming languages to a simple table such as this may mean that other important aspects are overlooked. You should, therefore, justify your choice of programming language in more depth, using a table like this to support your arguments.

 ## 6.11 Top-down and bottom-up development

6.11.1 Introduction

If you are producing a conventional software system with a number of components (for example, modules, functions, screens) that can be broken down into lower levels of detail, you will have to decide whether to use a top-down or bottom-up approach for the development. These development approaches are applicable to third-generation languages (where the software may be constructed with a number of functions, subroutines or procedures), fourth-generation languages, web-based applications and multimedia applications (all of which could be broken down into different levels of screens and sub-screens from different menus). Figure 6.7, which is an example program breakdown structure, helps to illustrate the difference between these two techniques in the following sections. The program in Figure 6.7 is a data handling system that generates long- and short-term statistical results from a data set selected by the user.

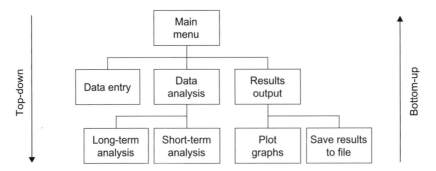

Figure 6.7 An example program breakdown structure

6.11.2 Top-down development

In a top-down approach you work your way down through the program structure, coding successively lower level modules of the program until the entire system is complete. You can achieve this in one of two ways – *vertically* or *horizontally*. In vertical top-down development you work down each branch as far as you can go before moving back up through the structure and working your way down again. In Figure 6.7, a vertical top-down approach would lead you to code the modules in the order shown in Table 6.3.

Horizontal top-down development involves progressively coding an entire level of the system before moving down to the next level and so on. Table 6.3 shows how the modules would be coded in the example program shown in Figure 6.7.

Vertical top-down development attempts to get particular components of the system working early rather than providing an overall working system. For example, in Figure 6.7, we would have the *Data Analysis* section of the system in place before any work on the *Results Output* section was even started. A horizontal top-down approach would test the look and feel of the system, only adding in lower detail when an entire layer of functionality was completed. In Figure 6.7 we would get an idea of how the *Main Menu* worked and how the three main options (*Data Entry, Data Analysis* and *Results Output*) would look, even though they would not actually work, before we began work on the lower working levels.

Order	Vertical top-down	Horizontal top-down	Bottom-up
1	Main Menu	Main Menu	Long-Term Analysis
2	Data Entry	Data Entry	Short-Term Analysis
3	Data Analysis	Data Analysis	Plot Graphs
4	Long-Term Analysis	Results Output	Save Results to File
5	Short-Term Analysis	Long-Term Analysis	Data Entry
6	Results Output	Short-Term Analysis	Data Analysis
7	Plot Graphs	Plot Graphs	Results Output
8	Save Results to File	Save Results to File	Main Menu

Table 6.3 Order of development for different approaches for example program shown in Figure 6.7

In order to test your system as you proceed with a top-down approach, you would have to develop a number of *stubs* in order to replicate the behaviour of lower level components of the program before they are actually written. According to Knott and Dawson (1999: 162), a stub can be:

- a dummy routine that simply returns, doing nothing;
- a routine that simulates the behaviour of a module by returning constant values; or
- a routine that simulates a module by asking the user to input suitable return values.

The advantages of using a top-down approach are that a working version of the system is produced quickly, enabling the user to get an idea of the overall look-and-feel of the system. In addition, by providing a working system early the user can spot any serious omissions in the top level design of the system. However, there are some drawbacks to this approach. First, some of the 'difficult' components of the system will probably be at the lower levels. Leaving these until later may prove costly if they lead to problems that are difficult to overcome. Second, as lower levels are often concerned with data input and output it may not be possible to get a feel of how the system is working until these components are written and the system is able to handle appropriate data.

6.11.3 Bottom-up development

The bottom-up approach is the opposite of the top-down approach in that you begin by coding the lowest levels first before bringing these components together to produce the fully working system. For example, in the case of Figure 6.7, you might begin by working on the Long-Term Analysis component of the system first. This may involve the development and implementation of a complex algorithm so you might want to ensure that you can get this working sooner rather than later in your project. You will probably understand that the higher level components (for example, the Main Menu) will be easy to complete, so it would make sense to tackle the harder parts of the system first rather than leave these until the end. Applying a bottom-up development approach to the program in Figure 6.7 results in coding the modules in the order shown in Table 6.3.

As you continue to build the lower-level components of your system, you need to consider how you will bring these together in the final system. This should be done incrementally, where the components are added to the system as they are completed and the system 'grows' over time. However, before a module is added to the system it should be tested in isolation to ensure that it behaves in the way it is intended. Quite often, developers will produce *test harnesses* – structures of code that enable lower level modules to be tested in isolation. However, these structures take time to write and you may be better coding higher levels of the system to act as harnesses to save time.

While the bottom-up approach enables you to test out the lower levels of detail in your program sooner, it does have a number of disadvantages. For example, there is no visible system until the end of the development when the higher levels are developed. This can mean that progress appears slow and may mean that any major design omissions are not spotted until near the end of the project when it is too late.

In theory, you could swap the implementation of some modules around and still be pursuing a particular top-down or bottom-up development approach. For example, there would be no harm in swapping over the implementation of Long-Term Analysis and

Short-Term Analysis. In this case, the Short-Term Analysis function may be more difficult to implement, so you might want to tackle this sooner in order to get it working. You will probably want to complete Data Entry before Data Analysis (although in theory they could be swapped in any approach) as you will want to have 'read in' some data to work with before you can implement and test the Data Analysis and its sub-functions. In practice you should mix and match the approach to the development you are undertaking. It may be appropriate, for example, to code some components from the bottom-up (to test out a difficult algorithm or routine) and then tackle the remainder of the system top-down (to provide the user with a tangible view of the system overall). Once again, whatever you decide to do, you should be able to justify this to your supervisor and examiners, and you may have to include some discussion on your chosen approach in your final report.

● 6.12 Verification, validation and testing

6.12.1 Introduction

There are three ways that you can deal with errors in your program:

1. **Prevent or avoid introducing them in the first place.** You achieve this through practice and experience, and following a development process such as those outlined earlier.

2. **You can detect and remove the errors.** You should hope to do this as early as possible as the longer errors remain in your code the greater the impact they will have and the greater effort will be required to remove them later when the code has grown even more. Verification, validation and testing (VV&T) are concerned with this issue.

3. **You can tolerate them.** There may be a certain level of quality that your client, user, supervisor and examiner are willing to accept or tolerate. You will know from your dealings with them what is acceptable and what is not. If a high level of quality is required it may be better to reduce the scope of your system in order to minimise the number of errors within it. However, if your user is demanding a high level of functionality, they may be willing to compromise a little on quality to get what they want. It is probably better to have an 80% functional system working 100% correctly than a 100% functional system working 80% correctly – the former appearing much more professional and robust. In addition, in the former case, the remaining 20% of functionality you have left out could always be identified as further work in your report (and the 20% of problems in the latter case may take a long time to sort out if the code is badly written). Discuss these alternatives with your supervisor and client so that an appropriate balance can be reached.

Of these three options, this section is concerned primarily with VV&T.

6.12.2 Verification

Verification is the process of checking that we are performing our development correctly. In other words, are we sticking to our project plan and are we performing the stages of the development process properly? For example, looking at the conventional waterfall model, verification involves checking that we are performing each of the stages correctly – by looking at what we know before a stage commences and whether (when we have completed that stage) that stage produces the things we would expect to the right level of quality. For example, after putting together our program's specification we would expect our design stage to produce an appropriate set of design documents based on this specification. Boehm (1979) summarizes verification as:

Are we building the product right?

You can use meetings with your supervisor to verify your development. For example, you may identify the completion of each stage in your development process as a milestone and use this as a verification point with your supervisor.

6.12.3 Validation

While verification checks that you are developing your system correctly, validation is checking to see if that system is really what the client/user needs at all. Referring back to Figure 6.2, you will remember that a user's problem is not stationary and will evolve over time as you undertake the project. Validation is concerned with re-visiting the requirements with your user at regular intervals and checking that you are still developing what your user needs. Certainly if the user was naïve or had limited understanding of the problem, validation becomes vitally important to ensure that you eventually deliver a system to them that solves their problem. In a similar definition as before, Boehm *(ibid.)* neatly summarizes validation as:

Are we building the right product?

Validation will also include a deeper evaluation of your system when it is finally completed. For example, you should, if possible, evaluate your system against other similar systems – how is yours better, worse, different? How does it compare with commercial software systems, freeware and others? How will your system improve things for the client/user – what impact do you see it having? Is your system developed from an existing system? If so, what enhancements does it include and what benefit are these to the user? Does your system include any innovative aspects – new algorithms, coding techniques, user interface designs – that can be applied in other areas?

These kinds of evaluation show that you are thinking much more deeply about your project. They provide your project with **academic** content – a deeper insight into the project than the mere writing of a piece of code.

6.12.4 Testing

Testing refers to the testing of the program itself to see if it works or has any bugs or errors within it. You can test your program as you go along, testing individual components before bringing these together into the whole system which must also be tested thoroughly. Testing can take place at a number of levels:

- *Unit testing* – of individual modules. You may have to build some form of program harness to test these sub-components.

- *Integration testing* – of sub-systems and the system as it is drawn together. Do the components of the system interact correctly?

- *System testing* – this is the final testing of the complete system against the specification and possibly the user manual.

- *Acceptance testing* – by the user/client with or without you present. They will be interested in how the system operates in its live environment, with real data and performing in real time under normal working pressures.

- *Regression testing* – involves testing the system after you have made significant changes to ensure that new bugs, not present in previously working parts of the system, have not crept in as a consequence of the change. Regression testing is particularly important when working on group projects where individual members of the team are developing different parts of the system. It is important to ensure that, as components are integrated and members of the team work on different parts of the system (perhaps not understanding how other programmers implemented certain parts of the system), new errors are not introduced and/or old bugs are not reintroduced.

You should test your code both *statically* and *dynamically*. Static testing does not involve running the program but inspecting the code (either on screen or a printed copy) or the designs, specifications or other documentation (for example, the user manual). This technique can be used to assess the content and level of comments in a program, the scope and declaration of variables, the overall structure of the program, how the program matches the design and the layout of the code (have you used tabs to indent statements, line breaks to separate different sections of the program?).

Dynamic testing involves running the program in order to identify any errors. In large software developments, dynamic testing involves *white-box* and *black-box* testing. White-box testing means you know how the code is programmed and structured so that you can test out potentially error-prone parts of the system. Black-box testing means that you only know what the program is supposed to do, not how it is programmed to do it. For your own program testing you will be undertaking white-box testing as you know how the program is structured. However, you may wish to involve others in black-box testing of your software if you feel this is appropriate.

Some useful tips for dynamic testing are presented below.

- **Create appropriate test data sets.** Try to create test data for your program that includes both extreme values and normal data. It may also be appropriate to generate test data that includes 'bad' data – i.e., data that the program would not normally be expected to handle (for example, text data instead of numeric data). How does your program cope with this? Does it need to deal with extremes or bad data, or can these anomalies be ignored (is the user ever likely to enter something like this?)?

  Your test data should include *boundary values* and *equivalence partitioning* can be used to minimise the size of test data sets. Boundary values are input values at the boundaries of what the system is expecting. For example, if the system is expecting an input between 1 and 10, the test data should include 0, 1, 10 and 11, as well as a number in between (5, for example). Equivalence partitioning splits the test data into categories (whatever might be appropriate) that represent different aspects of the data. You then need only test the program with one sample from each category rather than all the data.

- **Break points.** Many compilers allow you to insert break points into a program before it is run (alternatively you could code them in yourself). This allows you to run the program part-way and inspect the values of variables at certain points. If your program is crashing you can use break points to 'home in' on the guilty portion of code.

- **Dynamic data entry.** You may wish to see how changes to variables affect your program's performance. Some compilers allow you to stop programs and change the values of variables before continuing. Alternatively, you may wish to include some statements in your code that allow you to enter a variable's value part way through the program.

- **Displaying variables and markers.** You can add code to your program that informs you of the value of variables as the program is running and also how far the program has reached (for example, printf("here1") or writeln("here2")). This can be useful in tracking down faults or determining just how far a program has reached before crashing.

6.12.5 Who is involved with testing and evaluation?

Although you will be primarily involved with the testing of your own program, at some point you will need to get additional feedback on your program's performance. Not only are you interested in whether you have identified and removed any bugs, but you will also be interested in whether the system meets the user's needs, if the interface is appropriate, whether it flows logically, etc. You will need to get a number of people involved in the evaluation of your system and answer some of the following issues:

- **The user(s).** Is there going to be just one user of the system or many? If there are many, can you get an appropriate cross-section of users to look at your program and assess it? Will you be present during testing (known as *alpha* testing) or will you leave it to them to feed back their thoughts to you (*beta* testing)? Will you have a structured system test with them (where they look at specific parts of the system in order) or will you allow them just to 'play around' with the system as they feel fit? Are there specific parts of the system you want them to focus on? Will you gather feedback from them formally, through a questionnaire or interview, or informally?

- **The client.** Quite often the client and the user(s) of a system are not the same. For example, you may have developed a multi-media sales DVD for a company. While the company is your client, it is their (potential) customers who will be the users. In this case, can you get access to any potential users of the system for evaluation? If the client is happy does this mean the user will be happy? If the client wants one thing but you feel (know) that the user requires something else, who should you attempt to satisfy?

- **Novice.** It might be worth getting someone who is a complete novice (in terms of both IT and/or the problem area) to look at your system. They may identify issues you had never considered. For example, simple things like your colour-scheme or interface might be inappropriate; your system's data input may be illogical, etc.

- **Expert.** Will you be able to get someone who is very familiar with the problem area or the type of system you are developing to evaluate it? They can be very useful in identifying technical issues with your system. For example, they may ask you if you have anticipated particular inputs occurring or whether your system can handle rare events that you had not thought of.

■ **Your supervisor.** Is it appropriate to involve your supervisor in the assessment of your system?

■ **You.** There are some drawbacks to testing your system yourself. You know how the system works and may not test it with data you know it cannot handle because you could not imagine anyone being so stupid as to enter such data. You may steer away from parts of the system you know to be weak (consciously or subconsciously). However, it is up to you to evaluate certain parts of the system – particularly the validation of your system as noted in the previous section.

As you can see, a number of people can be drawn in to the evaluation of your system. You should ensure that you select an appropriate sub-set of these and be able to justify why you did not test the system with a certain group. For example, your examiners would be keen to know why you didn't get your multimedia DVD evaluated by potential users and only tested it on friends from your course.

All this evaluation will take time. You must make sure that when you plan your project you allow sufficient time for this evaluation to take place. Your project would be significantly weakened if such an evaluation did not take place.

6.12.6 Test plans

As part of your development you may well want to put together a **test plan.** This will identify what aspects of your program you are going to test, what inputs you are going to make, how you expect your system to perform and how it actually performs. You would also use test plans to separate out testing the functionality of the system (i.e., does the application behave as the client/user intended – validation) from testing for errors/bugs (for example, if I enter this value, does the software deal with it appropriately?).

Table 6.4 presents an example test plan for a student project. It is based on the simple project outline in Figure 6.7. This test plan shows that you have put some thought into your system's evaluation, the aspects that you feel are important, and not merely tested it 'on the fly' as the program developed.

The test plan shown in Table 6.4 may have too much or too little detail for your own purposes. For example, the tests for Data Analysis – Long-term are rather broad. You may want to identify specific periods, test data or selections within this. This test planning is more useful if you have designed it from the start of your development when the system requirements were drawn up. If you design your test plan at an early stage you are more likely to test that the system is doing what the user wants it to do rather than designing the tests to match what you have actually developed.

6.12.7 Miscellaneous testing types

The nature of your project may dictate that other factors are important and require additional types of testing:

■ **Volume testing.** Will your system be handling large quantities of data or processing lots of numbers? Your program may work well during testing with a small data set, producing the correct results, but can it cope with the larger data sets that it might

Section	Test Input	Expected Result	Actual Result	Comment
Main Menu	All option buttons	Correct sub-menu selected	Correct	
Data Entry	Back button	Return to Main Menu	Fault – jumps to splash entry screen	Corrected – 25/04/09
	File selection	Selects appropriate file and displays on screen	File selected but also shows file directory	User happy with file directory being displayed
	Selecting sub-set of data for processing – out-of-range selection	Error message showing user incorrect range selected	Correct	
	Select appropriate sub-set of data	Correct sub-set identified for analysis	Correct	
Data Analysis	Select either long- or short-term analysis	Correct analysis selected	Incorrect – both options go to long-term analysis	Corrected – 25/04/09
Data Analysis – Long-term	Process data correctly on long-term forecast	Calculates suitable long-term results	Works for periods up to 99 years	User needs 50 years so this is acceptable

Table 6.4 Example of a system test plan

encounter after its release (or does the system crash or take too long to process the data)? Volume testing is used to assess the ability of a system to deal with large quantities of data. Even if you don't have a large, real data set available for testing, you could soon generate a test data set using a spreadsheet, a text editor or a simple program you write specifically for that purpose.

■ **Usability testing.** The interface to your system may be particularly important – for example, if you were developing a system to be used by partially sighted users. Usability testing focuses testing more on how easy the system is to learn and use rather than whether it is fully functional.

■ **Installability.** Your system may have been developed to run on different platforms – Macintosh, Unix or PC-based systems (for example, a multimedia DVD). Installability involves testing your program to see how easily it can be installed and run by users on their own systems.

- **Recovery testing.** Because your system may be handling inconsistent or error-prone data it may be important that your system is robust and does not crash when it encounters such problems. Recovery testing involves testing how well the program recovers from 'bad' data, an overflow, a crash, etc. You can test your system in this way by generating 'bad' data that can be used during testing.

- **Documentation testing.** Your client/user may have requested comprehensive documentation to support your software and this may be assessed as part of your overall project mark. Documentation testing involves evaluating how good the supporting documentation is for your system. This can be performed by users, non-expert assessors (naïve testers), the client, yourself and experts. It can be performed *off-line* (i.e., assessed without the software system to hand), in which case you will be checking for things like readability, layout and clarity or *on-line* (assessed with the program to hand). During on-line testing you will be assessing how well the documentation supports the user in using the system: Do any tutorials match the program?; Is help available if things go wrong?; etc.

- **Interface testing.** This is particularly important in web development projects in which the user can be very critical of the overall look and feel of the site and has many other web sites with which to compare it. The home page of a web site is effectively the site as far as the user is concerned so getting this right is important. Interface testing also checks whether the system is usable from a functional perspective. The system you have developed may perform some quite complex, interesting functions, but if the interface is clumsy, difficult to use, or not intuitive it may well put the user off. You should consider reading guidelines on HCI (Human-Computer Interaction) principles when designing your system to ensure it is user-friendly and accessible.

● 6.13 Quality

6.13.1 Introduction

In Chapter 4 we introduced a generic model of the project process and showed that any product produced by a project will have a certain level of scope and *quality* (see Figure 4.1). Although scope (what the product does, its functionality, capability, etc.) has been defined separately, it is sometimes subsumed within the concept of quality – being one of the aspects that define a quality product. In student projects quality can refer to a number of things – the quality of the report (content and presentation), the quality of the underlying research, the quality of the contribution the project has made, the quality of a software system developed, etc. While the quality of your project is assessed by the examiners and measured by the mark you receive, in this section we focus on software quality and how software development projects control and manage quality. To begin this discussion we need to determine what is meant by software quality as it means different things to different people.

6.13.2 What is software quality?

The first point to note is that a high-quality product might not necessarily be appropriate for our needs. For example, a small system with limited functionality may provide just the functionality a user needs, while a more complex system (with lots of 'bells and whistles'), although doing what a user requires, might be so complicated as to make it unworkable.

Example

Take the example of a top performance sports car worth many tens of thousands of pounds. You could argue that this was a high-quality car but in terms of fitness for purpose it might be sadly lacking. If you needed to pop to the shops or visit your friends, your top performance sports car may well be impractical (small boot space so you could not buy much or carry a lot of luggage; high petrol consumption; expensive to insure, maintain; etc.). In terms of fitness for purpose, it would not be very good (unless your purpose was to drive quickly and look good).

It is generally accepted that an appropriate definition of software quality is *fitness for purpose*. This does not mean the product has to be of high quality.

When a customer buys a product they are selecting that product based on a number of quality criteria. Some of these criteria will be more important to some customers than others – some criteria may, for example, be of no concern at all.

- **Product quality.** This is probably the most important quality characteristic that buyers will focus on. In terms of product quality the customer will be concerned with the product's fitness for purpose – does it do what I need it to do? Does the product provide any additional functionality that I would like (in addition to my needs)? How reliable is the product – will it last me or will it need lots of maintenance, support, repairs, replacement, etc. (including spare parts, batteries, etc.)? Is the product environmentally friendly (will it have any impact on the environment through its every day use and eventual disposal or replacement)?

- **Company quality.** This refers to a consumer's confidence in the company. How well will they deal with any problems I have? What is their returns policy? Will I be able to get a refund or exchange a faulty or unsatisfactory product? What is the company's reputation?

- **Business quality.** These days consumers are very keen on knowing the environmental impact of the supplier. Is the company ethically sound (is the product produced by slave labour overseas, for example)? What has been the environmental and social impact of the manufacture of the product?

- **Value quality.** What is the product worth? What am I willing to pay for it? Does it represent good value for money or does it seem expensive for what it is? If it is expensive, is there an alternative that might satisfy my needs?

6.13.3 Quality assurance and quality control

Quality assurance is about getting procedures in place before a system is developed and delivered to ensure the system is of acceptable quality. By getting an appropriate development process in place beforehand, and monitoring and controlling this process, you will be laying the foundations towards producing a reasonable system. Without an appropriate set of processes in place, producing a system of reasonable quality will be subject to chance.

Quality control is about measuring quality of the product as it is completed and ensuring it meets the quality standards defined. In Section 6.12 we looked at verification, validation and testing. These techniques are a type of quality control – checking that the system you have produced meets the requirements, works well and satisfies the client's needs.

6.13.4 Quality standards

In developing commercial software systems, businesses invariably use (and are certified to) a quality standard of one kind or another. In this section we briefly discuss three of the most common quality standards that are used by organisations in product (and particularly) software development.

- **ISO 9000.** ISO 9000 is a series of standards for a quality management system. If a company is ISO 9000 certified, it means the company (following an independent audit) has a quality management system in place. This quality management system should, amongst other things, ensure that adequate records are kept of the business processes (in terms of definition and monitoring and control), processes are continually reviewed, and there is a quality control process in place. ISO 9000 includes a series of standards such as ISO 9001 (which is aimed at companies that design, develop, manufacture, supply and maintain products) and ISO 9004 (which covers continual process improvement). Although not specifically aimed at software, the ISO 9000 series of standards is often adopted by software development companies to improve their performance and marketability.

- **ISO 9126.** Introduced by the International Organisation for Standardization (ISO) in 1991, ISO 9126 defines six quality characteristics for software. These include: functionality, reliability, usability, efficiency, maintainability and portability. These characteristics can be broken down further depending on the nature of the system being developed (for example, reliability can be broken down into fault tolerance, recoverability, etc.). By applying numerical ratings to each of the characteristics (using Likert scales for example), it is possible to obtain relative measures of quality between systems.

- **Capability Maturity Model (CMM).** Unlike the ISO 9000 series of standards, CMM was developed specifically for the software development industry. Developed by the Software Engineering Institute it focuses on software process improvement. Organisations are graded on a five point scale according to their software process maturity. The levels range from 1, referring to organisations that have no defined software process in place and develop systems more by luck than judgement, to 5, which applies to organisations that not only have a well defined process in place but also invest in process change management.

Although these quality standards are aimed at organisations, some of the principles underlying these standards may be applicable to your own software development project. For example, the principles of ISO 9000 in which you should have effective and recordable development processes in place is good practice to follow. The quality characteristics of software defined by ISO 9126 can be adapted to your own system evaluation. The principles of CMM in which you manage your development process and look at ways of improving your processes are also worthwhile.

● 6.14 Summary

This chapter has introduced the following topics:

- software development processes;
- the generic software development life cycle;
- the original build-and-fix model;
- the conventional stage-wise and waterfall models;
- the incremental model;
- prototyping models – throw-away and evolutionary;
- choosing an appropriate development approach for your own project;
- top-down and bottom-up development;
- verification, validation and testing your software;
- software quality.

● 6.15 Further reading

Davis, A.M. Bersoff, E.H. and Comer, E.R. (1988) 'A strategy for comparing alternative software development life cycle models', *IEEE Transactions on Software Engineering*, Vol 14 (10), pp. 1453–1461.

Hughes, R. and Cotterell, M. (2006) *Software project management* (4th Edition), McGraw-Hill, London.

Turner, J.R. (1993) *The handbook of project-based management*, McGraw Hill, Maidenhead, UK.

● 6.16 Exercises

1. What development approach would be suitable in the following cases?

    i. You are undertaking a project that has been specified quite precisely by your project supervisor. The project requires you to develop a software system, written in C, to solve a problem specified by your supervisor. You will meet your supervisor every one or two weeks to discuss progress.

    ii. You are undertaking a research-oriented project that involves the development of a new algorithm to solve a particular mathematical problem. When you complete your project you will be expected to present a software system that incorporates this algorithm and illustrates how it works.

    iii. You are developing a multimedia DVD for a business client that will be used as a marketing device to 'sell' that company's products to potential customers.

    iv. You are developing a web site for a local sports club.

2. Given the following simple software specification, produce a set of test cases for the resulting software system. What kind of testing would you undertake for this?

The system must convert Celsius into Fahrenheit temperatures. The user should enter a numeric value (representing the temperature in °C) and the system should respond with the equivalent temperature in Fahrenheit.

3. Identify any omissions in the simple specification above.

6.17 Action points

■ Choose an appropriate development approach for your own project. If you are already pursuing your project, is your approach appropriate in light of what you have learnt from this chapter?

■ Justify why you have chosen the development approach you are using in your own project.

■ Think about how you will evaluate your chosen development approach at the end of your project.

■ Put together a test plan for your own project and discuss its content with your supervisor. Have you gone into too much or insufficient detail?

■ Think about how you will be evaluating your system towards the end of your project. Check that you have allocated sufficient time for this evaluation in your project plan and confirm that you have access to the right people to test your software when the time comes.

Solutions to selected exercises

1. i. As this project is quite clearly specified and you will be having regular meetings with your client (your supervisor), a conventional waterfall-type development approach could be used here. Alternatively, if the system can be broken down into a series of sub-systems, you might consider an incremental approach, adding components of the functionality as the project progresses and discussing these with your supervisor.

    ii. An experimental prototype would be suitable in this case to explore any feasible ideas you have and how these might be implemented. This might be written in a 3GL such as C, C++, Pascal or Fortran. This prototype may well be discarded, when you are satisfied that the algorithm works, and the final system can then be developed in a more graphical language (for example, Visual C++™) so that a user-friendly front end can be developed for the system.

    iii. An evolutionary prototype would be suitable in this case as the requirements are quite broad and the technology may be new to you.

    iv. Evolutionary prototyping would be suitable in this case. The technicalities of the project are fairly basic but the user-interaction issues are paramount. Alternatively, you might wish to develop two or three throw-away prototypes at the project's outset using an alternative platform from the final system (for example, page mock-ups in a drawing package) to provide the client with some different interface ideas. Having chosen a suitable interface you could then move onto an evolutionary approach to develop the final system.

2. As you do not know how the code was written, this is black-box testing; you only know the overall functionality of the software. You should therefore run the program to test it with a test set of input values. During these tests, have you included tests for the following?

    ■ Do you test a number of 'reasonable' input values – for example, 0, 10, 100, –1, –10, –200? Do these provide the correct results?
    ■ Do you test for extreme values – for example, values below –273.15, values above say 10,000? How should the system react in these cases?
    ■ Have you tested real and integer values?
    ■ Have you tested non-numeric data entry – for example characters or strings?
    ■ Have you tested the sensitivity of the system – for example, does 1.0 produce the same result as 1.000001?
    ■ Have you tested negative and positive values (for both the input and the output)?

3. If you were given this simple specification, there would still be a number of questions you would need to answer in terms of its implementation. You could make a number of assumptions yourself as to what is appropriate or you could return to the user for clarification. In some cases, the user may be happy to respond to these questions; in other cases they may be annoyed that you cannot make simple decisions for yourself – so tread carefully.

    Although we haven't even touched on the interface for this system in this example (which would throw up another series of questions), the following are things you would need to clarify:

    ■ How should the system deal with incorrect data (for example, character input, data outside the acceptable range, etc.)?
    ■ Should the system ask the user for another number after it has provided a result or should the program terminate?
    ■ Should the system end after an incorrect input, or should it allow the user to have another go?
    ■ If it allows the user another go, how many times should it allow this?
    ■ How should the results be displayed – for example, how many decimal places should be displayed? Should °F or Fahrenheit appear after the result?
    ■ What range of inputs should the system cope with? Does it need to provide a message to the user informing them of this?
    ■ How accurate/sensitive should the system be? This largely depends on the sensitivity of the input data – so how many decimal places are allowed for the input data?

    It is worth noting that even a simple program specification such as this has a significant number of ambiguities or areas where clarification is needed. Imagine the number of questions that will arise from much larger specifications.

Controlling your project

Aims:

To introduce the skills needed to manage yourself and your project effectively as it is progressing.

Learning objectives:

When you have completed this chapter, you should be able to:

- Control the five elements (introduced in Chapter 4) in your project as it progresses.
- Understand problems that can occur and be aware of ways of dealing with them.
- Manage your time effectively.
- Know how to use your supervisor effectively.
- Work efficiently in a project team.

- This chapter is relevant for both undergraduate and postgraduate projects.
- Section 7.5 (Working in teams) can be skipped by those undertaking research degrees and those not involved with group work.

● 7.1 Introduction

7.1.1 Overview

Although you may have proposed an interesting and worthwhile project and planned it well, once your project is underway it needs to be carefully managed and controlled or it **will** fall apart. You cannot assume that, having completed a detailed project plan and a solid literature survey, the project itself will be plain sailing and you can relax. You need to be aware of problems that might arise, remain motivated, manage your time effectively, make effective use of your supervisor and deal with other stakeholders appropriately. This chapter deals with these issues.

7.1.2 Getting started – project initiation

Once you've planned your project (the focus of Chapter 4) you are ready to start work on the actual project itself (the product-development activities of Figure 4.1) – called project *initiation* or *getgo*. In large industrial projects, initiation can be a major task. It might involve a launch workshop, where stakeholders are introduced, the project plan discussed and work assigned. It might involve bringing the project team together, inspiring a shared vision for the project, establishing a project office, working practices, booking rooms and other tasks. While these issues are more important in large projects, you can adopt some of these ideas for your own project.

You will want to establish some working practices, a work area or working environment in your home or at your institution (perhaps with a notice board on which you can pin important items – your project plan, for example – and a white board where you might note down ideas or list tasks to complete). You will want to set up an initial meeting with your supervisor and establish your relationship and rules of engagement (how often you will meet, how you will communicate, what sort of things you can ask of them and so forth). If you are undertaking a project for a client, you will want to meet with them and establish your ground rules early (similar to your first meeting with your supervisor, but perhaps contact and access to them might be more critical). If you are working on a group project, you will want to establish the team structure (leader, secretary, etc.), communication links, meetings and the like. A discussion on the issues surrounding project teams is presented in Section 7.5.

It is also a good idea to put together a project folder. This will contain important information such as your project plan and risk plan (see Chapter 4), your PID (project initiation document), contact details of other team members if you are working on a group project, etc. It is also where you might keep your references or useful papers, articles, newspaper/magazine clippings and other documentation. You might also want to define some programming and report standards to adhere to. You may also want to set up a work area on your computer (for example, work directories, folders for references, the report) and arrange passwords and access to whatever computer resources are required.

Once you have established your project in this way, you are ready to move on to actually doing the work. Controlling your project as you now progress is the focus of this chapter.

7.1.3 Managing the five project elements

In Chapter 4 we saw that a project consists of five elements – three consumables: *time, resources* and *money* (which are used to develop the project's product); and two attributes of the project's product; *scope* and *quality*. These five elements need to be managed and controlled as your project is progressing.

Within academic projects students will often argue that *time* is the most important of these elements. It is an element that you will always seem to be in need of. In virtually all academic projects you are limited in the amount of time you are allocated and, consequently, it has limited flexibility that you can control. All you can really do with respect to this element is to manage the time you have more efficiently – generally speaking, you cannot increase the amount of time you have available.

Money (*cost*) is another factor over which you have little control. However, in most academic projects, costs aren't usually a concern. All the facilities you require are generally available; if not, your project would probably not have been accepted in the first place. If you require additional hardware, software or literature material, you will either be provided with these or not – it is probably beyond your control to arrange their procurement and it something your supervisor will normally be responsible for.

Quality and *scope* are those elements over which you have most control and appropriately have the greatest responsibility for. Quality refers to the quality of your project itself; how good is it? Is it at the right level (postgraduate or undergraduate level)? Is it of an acceptable standard for your course? Is it worth an Honours degree or just a Pass degree?

Whereas quality can be measured by the depth of your project (for example, how well you develop or investigate a particular aspect of study), *scope* is an indication of its breadth. Sometimes scope is viewed as an attribute of quality. It represents the final outcome of your project, what it actually achieves, its contribution, its magnitude and its limits.

Resources are probably the most important element of all. Without resources there will be no project. In this case interest falls on the human resources that are available – i.e., you, your supervisor and possibly a project team. Making effective use of your supervisor is discussed in Section 7.4. In some cases you might be working in teams where colleagues need organising, tasks need to be assigned, and people's contributions drawn together. Working in teams is the subject of Section 7.5. For individual projects, organising yourself boils down to your ability to manage your own time. Managing time is discussed in Section 7.3.

Figure 7.1 emphasises the leading role resources play with all these five elements – shown at the crown of this diagram. It is through your own organisation that the elements within your project are balanced with respect to each other and with respect to your project's aims and objectives. The figure emphasises the fact that each of these elements is related to all the others in some way and tradeoffs can be made between them. How tradeoffs are made between elements is discussed in the following section.

7.1.4 Project control

The five project elements require managing and controlling through the five main project stages identified in Chapter 4: *definition, planning, initiation, control* and *closure*. Focus on these five elements changes as the project progresses through these stages. For example, during your project's inauguration you won't be too concerned about time and will probably concentrate more on identifying your project's scope. During this

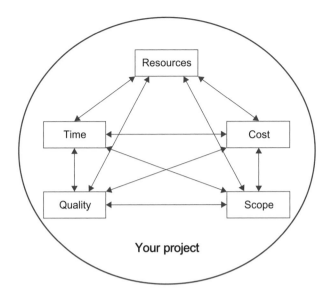

Figure 7.1 Balancing five project elements against one another

stage you will feel that there is an eternity before the final report is due to be handed in. You may have many ideas you want to pursue and you might wish to investigate and develop various aspects within the field of computing. However, two weeks before you are due to submit your dissertation, time will suddenly become a very rare commodity and a serious concern to you.

As your project progresses into the initiation and control stages emphasis moves from project management activities to product-oriented activities. In other words, you will begin to focus on the actual work of your project itself and direct your efforts towards investigating, developing and producing your project's deliverable, whatever you have identified this to be.

As your project progresses through these working stages, you will still need to perform certain project management activities. For example, you should monitor and control all the project elements with respect to your project plan. You will control time by checking to see if you are completing tasks in line with the times planned on your Gantt chart. If you are, you are on schedule and should have no worries. If not, you might be falling behind schedule and you will need to do something about it. Not only should you monitor time as your project is progressing, but you should also keep an eye on your project's scope and quality. Are you, for example, meeting the objectives of your project satisfactorily or have you had to make some compromises along the way?

Project management will often involve deciding how to trade each of the five project elements off against one another as your project progresses. For example, you could reduce the scope of your project in order to improve its quality. Conversely, you may decide to expand the scope of your project (for example, by increasing the functionality of a program you are developing) at the expense of some quality (by introducing more bugs). Time is always limited so you will often find yourself trying to trade it with other elements – for instance, saving time by reducing quality and/or scope, particularly towards the end of your project. However, you must always ensure that you do not

Time v Quality	Save time by reducing the quality of your product. If you wish to improve your project's quality this will clearly take longer.
Time v Scope	Save time by reducing the scope of what you intend to do. Increasing the scope of your project will take longer.
Scope v Quality	Improve quality by reducing scope; reduce scope to improve overall quality of the project's product.
Resources (i.e., you) v Time	Improve your own time management to give yourself more time on your project. If you want to spend time doing other things, you will have less time to spend on your project – see Section 7.3, 'Managing your time'.
Resources v Quality	Improve your time management to so that you can spend more time on your project and improve its quality.
Resources v Scope	Improve your time management to so that you can spend more time on your project and improve its scope.

Table 7.1 Summary of tradeoffs between the elements over which you have control

compromise your project and submit, on time, what you feel has been your best effort. Table 7.1 summarises the tradeoffs you can make between those elements over which you have control (i.e., all but cost).

7.2 Dealing with problems

7.2.1 Introduction

Chapter 4 introduced a risk management process that enables you to identify, prioritise and control risks in your project. In this section we look at specific things that can go wrong with projects and ways of dealing with these issues. If your project progresses to completion smoothly without any problems, you are probably very lucky indeed. Virtually all projects encounter problems at one stage or another; whether they are performed by leading academics at the cutting edge of science, first year undergraduate students pursuing a small assignment, or large industrial project teams whose work can last for several years. It is not really the nature of the problem that you encounter that can lead to project failure, but **how you deal with the problem** that counts.

The key to successfully overcoming any problems is not to panic, tackle them objectively and professionally and make best of the situation. Problems don't usually solve themselves. A problem will often require some action from you in order to be resolved. The following six points encapsulate perhaps the most likely problems you will encounter when performing your project, with suggestions on how they might be overcome.

7.2.2 Weakening

Weakening is something that can happen at any stage of your project. It can stem from a lack of motivation, a lack of confidence in what you are doing, losing your direction, working yourself too hard and burning yourself out or the feeling that you have attempted to do far too much in the time available. Weakening is something that can usually be traced right back to the first stage of your project – its *definition*. Did you decide to pursue a project you weren't really interested in? When you planned your project did you plan to do too much? Were the aims and objectives of your project too vague leading you to lose faith in what you are doing because you don't appear to be heading anywhere?

The first solution to dealing with this problem is clearly to address its root cause – i.e., tackle it at your project's outset. Make sure that you select a topic in which you are really interested, define and plan it thoroughly and ensure that you have planned some flexibility into your project so that you can expand or contract its scope depending on the time available. This can help to address weakening caused by feeling you are doing too much. Think about ways you can reduce the scope of your project without compromising its quality. Alternatively, deal with large chunks of work by breaking them down into smaller, more manageable pieces.

Another way to overcome a lack of motivation towards your work is to move on to something else. It may be that you are getting bogged down with a particular part of your project and are working at too fine a level of detail – you have spent too long on one aspect and ground to a halt with that component. Try to identify from your project plan other areas of work you can do instead. You may then return to the area you are struggling with later when you are refreshed from your break. If you have come to a halt because of a lack of confidence in what you are doing, meet with your supervisor to discuss this as soon as possible. S/he may well provide the encouragement that you need and highlight the contribution your work is making – something you may have lost sight of as you worked on the fine detail. Other ways to deal with weakening are addressed in Section 7.3 (Managing your time), where *procrastination* is discussed.

7.2.3 Personal problems

Over the period of your project, be it six months, a year or more, chances are that you will experience a personal incident of one kind or another. This can range from happy occasions such as getting married, having a baby, a significant birthday celebration and so on, to sadder, more difficult events to cope with such as illness, family bereavement, splitting up with your partner, etc. Other personal 'problems' you might encounter include moving house, changing jobs, being selected for a university sports team and so on. These kinds of changes might be good or bad but one thing is certain, they will be a drain on your time and your emotional energy. Although it is beyond the scope of this book to discuss how you deal with these problems from an emotional level, their impact on your project and what you can do to deal with this impact is of concern.

The most important thing to do in any of these situations is to tell somebody what has happened – be it your supervisor, personal tutor or course leader. Your own institution should have guidelines on whom to approach first with problems of different natures and you should follow these suggestions. You may then be guided towards other departments within the university that can deal more effectively with your difficulties; the students' union, counselling services, local doctors, hospital or chaplaincy and others.

Chances are that your institution also maintains some form of 'extenuating circumstances' or 'impaired performance' procedures. These procedures enable you to inform your institution officially of what has happened, enabling them to consider how to deal with you and possibly how to help you with your project. This will probably involve completing a form and providing evidence of some kind, such as a doctor's note. Note, however, that your institution will have guidelines on what is an acceptable reason for claiming extenuating circumstances – such as illness – and what is not – for example, going on a holiday with your friends for two weeks during term time. Also make sure that you follow your institution's guidelines on this issue. For example, some institutions require that these sorts of claims need to be made within a certain time frame. Your supervisor should advise you on the regulations.

By following your institution's procedures you are at least going some way to dealing with your problem. Not only will they be able to help you on an emotional level (for example, with counselling services) but you may well be awarded extensions to complete your work. Above all remember that if you do not let anyone know what has happened then nothing can be done to help.

7.2.4 Hardware failure

In almost all projects these days, computers are used to a greater or lesser extent. They might be used simply to word process your final report or they might be used throughout the entirety of your project as you develop a program or use them to analyse data. Whatever the case you may well find that the computer you use fails and that data and files you are using are lost or erased forever.

The only answer to these kinds of problems is to make numerous and frequent back-ups. These can be made onto memory sticks, so you can take them away with you, or onto your institution's own file server. It is up to you how often and how many back-up copies you make – you know the reliability of the system you are using. However, to make no back-ups at all is ill advised. Certainly, towards the end of your project, daily back-ups will be essential. Losing an entire week's work at the start of your project is not too serious, but at the end it would be disastrous. Take the following example as a cautionary tale:

Example

Jane was a final year undergraduate student on a computer studies course and kept her work backed up on memory sticks that she carried around with her. She was reasonably well organised and as such made **three** back-up copies of her work every day. One day, when she was working on her dissertation, she found that she couldn't read any data on her hard drive – her PC had crashed. Fortunately, she had her back-up memory sticks with her and loaded one of these into her machine. The PC claimed the memory stick was unreadable and she tried one of the others. Again, the PC claimed that the stick was unreadable. At this point Jane realised something was terribly wrong with the machine she was using. Moving onto another machine and using her third back-up memory stick, she was able to save her work.

What had happened was that Jane's PC had become infected with a virus and was erasing any memory sticks that were connected to it. Had Jane only made two back-ups of her work she would have lost everything. Fortunately, with three back-ups, all was not lost and she was able to complete her project on time on another machine.

7.2.5 Data availability

Data availability is often a problem with student projects. Either a journal or a book you require is unavailable, you can't get hold of some data, you lose your contact in a local company where you hoped to perform a case study or you receive a poor response from some questionnaires you issued. Whatever the problem, your project looks as though it will suffer from a lack of available data.

In a similar vein to *weakening* discussed earlier, problems with data availability can often be traced back to your project's early stages. If you had thought about your project more thoroughly during its inauguration, you might have identified that a book/journal was difficult to obtain, questionnaires were likely to prove unreliable and so on. Bearing these things in mind you might well set up contingency plans at an early stage – for example, changing your project's direction so that it doesn't rely entirely on a particular set of data.

If, however, data availability problems only become apparent well into your project they must be dealt with there and then. Simply put, either the data are available or they are not. Begin first, with the help of your supervisor, considering whether you can obtain the information you require from another source – is there another company you could use as a case study, for example? Have you time to chase up the question-naires you sent out or send out new ones? Does your supervisor or your colleagues have alternative data you could use? However, if no other options are forthcoming, the sooner you accept this, adjust your project and proceed the better.

7.2.6 Discovering your work/research has been done before

 On a taught degree you will not be expected to make a contribution to world knowledge, but this is not the case for research degrees, particularly for PhDs (see Chapter 5). At research degree level, students often worry if their work is truly unique and is not merely repeating the work of others. They worry if the project they are pursuing has not been undertaken by someone else before and, as a consequence, are not making that contribution that is vital at PhD level (they are perhaps in the *Demoralised* quadrant of Figure 2.2).

The first means of avoiding this problem is to ensure that you have conducted a thor-ough literature survey in the first place. Not only should you read all the relevant journals and books associated with your topic area but you should find out about (and/or attend) conferences in your field, too. It is at conferences that cutting-edge work may be presented first and ideas are discussed that are not yet published elsewhere. Try to get hold of conference proceedings early and use the Internet to access conference schedules and programmes. Through these sources you will keep track of who is doing what in particular areas and where the latest thinking is heading. It is also useful to build up contacts with other departments, research groups and institutions that are working in your field. Through the literature, conference announcements and your supervisor, you should be able to identify the 'key players' in your field. Try to make contact with them and keep track of what they are currently working on. The Internet and mail (discussion) groups are usually a good source of information in this area.

If you are satisfied that the work you are doing is unique, there is still a worry that someone else may publish your ideas/results first. One way to overcome this is to submit internal reports within your own department. Quite often, departments have an internal report mechanism to which staff and research degree students can submit working documents. There is then a time-stamped record of your work/ideas that you can refer to into your final dissertation which shows that, despite someone publishing something similar, you had thought of the idea and got it into print first. If you have a good idea and some new results, however, the sooner they are in the (more) public domain the better. In this case you can refer to a public document which shows you were the originator of the contribution. Aim to submit your work/findings to conferences at the earliest opportunity and prepare more detailed journal articles as your ideas mature.

At research degree level, your supervisor should be an expert in your field of study. They should know about developments in the field and what contribution your work is going to make. Discuss with them any concerns you have with repeating the work of others – they should be able to advise you.

7.2.7 Other things taking priority

Your project will never be (and shouldn't be) your only interest. You will have other subjects to deal with, coursework, your part-time or full-time job, a social life, a personal life and so on. All of these things take time and often you will find that your project takes second place to all of them at one stage or another. The only way to deal with this problem is through better time management. This is the subject of the following section.

● 7.3 Managing your time

7.3.1 Introduction

Everybody is limited in the amount of time they have available – there are only 24 hours in a day and seven days in a week, no matter who you are. Although everyone needs to use some of this time for essential activities such as sleeping, eating and dressing (referred to here as *essential* time), some people make more effective use of the remaining *serviceable* time than others. How you become more efficient in your use of serviceable time is the focus of *time management*.

Although there are some specific techniques you can employ to save time, the only way to make dramatic improvements in your use of time is to approach time management from a fundamental analysis. This fundamental analysis is a *process* that involves three stages and is summarised in Figure 7.2:

1. Decide what you want to do.
2. Analyse what you are currently doing.
3. Change what you are doing to achieve your aims.

Many people might try to improve their use of time by employing specific techniques that are identified in the third stage of this process. However, failure to comprehend your existing use of time, by omitting stages one and two of this process, will lead to only minor improvements in your time usage.

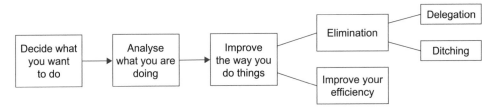

Figure 7.2 The time management process

The time management process, shown in Figure 7.2, is similar to the concept of personal development planning (PDP), briefly mentioned in Chapter 3 as an aid to project selection. In recent years, PDP has been promoted and supported by higher education institutions. PDP is about identifying your aims in terms of personal development, putting a plan in place to achieve these aims and monitoring your progress as you strive towards those goals – much like the time management process introduced here. For further information, the Higher Education Academy provides some useful material on personal development planning, including case studies, newsletters, surveys and links to other PDP web sites (see, for example, Higher Education Academy, 2008).

Each of the stages of the time management process will now be addressed in turn before some specific ideas are introduced that can help you improve your use of time.

7.3.2 Decide what you want to do

The first stage of successful time management is to decide exactly what you want to achieve in terms of goals and objectives. Most time management texts and courses will recommend that you identify both your short- and long-term goals as part of this process. Short-term goals represent those things you want to achieve during the following year. Long-term goals stretch much further into your future, such as five, ten or twenty years hence. For the purposes of this book, the main focus is your short-term goals and it is assumed that completing your project is one of these goals.

It is far easier to categorise your goals according to their different types, rather than just attempting to identify broad objectives. Ferner (1995: 11) defines four categories you can use to identify your goals: *Work Goals, Family Goals, Community Goals:* and *Self Goals*. Thus, if you were to categorise your goals for the year ahead, they might include targets such as:

Work Goals   Complete my degree with at least an upper second

Family Goals   Spend more time with my partner
                        Start a family
                        Teach my children to swim
                        Visit my parents at least five times this year

Community Goals Help out at the local youth club
                        Train the local football team
                        Do a sponsored walk for charity

Self Goals   Achieve grade 5 piano
                        Get my golf handicap down to 10
                        Learn to swim

> Join a local quiz team
> Complete a marathon
> Go on holiday to Hawaii

The goals you identify should be as specific as possible. For example, rather than just identifying a self goal as 'be happy', you should identify how you will achieve this, for example, 'go on holiday to Hawaii', 'complete a marathon' and so forth.

Chapter 4 introduced project planning and discussed how to identify objectives that are steps towards your project's ultimate goal. The same is true here. For example, one of your goals for the following year might be to complete your degree course successfully (i.e., with at least an upper second). To achieve this goal you need to complete a number of objectives: complete your project successfully, pass your exams in subjects x, y and z, complete assignments a, b and c and so on. You are thus identifying that your project is something that is important to you. Just like all the other activities and events on your list of goals, it is identified as something to which you wish to commit yourself and something that you are willing to spend your time pursuing.

In this stage of the time management process you have identified the things that you hope to achieve. The next stage of the process involves checking to see if what you are currently doing and spending your time on is helping you fulfil these goals.

7.3.3 Analyse what you are doing

Analysing how you are currently spending your time is achieved through two activities. First, you need to identify *how* you are spending your time and, second, you need to *categorise* the time you have identified. There are a number of techniques that you can use to identify your use of time, each technique doing much the same thing but in a slightly different way. *Time logs,* which are probably the most popular technique for recording time usage, are introduced here.

Time logs are simply a way to chart how you spend your time. They identify the activities you perform during the day, how long you spend on them, how efficient you were at performing them and, perhaps, ways in which you can improve your use of that time in future. You should continue making time logs for about a week to see if any patterns emerge. Table 7.2 illustrates how James, a 'typical' student, described a day in his daily time log

This is perhaps an extreme example of a 'day in the life of James'. You should also remember that this is just a snapshot of one day; James may well be doing other things differently on other days of the week. This is why you should use time logs for a full week as individual days may provide spurious indicators of your time use.

Having a look through this time log can certainly help to identify some room for improvement (depending on the person's goals). If James's main goal is to socialise, his use of time is probably quite effective. However, if James wishes to do well in his exams and assignments, then some adjustments need to be made.

One important outcome from your daily time analysis is to identify your work performance. During the course of a day you will find that there are times when you work more effectively than others; for example, early in the morning, late at night and so on. You can plot these daily 'rhythms' on a work performance chart such as that shown in Figure 7.3. Figure 7.3 shows that this person works more effectively during

Time	Activity	Effectiveness	Comments/ Improvements
7.00–8.00	Get ready for university	50%	Could probably do this in 30 minutes but I'm always tired
8.00–8.30	Walk to campus	80%	Could get the bus but I need the exercise
8.30–9.00	Meet friends in canteen	10%	Need to socialise
9.00–10.00	Lecture	70%	Quite good today!
10.00–10.15	Coffee break	10%	I need a break
10.15–12.00	Tutorial/seminar	50%	Could have done this in half the time
12.00–1.30	Lunch – students' union	20%	Far too long but I need to eat
1.30–2.00	Library hunting for books	40%	Couldn't use the computer
2.00–2.30	Meeting with project supervisor	80%	Useful
2.30–3.00	Coffee with friends	20%	I need to socialise
3.00–4.00	Library hunting for books	20%	Not finding what I wanted and getting distracted
4.00–4.30	30 minutes on assignment	30%	Wasted time getting started – should spend longer on this
4.30–5.00	Walk home	80%	As before
5.00–5.30	Have a coffee	0%	No comment
5.30–6.00	Watch TV	0%	No comment
6.00–7.00	Get tea	50%	I need to eat
7.00–8.00	Work on assignment	90%	Get a lot done
8.00–11.00	Go to pub	40%	I need to socialise but should have done more work first
11.00–1.00	Work on project then go to bed	50%	Too tired to achieve much – must tackle this kind of thing earlier in the day

Table 7.2 A 'typical' student's daily time log

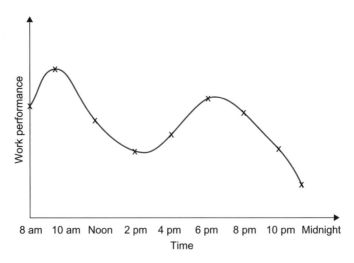

Figure 7.3 A daily work performance chart

the morning and early in the evening than at any other time of day. Thus, it would be better for this person to schedule difficult tasks (for example, reading journal articles) during those peak periods, and schedule easier tasks or socialising for other times. You can extend this concept to weekly work performance charts. For example, you may find that you work more effectively on Tuesdays and Wednesdays than on Friday afternoons. Consequently, you will schedule your weekly work to coincide with this performance.

Having identified how you are spending your time, you should then categorise your use of serviceable time. Time is categorised, according to the goals you identified earlier, into the following two components: important/unimportant and urgent/non-urgent. Table 7.3 summarises these categories:

Important activities are those activities that are important **to you** based on your own goals and objectives, while unimportant activities are those that will not affect your goals and aspirations if you don't do them. Urgent activities are those that must be done now and will not wait, while non-urgent activities are those that you could put off until tomorrow without causing any serious consequences.

Note that Table 7.3 covers only serviceable time. *Essential* time, which is time that you need to spend on essential day-to-day activities such as sleeping, eating, washing, dressing and food shopping, is not covered by these categories. Essential activities must be performed in order for you to function properly and to sustain you for everything else. However, although quite a number of activities you perform may appear essential, you might find that you could reduce the time you spend on them to some extent (for example, by taking shorter lunch breaks or persuading someone else to do your shopping for you).

	Important	**Unimportant**
Urgent	Do	Minimise/Avoid
Non-urgent	Don't Ignore	Abandon

Table 7.3 Categories of time use (adapted from Jones, 1998: 62)

All the activities you identify in your daily and weekly time log will fall into one of these categories. For example, completing an assignment that is due the following day would be important **and** urgent. At the start of the year your project would be important but at that stage it wouldn't be urgent. However, it would certainly become urgent towards the end of the year as its deadline approached.

An example of unimportant and non-urgent activities might be surfing the Internet or sorting your books into alphabetical order. Urgent and unimportant activities might include answering the phone, being interrupted by visitors, attending a meeting and so on.

Important and urgent activities are those that you must do and you must do now. If none of these activities are pending, you should focus on important and non-urgent ones. Avoid any activities that are unimportant and non-urgent and try to minimise, as much as possible, activities that are urgent but unimportant.

7.3.4 Change the way you do things

'What you can't dump, delay... *What you can't delay,* delegate.... *What you can't dump or delay or delegate,* do.'

(Turla and Hawkins, 1994: 58)

There are only two ways to improve your use of time to achieve the goals you have set yourself:

1. eliminate activities you don't need to do; and
2. be more efficient doing the things you have to do.

You can eliminate activities in one of two ways. First, if they are unimportant, you can ditch them and should do so straight away. Second, if they are important, you might be able to delegate them to somebody else. For example, you may be able to persuade your partner or a friend to proof read your dissertation for you or help you trace some references in the library.

If you cannot eliminate tasks, you are left with only one option: become more efficient in doing the things you have to do. This is achieved by planning how best to use your time and dealing effectively with any problems that arise. Planning how to use your time is usually done at two levels: weekly and daily. The first stage to time planning, however, is to set your priorities. The activities you need to perform on a daily and weekly basis are prioritised according to the categories introduced earlier (adapted from Ferner, 1995: 126):

■ High Priority – Must Do – urgent and important.

■ Medium Priority – Should Do – important but not (yet) urgent.

■ Low Priority – Nice To Do – unimportant and non-urgent.

■ Scheduled – Low/Medium/High Priority scheduled activities – for example, meetings.

Depending on how you structure your week, weekly planning is best done either first thing on Monday morning or last thing on Sunday night – in other words, before the week ahead begins. When planning what you want to achieve during the week ahead, you will focus on high-priority activities. Schedule time to deal with high-priority work and identify what you want to complete by the end of the week. Only when these activities are completed can you think about medium-priority work. During the course of a week and during each day, you will have scheduled events to deal with. Once again, only attend these if they are medium or high priority. Try to avoid scheduling low-priority events if you can.

It might be worth reviewing the previous week's activities as you put together your weekly time plan. For example, did anything take longer than expected? Is there anything left hanging over from the previous week that needs finishing off?

Having decided what you want to achieve during the week you should plan what you want to achieve each day. Make a list of things you must do, scheduled activities for that day and things you can do if you find you have some free time available. Make sure that you allow plenty of time for high and medium priority tasks and schedule your day according to your daily work rhythms (see Figure 7.3). Try not to be too rigid with daily plans as unexpected events always arise and you should allow flexible time to deal with these things. Making a list of tasks that you need to perform provides a motivation for tackling those tasks. Seeing a task on a 'to do' is a motivation in itself and there is always a sense of achievement when you are able to cross something off the list and reduce it.

You will find that your *to do* list will contain large tasks and small tasks that need to be performed. A good way of working through these different kinds of tasks is to tackle 'chunks' of a large task first. As you become tired or bored with this work, you can give yourself a break by tackling some of the smaller tasks on your list. You will therefore switch from longer-term important, but not urgent, large tasks to smaller tasks and back again as the day continues. This is probably a better way of working than trying to complete all of a large task in one go or all of your small tasks in one go.

Although you may plan your weekly and daily time commitments thoroughly, problems and unexpected events will occur. These are addressed in the following section.

7.3.5 Time management tips

Procrastination

Procrastination means that you put off until tomorrow what you can do or should be doing today. The same might happen tomorrow and things that you ought to be doing never get done properly. There are various reasons why you might procrastinate – for example, you have lost your motivation, the task appears too great, you don't want to trouble somebody because you are nervous of the response you might get, etc.

There are various ways you can deal with procrastination. The first thing to do is to decide that you really do want to deal with it. If this is difficult, you can make a list on a piece of paper of the reasons for and against dealing with the work you need to do. By analysing the work in this way, you often convince yourself that the benefits of dealing with the task outweigh the negatives. If the task appears too great, the obvious answer is to break it down into manageable chunks and deal with each in turn.

Other ways you can deal with procrastination include the carrot and stick approach. Get somebody to monitor your progress – a colleague, your partner, a friend, your supervisor – and ask them to keep prompting you for progress reports on your work. Quite often, if you aren't motivated to work for your own benefit, knowing that some-one else is interested in your progress does help. Another alternative is to reward your-self. Promise yourself some kind of treat if you complete the work; a trip to the cinema, a meal out or whatever.

Grains of time

Grains of time are those small periods of time you gain during the day that you don't use effectively – for example waiting for someone to turn up to a meeting, finding your tutorial has been cancelled, sitting on the bus to college for 30 minutes and so on.

Make sure you don't waste these grains of time. Have something that you can pick up quickly and do to fill these periods – for example, some revision notes with you that you can read on the bus, a notebook (log book) so that you jot down some ideas, the morning's post that you can sort through. You'll be surprised at how productive you can be when you make good use of those grains of time.

Email

You will undoubtedly use email during the course of your project – contacting friends, clients, users, your supervisor and others. Although email is an invaluable tool for communication, it can waste a lot of your time too. You will probably receive a lot of junk email or spam that takes time to deal with, and you might also spend a lot of time composing messages or replies when a simple response or telephone call would do. Following are some useful tips for managing your email effectively:

- Make use of mailboxes to store messages that you have dealt with. Try to keep your email *inbox* as small as possible. If you receive an email that can be dealt with quickly (something needing a quick reply, for example), do it there and then. The message can then be deleted or moved to an appropriate mailbox if you want to keep a record of it. In this way your inbox should only contain five or six long-term items that you need to keep an eye on or do something about.
- Make use of your email system's filtering and anti-spam facilities.
- Some email systems provide two windows when viewing emails – one with a list of emails recently received (the inbox), and another showing some of the content of the currently selected message. You can skip through your list of recently received emails in your inbox and glance at their content in this other window. In this way you should be able to read most of what you need from a message without actually opening it and you should also be able to spot spam or junk email which you can delete straight away.
- Set up signatures so that you can quickly add your name and contact details to an email you are composing without having to type these details out each time.
- Keep your list of contacts up-to-date in your address book so you can quickly compose an email to someone you know rather than having track down and type out their email address each time.
- If you have been away for some time and you find you have a large number of emails in your inbox, you can quickly sort out junk mail and spam by ordering the messages according to who sent them. You may well find that the same company or organisation has sent you several unwanted messages (sometimes the same one several times) and you can quickly select these and delete them all in one go.
- If you are away from your email for some time (over a week, for example) you may want to set up some sort of message forwarding or auto reply system that informs people that you are away. In this case, if people are expecting an urgent response from you, they will be informed of your absence.

Unfinished business

It may appear obvious, but until a task is completed, it is never actually finished. Don't start things that you will not finish. All the time you commit to half completing a task is wasted unless you finish that activity off.

Interruptions

Everyone is subject to interruptions of one kind or another in their work: people calling in to see you, the phone ringing, people asking you to do things, etc. Some of these are unavoidable, but it is how you deal with them that counts. One way to deal with interruptions is to avoid them by finding a 'hide away'. This might be a quiet place in your university's library where you know you won't get disturbed. You might want to put a notice on your door saying 'do not disturb' or go away for the weekend to get away from it all. If you do find that you are constantly being asked to do things you also need to learn to say 'no'. Don't deal with junk mail – just bin it. Remember your priorities, and if your project is due in, you must avoid doing other things and focus all your energies on it.

Perfectionism

Don't fall into the trap of trying to be perfect at everything you do. It can take a lot of time to improve something you do from 'good enough' to perfect. This time is wasted. For example, if you need to reply to a letter, don't waste time drafting out and redrafting a reply on a word processor with figures, clever fonts and letter heads. If you can, write a brief reply on the letter itself and post that back. If a brief reply is all that is required, do it.

Losing things

You can often waste a lot of time through your own inefficiency with data, files, documentation and papers/articles. Keep things in good order and references up-to-date, and have a means of managing all your paperwork. Gather together things you will need for a task before you start work. This will stop your concentration being broken and wasting time getting back 'up-to-speed' when you return from finding the thing(s) you need. Think about ways of managing your software back-ups too – for example, by using date-stamping or version numbers. Section 6.9 presented some ideas on this issue.

Short breaks

Sometimes work can get too much for you and you need to take a break. A useful tip here is to make a note of where you are up to and what you were intending to do next when you take a break from your work (for example, when you have finished your work for the day). This will save time later when you return to work and you try to remember what you were doing.

Long breaks

Because student projects can last for six months or longer, it is often the case that you will be away from your university for holidays, term breaks and field trips, etc. – times when you will not be able to do any detailed work on your project. While it is useful in this case to make notes as outlined in the 'Short breaks' section above, it is also useful to try to keep your project 'ticking over' during longer breaks from your work. For example, is there a book or journal article you could be reading while you are away? Could you work on some designs or requirements or could you proof read your report, etc.?

Make sure you do not completely forget about your project for one or two months away. You will find it much easier to pick up where you left off when you return if you have managed to do something (no matter how small) to keep it in your mind while away.

Log books

Many institutions insist that students maintain a log book during the course of their project and this can prove to be an invaluable resource. It will help you keep track of how your project has progressed and where you are up to (useful for short and long breaks). It can be a useful place to jot down ideas as they come to you (whether you are on the bus, in a lecture or wherever). It can be used during meetings with your supervisor – to minute the meeting, show what you have been doing and what ideas you have. You can use it to record literature you have read and to note important references.

Log books can take many forms – from detailed diaries to loose-bound notes kept in a folder (see Section 7.1.2). If your department has no formal requirements for a log book, use an approach with which you are comfortable. You should ask your supervisor for their advice on this issue during one of your first meetings with them.

● 7.4 Working with your supervisor

7.4.1 What is a supervisor?

A 'supervisor's primary professional responsibility is to develop his or her research students so that they can think and behave as independent academic and scholarly researchers in the field of study concerned.'

(Cryer 2006: 47)

One of the main resources of your project is your supervisor and, as such, how you get along with and how you use this individual needs effective managing. Chapter 3 discussed some ideas on how you should choose your supervisor (if this is possible within your own institution) and what to look for in him or her. The purpose of this section is to discuss ways in which you can make effective use of your supervisor during the course of your project.

Although most institutions have similar guidelines for the supervisor/student relationship at the research degree level, for taught degrees institutions have quite different rules, expectations, roles and responsibilities for supervisors. Some institutions will expect you to work very closely with your supervisor, perhaps meeting with him or her regularly each week during the course of your project. Other institutions prefer to emphasise the independent nature of project study and would only expect you to see a supervisor on rare occasions for advice and guidance. The role of your supervisor can also differ. Blaxter *et al.* (2006: 138) identify two roles that a supervisor can perform:

- A *manager*
- An *academic advisor.*

As a *manager,* your supervisor is responsible for managing your project in 'a more general sense'. S/he will be concerned with your overall progress; are you meeting the milestones you have set for yourself? Are you coping with your project and balancing it with other commitments? Your supervisor will also be concerned with ensuring you are following institutional guidelines as part of this role. For example, are you aware of all the guidelines, regulations (plagiarism and copyright issues, for example) and assessment requirements relating to your project? Are you producing the right documentation at the right time? As a manager, your supervisor should also advise you on which procedures to follow to submit your dissertation, what forms to complete, how to lay out the report and when to hand material in. A supervisor also arranges access to appropriate hardware and software for you as well as for you to attend appropriate courses, seminars and conferences.

As an *academic advisor,* your supervisor is more concerned with the 'academic' or technical content of your project. Are you reading the right journals and books? Are you following the correct research and data gathering methods? Are you performing the right analyses? Are you developing your software in the correct way, etc.? You may need your supervisor's academic expertise to advise you where to go next, what areas to develop further, to clarify particular topics, provide technical help with programming or design issues, to advise you which techniques and tools to use, and to discuss recent developments in your technical field. You should also expect your supervisor to tell you where you are going wrong; for example, is the academic quality of your work not up to the standards required for your course?

The University of Warwick (1994: 24) list the following areas which your supervisor should be able to advise you on when acting in an academic capacity:

- research design and scheduling
- literature surveys
- theoretical and conceptual development
- methodological issues
- development of appropriate research skills
- data collection and analyses.

Sometimes you will also need your supervisor to act in a *pastoral* role for you. Under this role your supervisor will be more concerned with your emotional and general well being. Are you maintaining your motivation? Are you under pressure from other work? Have you any personal problems that s/he can help you to deal with?

Combining academic expectations with managerial requirements, Phillips and Pugh (2005: 145–151) list the following expectations students have of their supervisors:

- 'Students expect to be supervised'.
- 'Students expect supervisors to read their work well in advance'.
- 'Students expect their supervisors to be available when needed'.
- 'Students expect their supervisors to be friendly, open and supportive'.
- 'Students expect their supervisors to be constructively critical'.
- 'Students expect their supervisors to have a good knowledge of the research area'.

While your supervisor has responsibilities towards you, s/he will also expect some obligations from you in return. According to the University of Warwick *(loc. cit.)*, some duties expected by supervisors of their students are:

- to arrange regular meetings;
- to maintain a regular work pattern; and
- to discuss progress and problems fully.

In addition, Phillips and Pugh (2005: 97–101) identify the following obligations of doctoral students, which are also relevant to undergraduate projects:

- 'to be independent';
- 'to produce written work that is not just a first draft';
- 'to be honest when reporting on their progress';
- 'to follow advice that is given'; and
- 'to be excited about their work'.

7.4.2 Using your supervisor effectively

The main contact you have with your project supervisor will be through prearranged meetings. These meetings may be at a regular time each week or more infrequent, perhaps only occurring every four or five weeks or more. As academic staff tend to be extremely busy, they are often difficult to find at other times and unlikely to be able to see you. You therefore need to make optimum use of the time you do see them during these meetings.

- Prepare for your meetings. Don't just turn up to a meeting with your supervisor without any ideas on what you want to get out of it. Think about what you want to discuss, decide what advice you want from your supervisor on which aspects of your project, and go prepared to present some of your own ideas and plans to him/her.

  Ricketts (1998: 17) suggests using the minutes of your previous meeting as a starting point for discussion each time. This helps to remind everyone of the current state of your project and identifies the work you were expecting to complete since the last meeting.

- As part of your meetings you may well want to discuss the following topics each time:
  - What progress you have made since the last meeting – work you have done, articles you have read, literature found, plans made, interviews conducted, requirements captured, designs drawn, programs developed, etc.

- What problems have you encountered? How did you overcome them or do you need help?
- Whom have you met – what did you discuss with them?
- What do you intend to do next – is this suitable? Has your supervisor any other suggestions?

■ Make notes during your meetings. It is unlikely that you will be able to remember everything that is discussed. Make notes as you go along and clarify things that you are not sure about before you leave. If you don't understand something that your supervisor is saying you must tell him or her. It is far better to get things clarified at an early stage than six months later when you realise you haven't investigated an important topic and perhaps omitted something vital from your project.

■ Arrange your next meeting. It is usually a good idea to arrange the time and date of your next meeting before you leave. Agree some goals and targets with your supervisor that you intend to complete before your next meeting. This will give you something to work towards and will provide some motivation as you know your supervisor will be checking up on your progress at the next meeting.

■ Follow your supervisor's advice. There is no point in meeting if you are going to ignore any advice given. Clearly, there are times when your supervisor will make *suggestions* that you might not want to follow. However, your supervisor will generally provide you with invaluable advice that you would be unwise not to take on board.

■ Be prepared to communicate with your supervisor through other means – by email or telephone, for example. If your supervisor is particularly busy these other means may be the best way to maintain regular contact and receive advice.

● 7.5 Working in teams

7.5.1 Introduction

Due to increasing numbers of students within higher education, group working for projects and assignments is becoming more and more common. However, it is also recognised that group work has a number of educational and practical advantages for students as Blaxter *et al.* (2006: 45) identify:

■ It enables responsibility to be shared.
■ You are able to specialise in areas you are comfortable with and good at.
■ It provides experience of teamwork.
■ You can perform much larger projects than you could achieve on your own.
■ You have a 'support-network' of colleagues.

In addition, working in teams will provide you with an invaluable experience in interacting with others, sharing work, overcoming joint difficulties and introducing you to the working practices of the 'real world'.

Many students resent working in teams as they feel their grades may be adversely affected by other people over whom they have no control. Others enjoy the experience and feel their team achieves far more than they could have done as individuals. Whatever the case, at one stage or another you may well find yourself conducting a project as part of a team. This section discusses the issues involved in teamwork and presents some tips to help you successfully complete team projects.

7.5.2 Team roles

Different institutions have different regulations for establishing project teams. Some departments will arrange you into teams (perhaps attempting to mix abilities and skills) while others will allow you to form your own teams. Be aware that if you form your own team this is not how things operate within industry where you often find yourself working with people you don't get on with or people lacking appropriate skills for the project.

Whether you can choose your own team or whether your group is assigned to you at 'random', all your team members will bring two kinds of skills into your group; *personal (team) skills* and *technical skills*. An imbalance within either of these skill areas in your group will probably lead to a poor team performance. Consequently, it is not always a good idea to form a group with your friends who may all have similar interests, personalities and technical skills to you. If you can, take careful note of the following skill types and select a group with a good balance of these skills.

Belbin (1993) identifies nine personal or team skills that people bring to a project. These skills or roles are grouped into three categories as follows:

Action oriented roles

- **Shaper** – Dynamic, thrives under pressure and overcomes obstacles. Can be argumentative and annoy other team members.
- **Implementer** – Disciplined, reliable and efficient. Takes ideas from others and acts on them. Although willing to take on jobs other people dislike, often set in his or her ways and does not like change.
- **Completer-Finisher** – Conscientious, attends to detail well and finishes work on time. Has a strong attention to detail and aims for the highest standards. Finds it difficult to delegate work and can annoy other team members by attention to detail and worrying about things.

People oriented roles

- **Coordinator** – Good manager, delegator, chairperson. Able to see the wider context of the project and understands other team members' strengths and weaknesses. Sometimes resented because only seems to delegate work to everyone else.
- **Resource investigator** – Extrovert communicator – good for making contacts and working with external stakeholders. However, loses interest easily and needs refocusing on the task.
- **Team worker** – Cooperative, diplomatic and good listener. Helps to keep the team together and working well but can be indecisive: does not like to take sides.

Thought oriented roles

- **Plant** – Creative, imaginative, can solve difficult problems. Does not like criticism; often introverted. Often so preoccupied with problems that s/he doesn't communicate effectively.

- **Monitor evaluator** – Sees all options and maintains a strategic view of the project. Tends to be quite shrewd and objective in decision-making. Because of focus on strategic issues, can appear quite detached from the day-to-day operations of the project and does not really inspire others.

- **Specialist** – Narrow specialism and viewpoint but dedicated. While essential to certain parts of the project, contribution can be limited. Often uses a lot of jargon in communications.

Chances are that you will not be working in a team with this number of members. However, individuals within your team may well possess two or three of Belbin's skill traits, giving your group a reasonable skills balance. Having a good cross-section of team skills within your group is, however, no guarantee of project success. Having said this, the more of these skills that are present within your group, the higher the chances are that the team will succeed. Individuals will work together well and the team will not suffer from clashes between the egos of several like-minded people.

These skill traits should be kept in mind when team roles are assigned. Three team roles, which are common to all project teams, irrespective of the project, include:

- *Team leader* – chairperson, coordinator. Responsible for time-tabling the work, assigning it, chasing team members' progress, chairing meetings, making difficult decisions, etc.

- *Librarian/secretary* – minutes meetings, coordinates paperwork and all literature.

- *Team contact (communications officer)* – liaises with external bodies – the client, supervisor, etc.

When assigning these roles, you might, for example, elect your team leader as the person possessing the skills of a *coordinator*. A *resource investigator* would perhaps be a good person to assign as your team contact, and the team's librarian/secretary may be best assigned to a *completer-finisher*. You might also assign primary and secondary roles to each member of the team. For example, someone may have the primary role of *librarian/secretary* and be supported by another team member who has this as their secondary role. Thus each team member is responsible for one aspect of the project, supported by one other team member, and each team member is supporting, in a secondary role, someone else.

Sometimes you may find that no one naturally fits into any of these roles or you may find that no one is willing to take on a particular role. In these cases the role might have to be divided so that different people are responsible for it, or that different people take on the role at different stages of the project. For example, team leadership could be split into coordinating team contributions, chairing meetings, planning, etc. This is a compromise and not an ideal solution as projects should ideally have a single leader.

Technical skills are particularly important within computing projects. Depending on the nature of your course, and the type of project you are undertaking, you will need team members with some of the following technical abilities:

- Programming – high level, low level, 4GLs, visual programming, etc.

- Databases – analysis, design, development

- Systems analysis
- Systems design
- Information systems
- Human computer interaction
- Networking
- Computer systems architecture
- Graphics
- Mathematics (including statistical analyses, etc.)

O'Sullivan *et al.* (1996) suggest using a SWOT analysis to identify team responsibilities. A SWOT analysis identifies everyone's *strengths, weaknesses, opportunities* and *threats*. For example, your own personal SWOT analysis might look something like this:

Strengths	**Weaknesses**
Strong leader	Poor relating to people I don't know
Technically sound	Writing skills poor
Good programmer	
Opportunities	**Threats**
Project is a chance to improve my systems analyse skills	Field trip clashes with project presentation

Not only must your team be well balanced with respect to technical skills and the team skills identified earlier, but your team must also *link* well. In other words, there must be good communication between team members in order for the project to succeed. This boils down to people's ability to get on with one another and is the main benefit of being in a group with your friends.

7.5.3 Team development

Teams do not form together in a consistent manner and generally evolve through five stages of development. Being aware of these stages can help you to understand why the team might be behaving as it is, prepare you for the types of problems the team may face during each stage and perhaps enable you to deal with these problems more effectively. These stages, originally identified by Tuckman in 1965, are:

- **Forming.** When the team first comes together as a group of individuals, the team members are keen to make an impression. The team become acquainted with one another, the goal for the project is defined, roles are established and communication channels are set up. During this stage the team leader must provide guidance and direction and be prepared to be challenged as the team begins to probe boundaries of acceptable behaviour within the group.

- **Storming.** Following initial formation most groups go through a period of instability as roles, personalities, hidden agendas and cliques come into conflict. Through this period realistic procedures are established and people determine how they can get along and work together. It is difficult for decisions to be made during this period as everyone seems to be pulling in different directions. Uncertainties exist and team members need to focus on the goal of the project and not the relationship and emotional issues that seem to be overtaking the team during this stage.

- **Norming.** This stage represents the settling down of the team following the chaotic storming process. It is during this stage that the team begins to stabilise into a working environment, patterns of work are established and people are committed to the project. The team now has a sense of identity, a team spirit forms and everyone knows what their roles and responsibilities are.

- **Performing.** The team can now achieve its optimum performance and really focus on getting the project completed. Performing can only be achieved if the previous three stages have passed successfully. Any disagreements can now be handled effectively within the team, all team members know their strategic direction and team members tend to look after one another.

- **Mourning** or **adjourning.** When the project is complete, the team might well be disbanded unless there is another project in the pipeline. To many group members this can be quite a culture shock for those that have been in a close-knit team for a long time. In an industrial context team members may move onto other projects, have to form new relationships or be returned to their original departments. For student projects it may mean the end of your course or a shift to other things such as exams or coursework. Whatever the case be aware that emotions you might feel at the end of a group project are not unique and you should reflect on your time in the team positively.

Some group projects require students to undertake a reflective summary of their project at the end. This will normally take place after the project has completed so occurs during the mourning stage. This is discussed in Section 7.5.6.

7.5.4 Managing the team

You have 'selected' your team and the project is underway – how should the group and its communications be managed? Group coordination will clearly rest on the shoulders of the team leader. It is his or her responsibility to coordinate effort by breaking a large project down into manageable chunks and assigning these chunks appropriately.

The main coordinating link that should be maintained within a group project is through frequent team meetings. These should be minuted, everyone should be in attendance and work should be agreed and assigned. When work is assigned you should all agree on what should be done **and** by when. Work should be assigned to individuals based on their technical skills and sometimes subgroups might form to work on particular parts of the project. The Gantt charts and activity networks, introduced in Chapter 4, can help you assign work to team members, as they provide a strategic view of workloads and responsibilities. It is useful to get people to sign up to their obligations at this stage so that everyone knows who is responsible for what. If problems do arise later, and the team falls apart for whatever reason, individual contributions can be identified for assessment purposes.

Frequent meetings also provide a useful means of project control. They enable progress to be monitored and provide a time and place for team members to meet and discuss ideas. Motivation of team members also becomes clear at frequent meetings and any problems can perhaps be dealt with sooner rather than later. Some points you should consider when arranging your team meetings include:

- **Location.** Avoid public areas for the meeting such as a café or bar. Try to find somewhere more professional to meet where you will not be disturbed and can access useful materials such as white boards, flip charts, wireless internet connection, etc.
- **Agenda.** Your meetings should have a clear agenda. You should discuss issues such as progress since the previous meeting and against the project plan, individual contributions, problems and solutions, other meetings (contacts with clients, supervisor, etc.), changes to the project plan, (re)assignment of tasks, target setting for the next meeting.
- **Chair.** Try to ensure you have someone in charge of the meeting who can control the discussions and make sure someone is also taking notes and minuting the meeting.

7.5.5 Resource allocation histograms

In order to identify which members of your team are working on which tasks at particular times, you could use a *resource allocation histogram* (RAH). RAHs are used by project managers to balance out work commitments amongst staff and resources and show, quite clearly, which resources are working on which tasks at any given time. A RAH is usually put together during the project's planning stage and is a useful tool for project control. An example of a RAH is shown in Figure 7.4 – in this case, showing two people working on a software development project over a period of 13 weeks. You can see from this figure that it is quite easy to determine who is working on which task at any particular time. The RAH can easily be extended to several team members (by adding extra rows) and can include non-project work too (for example, holidays, field trips, etc.).

7.5.6 Group work reports and the allocation of marks

Quite often, in addition to completing a group project, institutions expect individual students to reflect on their experience of teamwork and report on the conduct of other members of the group. Examiners may also want to know how to distribute marks amongst the team members – should everyone be given an equal share or have some members contributed more than others? The requirements for such reports will vary from one department to the next – some requiring little more than an honest percentage breakdown of each

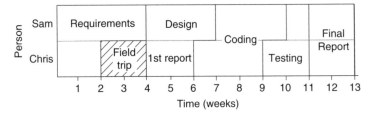

Figure 7.4 A *resource allocation histogram* of a simple development project

team member's contribution while others may require a more reflective review presented as an essay or a report. Examiners may also be interested in a reflective account of how the team worked together. For example, did you have a single team leader, how did the team communicate, how was work allocated, how was the team managed, what was your role and was this an appropriate use of your skills, what would you do differently next time, etc.?

Ideally, if the team has worked well together and everyone has done their fair share, each student will claim an equal share of the marks and the marks will be allocated evenly. However, when discrepancies appear the examiners must decide on a means of reaching a compromise. If the students are claiming similar contributions (but not exactly the same), a simple averaging of the claims may be fair. Examiners may adjust marks if at least two members corroborate a different percentage split. If the claims are wildly different (for example, one team member claims he did 80% of the work while the other team members think he did only 30%) the examiners may well interview the team (individually and/or as a team) to determine a compromise or identify why such discrepancies have arisen. It is at times like these that documentary evidence is important – so make sure you minute your meetings.

The following are some tips that should help you if you are asked to produce an appraisal of your team's performance (as a team and from an individual perspective):

- Be honest. If you write an honest account of your contribution to the team and the team performance it will be accurate and should be supported by your other team members.

- Try to come to an agreement as a team before you hand in your summative reports – so you are agreed on who contributed what to the project.

- Be willing to fight your corner if you feel you have been unfairly treated.

- Ensure you have documentary evidence to back up your claims – minutes of team meetings, for example.

- Make sure that all meetings are fully documented and people 'sign up' to work commitments. Not only does this provide people with a 'contract' which they feel obliged to fulfil but, also, if things go wrong, arguments won't start over claims that 'X said they would do this' and 'Y promised that'. These ideas should help you to deal with members of the team who don't seem to pull their weight.

- Try to monitor individual contributions as the project is progressing rather than at the end. At an interim meeting you could ask all team members to complete a contribution sheet – indicating what they feel each member of the team is contributing to the project (for example, for a team of five, an equal contribution would be 20% each). If there are discrepancies at this stage (for example, X feels she is doing the bulk of the work, while everyone else thinks work is split evenly), try to sort them out sooner rather than later. Get people to explain their reasoning as to why contributions appear to differ (you may find out, for example, that someone is doing a lot more work than you thought) or reassign tasks to try and even up the workloads.

7.5.7 Systems to support team work

There are a number of online systems available that can help your team perform more effectively. These systems include those that allow you to share documents, those that allow you to manage the team (arranging meetings, assigning work, etc.), configuration management systems that allow you to control changes to a system that several people are working on simultaneously and discussion forums. Configuration management was covered in Section 6.9. In this section we will look at tools to support group collaboration in other ways. Example of such tools include:

- **Wikis.** A wiki is a web site that users can access and contribute to – a type of interactive database of information like Wikipedia. Your team might want to establish one of these sites as a means of sharing information and ideas. For more information on Wikis see http://www.wikimatrix.org/ (a site for comparing Wikis) and Wikipedia at http://www.wikipedia.org/ – the largest online Wiki.

- **Blogs.** A blog is an online forum in which users post their ideas, thoughts, diary details, etc. You can set up a blog for your group and use it as a means of communication as well as recording conversations, comments, etc. For more information on blogs, see http://www.weblogmatrix.org/, which compares a number of blogging sites.

- **Project management systems.** These are online systems that allow you to manage your project and support the team. An example of such a tool is http://www.projectplace.com/, which provides facilities for managing documents, people (communicating assigning tasks, etc.), meetings, the project as a whole (tracking progress) and planning.

7.5.8 Teamwork tips

- Have a single project manager/team leader. It is often tempting in group work to have a rather democratic, leader-less structure. However, somebody *does* need to be in charge of your project's management and coordinate the effort of everybody involved, keep a strategic view on your project's progress and make 'unpopular' decisions. If the group has two or three members who would like to lead the team, perhaps this could be achieved on a rotational basis. This could be managed by rotating the team leader based on each team member's technical contribution and effort which will vary during the course of the project. Alternatively, as mentioned earlier, the team leader's role could be divided amongst those wishing to lead the group, but this is less satisfactory.

- Maintaining everyone's interest and motivation throughout the course of a large project can be difficult. For example, systems analysts would be busier at the earlier stages of a project than the end when, perhaps, programmers become overburdened. To overcome these problems try to plan into your project's schedule team responsibilities as well as technical activities. For example, the systems analyst might take over the group's secretarial/library activities as the project progresses; a programmer may relinquish the leader's role; etc.

- In line with the points made above, it is important to ensure that people aren't overburdened with technical *and* team roles. It can take a lot of time to manage a group alongside other activities. You should ensure that team roles are accounted for when work is assigned to each member of your group. For example, a good team coordinator, who can motivate and coordinate everyone's contributions, may be assigned this task as their only role.

- Maintain good communication between all team members. Make sure that a contact sheet for every team member is produced at the project's start with everybody's home address, telephone numbers and email address. Hold frequent short meetings, not long infrequent ones. Try to make full use of all the communication tools available to you. These can include facilities such as electronic diaries to plan meetings, email to support team communication, texting, etc. Email can also be used to transfer documents and files between team members as attachments. Also try to set up shared directories on your institution's computer servers so that all team members have access to the latest project files (but ensure some form of configuration management is in place).

- Try to create a team spirit. Create an identity with a team name and try to arrange some informal, social meetings as well as your formal ones

- Try to maintain a single person to act as a liaison with external bodies such as your client, technical support staff, supervisor etc. Even if two or three of you attend client meetings it should be made clear who the contact person is within the group. This ensures that a consistent message is presented to external bodies and contradictions are avoided. It also avoids contradictory information passing into your group from two or three team members who may have approached the client on different occasions and received contradictory requests.

- Split the report writing/documentation into appropriate sections and assign these according to each team member's abilities and what they have done. Make sure that team members know when they have to provide their particular contribution by; allow time for collating all the contributions; confirm an 'in-house' style that the team should adhere to for all documents produced. Get the team's librarian/secretary to coordinate this.

- Consider implementing some kind of configuration management process and system (such as that discussed in Section 6.9) to ensure, if several members of the team are working on different parts of a software system simultaneously, that the components integrate together seamlessly and version control is supported.

- Sometimes a team is dominated by one or more of its members who always seem to want to say something, no matter how irrelevant, about everything during discussions (monopolisers). Similarly, some members of the team may always seem reluctant to say anything or contribute to discussions (introverts). Divert attention from monopolisers by requesting ideas from other team members. Ask each member of the team to take a turn at providing a contribution (thereby including introverts and limiting monopolisers). Split the team into smaller working parties so that the influence of monopolisers is diminished.

● 7.6 Summary

- All projects have five elements that require managing to some extent as the project progresses: *time, cost, quality, scope* and *resources*. These elements need to be balanced against one another so that you achieve your project's aims and objectives.

- Of these five elements, cost is something over which you probably have little concern or control. Quality and scope are the two elements you have most responsibility for and control over. Resources are those that are available to accomplish your project – you, your supervisor, and your project team. The time you are allocated to complete your project cannot usually be extended so you need to employ time management techniques to manage this time more effectively.

■ Time management consists of three stages: decide what you want to do, analyse what you are currently doing and change the way you do things. There are only two ways to reduce the time you spend doing things; ditch them (perhaps by getting somebody else to do them – delegation) or use the time you have more effectively.

■ Your supervisor is an invaluable resource. You will probably only see your supervisor at prearranged meetings so these must be planned for and used effectively.

■ Working in teams brings a number of advantages and disadvantages. Each team member contributes two kinds of skill: team skills and technical skills. When work is assigned to team members, try to balance team roles with technical duties and assign work and responsibilities according to people's strengths and weaknesses. Meet regularly and maintain good communication.

7.7 Further reading

Dodd, P. (2008) *The 25 best time management tools and techniques: how to get more done without driving yourself crazy*, Capstone, Oxford, UK.

Evans, C. (2008) *Time management for dummies*, John Wiley, New York.

Forster, M. (2006) *Do it tomorrow and other secrets of time management*, Hodder & Stoughton, London.

Gleeson, K. (2003) *The personal efficiency program: How to get organized to do more work in less time*, John Wiley, New York.

Phillips, S. (2002) *Time management 24/7: How to double your effectiveness*, McGraw-Hill, London.

Rooney, K. (ed) (2004) *Steps to success manage your time: How to work more effectively*, Bloomsbury, London.

Tracy, B. (2008) *Eat that frog! 21 great ways to stop procrastinating and get more done in less time* (2nd Edition), Berrett-Koehler, San Francisco, USA.

7.8 Exercise

1. How could the student have managed their time more effectively in Table 7.2?

7.9 Action points

■ Identify how the five project elements (resources, time, cost, quality, scope) relate to your own computing project. Which of these elements is your main focus/concern at the moment?

■ Put together a time log for yourself during the coming week.

■ Categorise your use of time into important/unimportant, urgent/non-urgent, and essential types. How can you reduce the time you spend on unimportant activities?

- Plan for a meeting with your project supervisor.
- Establish and maintain a project log book.
- If you are working on a group project try to identify which of Belbin's (1993) team skills each of your group possesses. Have you assigned roles based on these skills? Are technical tasks and team roles balanced logically and evenly amongst your team's members? Put together a contact sheet for your team. Is everyone clear about what they are doing and what their responsibilities are?

Presenting your project

CHAPTER
8

Presenting your project in written form

Aims:

To introduce the skills needed to present your project effectively in written form.

Learning objectives:

When you have completed this chapter, you should be able to:

- Understand how to structure and write professional reports.
- Write clear and concise abstracts.
- Understand how to present data and results clearly.
- Understand how to reference material and avoid plagiarism.
- Document software, comment programs and write user guides.

- This chapter is relevant for both postgraduate and undergraduate projects.
- Section 8.6 (Documenting software) is background material for research degree students but highly relevant for taught degree software development projects.

8.1 Introduction

Chapter 2 identified the dissemination of your ideas and results as an important part of the research process. Quite often the report is the only evidence of your project when it is finished, unless you have developed a substantial piece of software (and even then,

181

people may only get to read your report rather than use the software). As the report represents your project, remember that the good work you have performed can be ruined by a poor report. There is no point in performing a tremendous amount of valuable and important computing work, research and development, if you cannot present your findings to other people. However, a bad project cannot be turned into a good one by producing a good report. Although you can improve a poor project with a good report, you must remember that your report is a reflection of your project and you *cannot* disguise sloppy investigation, development, implementation, analyses and method with a few carefully chosen words.

This chapter focuses on the presentation of written material for your project: structuring reports, writing abstracts, referencing material and presenting data. It also covers topics such as documenting software, commenting programs and writing user guides. How you present your project in oral form, through presentations and vivas, is the subject of the next chapter.

● 8.2 Writing and structuring reports

8.2.1 Considerations

As you begin work on your project's report, bear in mind two main considerations:

■ **What is the purpose of the report?** Is it to obtain the best mark you can achieve for your project? Is it to present your work in the best light? Is it to disseminate your ideas and results to others? Is it to provide a thorough literature review of the field? Is it to inspire others and to persuade them to get involved with your research? Is it to fulfil the requirements of your course?

■ **Who is going to read it?** What do they already know? What do you want them to learn? What do you want them to gain from your report? How do you want to influence them? Will it be read by people other than your examiners (future employers, other students, academics and experts, for example)?

These considerations will influence what you decide to include in your final report and also the style of writing and presentation that you adopt (for example, technically-oriented text for experts or more explanations and examples for the more novice reader). You should not include material merely for the sake of it as this might irritate the reader and appear like 'padding'. Similarly, you should not leave material out of your report if you think it is important for the targeted readership. Try to get the balance right – understand what it is you are trying to say, be aware of what the reader already knows, and include material appropriately.

Your institution may well have guidelines on how reports should be presented – for example, layout of the title page, word counts (upper **and** lower limits), font size and type, line spacing, binding, the number of copies of your dissertation/report to submit and so on. It is important that you follow these regulations; failure to do so may mean that your report is rejected.

One of the most difficult regulations to adhere to in many cases is the word count. When the regulations stipulate a word limit, students are often asked to put a word count on the front of their report. While minor indiscretions might be accepted (for example, 10,500 words when the limit is 10,000), major deviations from the limit might be heavily penalised. If you feel you are going over your allotted word limit, consider sections you could cut down, which text you could move into appendices (which will probably not be counted), or what text might be better presented in other ways – for example, in tables or charts. Berndtsson *et al.* (2008: 123) suggest that when you consider how long to make your report, you should really ask yourself "How short can you make it?" This will encourage you to focus on the important points while excluding all unnecessary material.

8.2.2 Approaches to writing

There are two main approaches that people tend to use when they write reports: the *top-down approach* and the *evolutionary delivery*. These two approaches are not mutually exclusive and you may well find yourself adopting both of them to one extent or another as you develop your report or dissertation. Whichever approach you use, do not expect to get it right the first time. Writing involves drafting ideas and rewriting the text. It may take a number of iterations before you are finally satisfied with what you have written.

The top-down approach is used to identify the structure of your report with a chapter breakdown structure – how many chapters it will have, what each chapter will contain and how each chapter will break down into sub-sections. With sub-headings identified, you can then go on to complete these sections at an appropriate point in your project when results are obtained and information is acquired.

Figure 8.1 provides an example breakdown for this chapter (covering the main sections). Identifying the content of this chapter as a number of component parts makes writing much easier and less daunting as individual sections can be tackled one at a time. By identifying the overall structure of a chapter, you can keep an eye on the overall target of that chapter so that you do not discuss extraneous ideas that are out of the chapter's context (the chapter breakdown structure will probably help you to identify a more appropriate place to enter the misplaced text). Chapter breakdowns also help with time management in that they provide you with a better understanding of the amount of writing you have to do. This stems from an understanding of the complexity of each section which will give you an idea of how long these sections will take to complete.

You might try to identify sections and sub-sections in your report early on in your project. However, as is often the case, it is not until you finally come to completing your project that you fully understand what you want to include and can identify the specific content of every chapter. Whatever happens, you will find that a report breakdown structure is a useful way of arranging your thoughts and ideas and identifying how they link together within the content of your report.

The other writing approach is the evolutionary delivery. Many people use this approach but are not conscious they are doing so. In this approach you begin to write parts of your report and rewrite these parts as your project progresses (drafting and redrafting). Each part thus evolves and matures over a period of time as new ideas emerge and your understanding increases. Thus, you do not sit down at the end of your

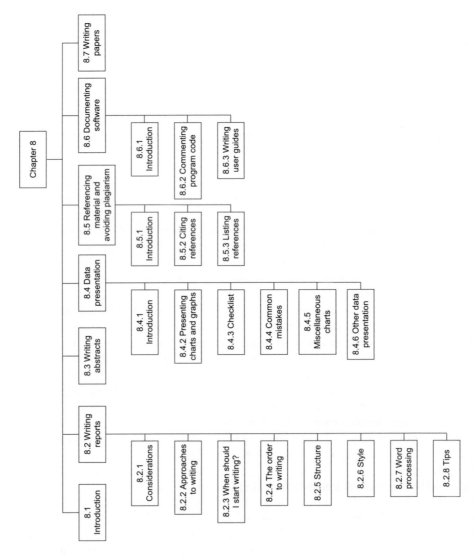

Figure 8.1 A chapter breakdown structure for this chapter

project and write your report as a one-off. You write it over a much longer period of time throughout your project.

The evolutionary delivery leads to a number of drafts of the report on which you may require feedback from your supervisor. It would be inappropriate to inundate your supervisor with draft after draft to read through – each one containing only minor changes to the previous version. This would be a considerable waste of your supervisor's time and slow your writing down too as you await feedback each time. A more sensible approach to presenting a series of drafts to your supervisor might be as follows:

- **A chapter breakdown structure.** This will allow your supervisor to check quickly if you are on the right lines, including all the appropriate sections and covering the appropriate material.

- **A completed major section** (perhaps the introduction or literature review). This will allow your supervisor to check your writing style, presentation, depth of discussion and referencing at an early stage.

- **A significant draft.** Most of the report should be in place at this stage before you obtain feedback from your supervisor. Any missing sections should be identified with descriptions.

- **Completed chapters.** As an alternative to presenting a significant draft to your supervisor, you might want to present your report one chapter at a time as you complete them. Your supervisor will probably have more time to read one chapter at a time than the entire draft report in go.

- **Final draft.** This should be virtually the final report and the last draft of the report your supervisor will see before it is completed and handed in. It will probably be too late for you to make any significant changes to your report at this stage, but your supervisor might spot some areas for final improvement.

The two approaches introduced above can be combined so that you identify, perhaps at the start of your project, the specific sections of some of your report's chapters. You can then begin to write these sections but will find that they evolve and change as your project progresses. You might also find that your report breakdown structure itself evolves over time as your understanding increases, your ideas change and develop, and you obtain your results.

8.2.3 When should I start writing?

Since personal computers became commonplace during the 1980s, students no longer leave the final *writing up* of their projects to the very end. Before the advent of the computer, students would spend, say, 80% of their effort working on the project itself (the research, development, experiments, etc.) before typing up their report/thesis on a typewriter. These days, however, it is possible to start work on your report when you start your project. This does not mean that you should start writing sections of the report during the first week, but you should at least be considering how your report will be structured and laid out using a word processing package. It doesn't mean that you will not have a final 'writing up' stage in your project. It will mean, however, that this stage is no longer a write-up of the entire project, but possibly as little as drawing together existing material that you have produced and the completion of, say, conclusions, an abstract and a contents page.

As you work on your project and produce word-processed reports, you should try to incorporate documentation (for example, requirements specification and design documents) and papers in your evolving dissertation. At the very least, you should be keeping good notes as your project progresses (a project log book, for example, as described in Chapter 7), so that when you come to the final write up, all the material and information you require are readily available.

 At research degree level you may have produced a number of academic papers during the course of your project (for example, conference papers, journal papers and internal reports). These might convert readily into the main chapters of your thesis, with minor changes to convert section headings to chapter headings and so on. If you have undertaken a software development-based project on a taught degree course, you may convert your requirements documents into a chapter, your designs into a chapter and so on.

Whatever the case, be aware that leaving your **entire** write-up to the very end (a 'big bang' approach) is unnecessary these days. Try to 'chip away' at your report as you go along and maintain good notes. This will mean you do not have to endure the stress of a prolonged writing phase when your project nears completion.

8.2.4 The order to writing

There is a particular order to writing that you should try to follow. This order breaks down into these ten stages:

1. **Identify structure.** This relates to the content of your report, using a report breakdown structure. Although a specific content structure might not be entirely clear to you at an early stage, you should attempt to produce as much detail for each chapter's breakdown as possible. Report breakdown structures were discussed in the previous section.

2. **Identify presentational style.** You should also try to set standards at this stage on the presentational aspects of your report, for example, its layout, font, numbering conventions, etc. This will save time later when you are trying to collate your chapters and sections and find they are presented inconsistently. Make sure that you follow any guidelines that your institution provides. If there are no guidelines, Cornford and Smithson (2006: 177) identify a number of points you should consider for your report's layout:

   ■ Avoid broad, open spaces or cramped layouts. Try to make sure figures and tables do not force large gaps into your text.
   ■ Use a clear 11- or 12-point font. Use something that is easy to read – a serif font like Times for the main text – and a sans-serif font like Arial for headings. Don't use too many fonts as this will look messy.
   ■ Use a single, justified column with adequate margins for binding. However, it is sometimes argued that two columns are easier to read than one as text lines are shorter. Check your institution's guidelines and ask your supervisor for advice.
   ■ Use page numbers centred at the foot of each page.

You might also wish to define your own presentation style such as line spacing (1.5 or 2 point), a section numbering convention (for example, '1.2 Section title') and paragraph styles (for example, start each paragraph on a new line tabbed in).

With colour printers commonplace these days, you might also decide how to use colours to enhance text and presentation within your report. Be careful not to introduce a complex style such as red text for chapter titles, blue for section headings and so on. This kind of presentation looks very messy and it is best to stick with black text for the bulk of your report. However, colours can be used very effectively to enhance tables and highlight certain points. For example, to distinguish different parts of a table presenting statistical data, you might wish to use colour to highlight significant results.

3. **Draft the introduction.** The introduction gives the reader an idea of the report's content so it should also help you to clarify your own ideas. At this stage, however, your introduction will only be a first draft as your ideas are bound to evolve and your emphasis change by the time you have completed your report. Remember that your introduction might include, or consist mainly of, your literature review. As such, it should be tackled early so that your grounding in the subject is complete.

4. **Develop the main body.** The main body of your report is the next part you should work on. You might include chapters such as methods used, analyses performed, etc. Clearly, the content of the main body of your report will depend on the project you have undertaken. You may find that you write parts of the main body of your report as your project progresses and you will not necessarily write each chapter or section in order. Examples of 'typical' chapters that form the main body of different project reports are presented in the following section.

5. **Articulate conclusions and make recommendations.** Quite clearly, your conclusions and recommendations should be one of the last things that you complete. Only when your project is complete will you fully understand what you have achieved and be able to present you final ideas and recommendations.

6. **Complete the introduction.** As part of the evolutionary approach to writing, you may well find that your introduction needs some reworking after you have completed the rest of your project's report. You may want to include some text alluding to your final results or introduce more background on a topic you have since focused on in more detail within your report.

7. **Write the abstract.** You cannot really write a clear abstract for your report until you know what has been included in it. How to write effective abstracts is covered in detail later in this chapter.

8. **Add references and appendices.** Although you will be collating references and appendix material as your project progresses, you should not complete their presentation until the rest of the report has been written. References may be added or deleted and you may decide to include or exclude material from the appendices.

9. **Arrange contents list, index.** Leave the completion of an index (if one is required) and your contents list until the end. Only then will you know the exact content of your report and all page numbers.

10. **Proofread, check and correct.** It is vitally important to proofread your report after it is completed. Quite often, because you have been so close to your report for so long, reading through your report straight away might mean that you miss glaring errors or omissions. You know what you meant to write so this is what you read, whether it is written or not. With this in mind, it is a good idea to leave your report for a day or two before proofreading it or, preferably, get someone else to do it for you. Bear in mind that if you do this, you will need to complete your report a few days before its deadline to allow time for proofreading and correcting or changing any points that emerge.

8.2.5 Structure

Your report should be structured into the following sections:

■ Title page or cover sheet – follow any guidelines provided (your supervisor should advise you on this issue). If there are no guidelines, as a minimum you should include: title, author, date and degree award (perhaps look at some past projects to see how they presented their title pages in your institution).

■ Abstract.

■ Acknowledgements – to people (and organisations/companies) you wish to thank for helping you with your project. Avoid acknowledging friends, relatives, people, gods, organisations and others that have had only indirect influence on you or your project (for example, 'Uncle Arthur, who taught me the importance of managing my time when I was 8').

■ Contents listing.

■ List of figures and tables – this is not compulsory and you should include these lists **only** if you feel they will add value to your report and will be useful for the reader. Otherwise, leave these out as they take time to compile and maintain.

■ The report itself (three main sections):

1. Introduction/literature review – the first chapter of your report should always be an introduction. Quite often, introductory chapters serve to present the literature review. Alternatively, the introduction serves as a brief overview of the project and the report, and the literature review is presented as a chapter in its own right later.

    Your introduction should set the scene for the project report, include your project's aims and objectives, introduce the project's stakeholders and the topic area, and provide an overview of your report. Berndtsson *et al.* (2008:129) also suggest that the introduction should include the 'purpose and situation – indicating why the report was written and what the purpose was.' They go on to suggest that you should also target the reader – i.e., you should state clearly at whom the report is aimed – who will be interested in the report.
2. Main body – the content of which depends on the type of project you are undertaking. Some examples are provided below.
3. Conclusions/recommendations – summarises the contribution of the work and identifies future work, etc. This is discussed in more detail below.

■ References – presented in an appropriate format. Referencing material is discussed in more detail later in this chapter.

- Appendices – labelled as Appendix A, Appendix B, Appendix C, etc. These may include program listings, test results, questionnaire results, interviews you have transcribed, extracts from manuals, letters/correspondence you have received and project details such as your initial proposal, your project plan (and other project management documentation) and meeting reports. You may also include a user manual and installation guide and perhaps extracts or examples of data or data sets used. Consult with your supervisor over what should and what should not be included in the appendices of your report.
- Glossary of terms – if required.
- Index – if required – but avoid if possible.

Following is a typical structure that many of my undergraduate students use for projects that have involved the development of a software system:

- Abstract
- Acknowledgements
- Contents listing
- Chapter 1 – Introduction
- Chapter 2 – Literature review
- Chapter 3 – Requirements
- Chapter 4 – Design
- Chapter 5 – Implementation and test
- Chapter 6 – Evaluation
- Chapter 7 – Conclusions
- References
- Appendices

Figure 8.2 provides an indication of how the chapters in this kind of report structure relate to one another (those of you familiar with software engineering may recognise this as an adaptation of the v-process model). For example, the *Conclusions* chapter evaluates the project overall – how well it achieves its aims and objectives (outlined in the *Introduction*) and how it fits in and supports existing work in the

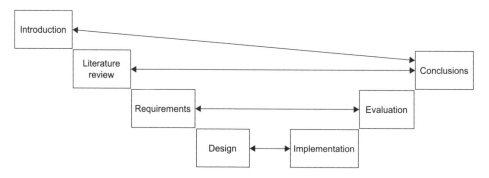

Figure 8.2 The relationships between chapters

field (covered in the *Literature review*); the *Evaluation* (of the software) chapter appraises the system developed with the original requirements and evaluates whether those requirements were appropriate; the *Implementation* chapter discusses how the software was implemented and how the implementation follows the design presented in the previous chapter.

Sometimes students will swap over Chapters 2 and 3 (*Literature review* and *Requirements*) to provide the reader with more information about what the project is about before setting it in a wider context. Another variation is to combine Chapters 4 and 5 into a *Design and Implementation* chapter and move all testing (of the software, including test plans and so on) and evaluation into Chapter 6. Chapter 6 (*Evaluation*) covers the evaluation of the **product** developed – i.e., what the user(s)/client think of the system, how it compares with other systems, how it matches the requirements, and so on.

The final chapter (*Conclusion*) presents an evaluation of the **project** – it summarises what the project has achieved (what has been its *contribution*) and how the project has met its initial aims and objectives (and if not, it explains why). How does this project fit into and enhance existing work in the field? This chapter also covers a number of other issues. For example, was the development process model used appropriate (if not, why not and what else should have been used?)? Was the programming language suitable? What problems did you face and how did you overcome them? What would you do next if you had more time? If you were to do the project again, what would you do differently? What have you learnt and experienced from doing the project? How do you recommend the project should be taken forward in the future?

For information systems-type projects, Berndtsson *et al.* (2008:128–131) suggest the following structure for the main body of a final year report:

- Chapter 1 – Introduction
- Chapter 2 – Background
- Chapter 3 – Problem description and problem statement
- Chapter 4 – Theory
- Chapter 5 – Methods
- Chapter 6 – Results
- Chapter 7 – Related work
- Chapter 8 – Conclusions

The *Introduction* and *Background* (equivalent to a literature review) are similar in nature to the outline for the software development project above. Chapter 3, in this case, identifies clearly the problem that the project is setting out to solve and why this problem is worth solving. Chapter 4 discusses any existing theories and ideas associated with the problem. Chapter 5 discusses the methods that were used (and, possibly, adapted in some way) to solve the problem. Chapter 6 presents the results and Chapter 7 goes on to show how these results fit in with existing work – how they contribute, complement and support (and perhaps contradict) the work of others in related fields. The concluding chapter works in much the same way as before although Berndtsson *et al. (ibid.)* point out that this chapter 'should *not* present any new details of the approach or results etc., which have not been explained in previous chapters.' They also identify a number of other issues that the concluding chapter should address:

■ *What can the results be used for?* In other words, how can the reader benefit from knowing what they have learnt from the report? To what can they apply your results?

■ *Can related research areas benefit from the results?* Is what you have discovered or developed applicable to other research areas? What are the limitations of the approach and of the results?

■ *Are the results theoretical or do they have a real-world application?*

■ *How do the results compare with related research?*

■ *Has the work identified new questions that need to be answered?* Has the work identified new areas of research?

The structure presented by Berndtsson *et al. (ibid.)* is much the same as that suggested by Chinneck (1999) for graduate courses (i.e., research degrees). Chinneck suggests the following chapter breakdown:

■ Chapter 1 – Introduction
■ Chapter 2 – Background
■ Chapter 3 – Review of the state-of-the-art
■ Chapter 4 – Research question or problem statement
■ Chapter 5 – How the problem was solved
■ Chapter 6 – Conclusions

In this case, Chapters 1 and 2 cover the introductory and background material as before and Chapter 3 is equivalent to the literature review. Chapter 4 is equivalent to Berndtsson *et al.*'s (2008) Chapters 3 and 4 (*Problem description and problem statement* and *Theory*) and Chapter 5 encompasses Berndtsson *et al.*'s Chapters 5 and 6 (*Methods* and *Results*). As this is a research-based report, there is more emphasis in Chapter 6 (*Conclusions*) on contributions and future work.

In a similar vein, Bell (2005: 234–238) proposes the following structure for the main body of a report for research projects:

■ Chapter 1 – Aims and purpose
■ Chapter 2 – Literature review
■ Chapter 3 – Method(s) of data collection
■ Chapter 4 – Statement of results
■ Chapter 5 – Analysis and discussion
■ Chapter 6 – Summary and conclusions

This structure is similar to that of Berndtsson *et al.* (2008) in which, once the background and literature review are completed, the report presents the method(s) of collecting data before presenting the results. In this case, the presentation of results is split across two chapters – Chapter 4 presenting a description of the data that were collected (including appropriate figures and tables to summarise results) with Chapter 5 analysing and discussing these results. Chapter 4 presents the factual results of the study, whereas chapter 5 presents the interpretation of these results.

In conclusion, there is no right or wrong way to structure a report into a series of chapters – you should do what is appropriate for your own project. You might want to adopt one of the structures presented here or some combination of these suggestions. It is advisable to consult similar (past) student projects to your own to get an idea of the structure used. Your supervisor should certainly advise you on an appropriate structure for your report.

8.2.6 Style

The style of writing that you adopt to present your report can be discussed from three points of view. First is the actual presentation style of your report – for example, its layout, font size and so on. This kind of style was discussed earlier. Second is the style of grammar that you use within your report. Quite often good reports can be ruined by poor grammar. The author's meaning is unclear as ideas and results are hidden within long complex sentences that include excessive words and jargon. The third point of view is overall content structure and this will be discussed further later.

A good writing style comes with practice – the more you write the easier it becomes. Reading also helps to improve your own writing skills as you learn elements of good practice and identify interesting ways of discussing and presenting arguments. Having said this, there are some simple rules that anyone can follow to improve their writing style for professional reports. Try to write in the third person – in other words, try to avoid using personal pronouns such as: *I, you, we, my* and so on – but make sure that you don't end up producing elaborate, complex sentences just to avoid this. For example, take the following sentence from a student report:

I interviewed seven people to see what they thought of the system.

This could easily be reworded to a less 'chatty' style and without the 'I' to:

Seven people were interviewed to determine their thoughts on the system.

Your supervisor should be able to advise you on this point and it may be that the nature of your project requires you to use a more personal approach.

Keep sentences short and to the point. Avoid making several points within the same sentence. Avoid abbreviations, jargon and slang. Use simple, rather than complex words; the latter is often irritating for the reader, it clouds the meaning of your sentences and is often used to hide your own lack of understanding about the subject which the educated reader will spot. Try to keep your report gender-free – for example, use 's/he' or 'they' rather than 'he'.

It is common practice to present your report in the past tense as the report represents the results of the project which you *have* completed. Having said this, Day (2006) suggests that the present tense should be used when referring to the work of others (just like this sentence does!). Referencing material will be discussed in detail later but bear this point in mind.

Avoid jokes and personal asides. Avoid shortened forms such as 'isn't' instead of 'is not' unless you feel that the report will not flow well without these forms. Make sure you know how to use apostrophes – for example, 'John's computer' rather than 'Johns' computer' or 'Johns computer'. Finally, make sure that you use a spell checker; sloppy spelling puts many reports into a bad light.

Chinneck (1999) notes two further tips when writing reports:

■ *Avoid terms like 'clearly' or 'obviously'.* You might understand the fact to which you are referring but it may not be clear to the reader. The reader may also feel they are being 'stupid' if they don't see the point clearly or obviously.

■ *Avoid red flags.* These are claims that are your personal opinion rather than accepted facts supported by the literature. For example, 'requirements capture is the longest stage of the software development process'. You should make sure that if you include these kinds of claims you support them with either an appropriate reference or a 'caveat word' such as 'often' or 'sometimes'. For example, the previous statement could be reworded as 'requirements capture is *often* the longest stage of the software development process'.

Moving away from basic grammar, the third style to consider when writing project reports is overall content structure. This was discussed in detail in the previous section but remember, at the top level, your report should be constructed so that it has a:

Beginning – the introduction and literature review which set the scene;

Middle – the bulk of your report where the main component of your project is discussed; and

End – conclusions, summary, recommendations and future work.

This kind of structure should also be evident within individual chapters of your report. They too should have an introduction (possibly a chapter overview), the main body of the chapter, and an end (possibly a chapter summary or conclusions from the chapter).

8.2.7 Word processing

For computing students it almost goes without saying that the best way to produce your report is with a word processor of one kind or another. These packages are far more effective than typewritten or hand-written work alone. Almost all word processors these days come with dictionaries and a thesaurus facility built in. In addition, many are equipped with equation editors that can help you produce neat equations embedded within your text. Alternatively, equation editors are available that can be used to 'construct' equations before pasting them into your report. The following is an example of an equation that has been pasted into the text (this was produced using Microsoft Equation 3.0 which was installed in Microsoft Word). Notice how this equation has been given a reference number (8.1 in this case) which you must always include to uniquely identify each equation you incorporate in your report.

$$f(N) = \frac{\sum N(N-1)}{\sqrt{S^2(N-1)}} \qquad (8.1)$$

Be careful when using in-built spell checkers. Many are based on American dictionaries and will change words to their American equivalent; for example 'center' instead of 'centre' (or vice-versa if you are an American reader!). Spell checkers might also change spelling 'errors' within verbatim quotes you have used from other authors.

Grammar checkers should also be used with caution. What might appear an elegant, well-constructed sentence to you might be changed automatically by a grammar checker. However, if you feel that your grammar is weak, these facilities are invaluable.

While most students will use a WYSIWYG (What You See Is What You Get) word processor (for example, Microsoft Word) for their reports, for those undertaking more technical reports with lots of mathematical equations, a text formatter such as LaTeX (pronounced LayTech) may be more appropriate. LaTeX is a text formatting tool that takes a text document prepared by you and converts it into a form that can be printed. The text document is encoded in a similar way to HTML in that different markers within the document format the text in different ways when it is printed out. LaTeX has facilities for automatically numbering chapters, sections, equations, etc. It is mainly used within the computer science and mathematics fields and by professional publishers.

Oetiker *et al.* (2008: 3–4) list the following advantages of LaTeX over conventional word processors:

■ The documents produced are 'professionally crafted' and look as if they have been 'printed';

■ Mathematical formulae are easily typeset;

■ You only need to learn a few commands that specify the structure of the document;

■ Footnotes, references, contents tables, etc. can be easily generated;

■ It encourages users to write well-structured reports because this is how LaTeX works; and

■ The tool is free and portable between systems.

For those of you using Linux or UNIX, the chances are that your system already has LaTeX installed (speak to your supervisor or technical staff for help). For those with Windows-based systems you can use a system called MiKTeX which can be downloaded from http://miketex.org/. Macintosh users can use a similar system called OzTeX which is also freely available from numerous sites on the Internet.

8.2.8 Tips

This section on report writing will conclude with a few report writing tips to help you. Bell (2005: 245–247) identifies a number of points that can help you discipline yourself and improve your writing skills:

■ Set deadlines. Your report will take a long time to produce. If you do not set yourself deadlines and stick to them, you will not finish on time. Using a report breakdown structure can help you to plan your time commitments more accurately.

■ Write regularly. Find your best time of day for writing and your favourite location. In other words, make sure that you 'write when your mind is fresh' and 'find a regular writing place' (Saunders *et al.*, 2007: 520–521). People often find they cannot write with distractions or when they are over-tired.

- Create a work rhythm. Once you are under way, keep going. Don't stop to check a reference if the text is flowing, keep going until you reach a natural break.

- Write up sections when they are ready – when they are clear in your mind. This will also save time towards the end of your project when your project write-up might be little more than a collation of your existing text and producing an introduction and conclusion.

- Stop at a point from which it is easy to restart. It can often take a lot of time to get going again after a break so try to stop at a natural break in your report – for example, when you have completed an entire section. Trying to pick up from where you left off the previous day or week can be difficult as you might have forgotten what it was you intended to write. If a break in your work is unavoidable, make a note of what you intended to do next so that when you come back to your writing later you can pick up from where you left off more easily.

- Collate all the material you need together before starting to write. Breaking your writing flow to search for a reference or visit the library to trace a vital book will not help.

- Allow time for revision. You will not produce a perfect report in one sitting. Make sure you allow plenty of time to check and improve what is written.

- Read out loud. By reading your report out loud to yourself it will help you spot grammatical errors, overly long sentences, poorly written sentences, odd punctuation and whether or not the text makes sense.

- Get someone else to read it. Another person will often spot errors you don't. Because you have been so close to your report you read what you expect to read rather than what is actually written. A different set of eyes will pick up mistakes that you have missed.

- Avoid perfectionism when writing your report. It is better to get something down that is approximately right to start with (and you can edit later), than agonising over each sentence trying to get them perfect. Don't keep trying to get one section/chapter perfect before moving onto the next. When you have said approximately what you want to say, move onto the next section/chapter – you can always return to them later if there is time. There is a well used phrase that is appropriate here – 'Don't get it right – get it written'.

8.3 Writing abstracts

Blaxter *et al.* (2006: 261) define the function of an abstract as to 'briefly summarize the nature of your research project, its context, how it was carried out, and what its major findings were'. The abstract provides the reader with an overview of your project and is the basis on which many readers will decide whether or not to read your report at all. With this in mind your abstract should be concise (preferably no more than one page long), clear and interesting.

Many abstracts are structured like a contents listing, but this is of little value to the reader who can refer to the report's actual contents list for this kind of information. Your report's abstract should be one of the last things you write; when you actually know what you have achieved and what the content of your report is. Avoid using references in your abstract as the reader will not necessarily wish to search through your report to find them or be familiar with the author(s) you have cited. In addition, avoid using jargon and acronyms – these should be introduced only in the main body of your report.

There are three possible components to an abstract; the inclusion and coverage of which depend on the nature of the report you are producing; *context, gap* and *contribution*. The context introduces the topic area in which your project resides; it can include coverage of related topics and issues, and generally sets the scene for the reader so they can comprehend your project's subject area. Particularly for research-based projects (MPhils and PhDs, for example) you will then want to identify any gaps or shortfalls within the topic area that your project is going to explore and, hopefully, contribute to. The final component covers the contribution or content of your report itself. In other words, what does your report contain that fills the gap you have identified or what does your report contain in relation to the context you have discussed?

To get a 'feel' for good and bad abstract presentation pay careful attention to the way others structure the abstracts of articles that you obtain. Take, as examples, the following abstracts for the same article – based on an artificial neural network approach to predicting software development costs.

Abstract 1

This article investigates the application of ANNs to software development cost estimation. It begins by discussing existing software prediction techniques such as COCOMO (Boehm, 1981) and Delphi (Helmer-Heidelberg, 1966). The article identifies the process of software cost estimation and uses this as a basis on which to apply the ANNs developed for this project. Equations are presented showing how improvements can be made to the backpropogation algorithm used in ANN training. ANN simulation is also discussed. An evaluation of the results from the ANNs is presented and these results compare favourably with existing techniques identified in the paper.

Abstract 2

One of the major problems with software development projects is that it is extremely difficult to estimate accurately their cost, duration and resource requirements. This invariably leads to problems in project management and control. Part of the problem is that during the early stages of these projects very little is known about the problem domain and, consequently, initial estimates tend to be best guesses by a project manager. Artificial neural networks appear well suited to problems of this nature as they can be trained to understand the explicit and inexplicit factors that drive a software project's cost. For this reason, artificial neural networks were investigated as a potential tool to improve software project effort estimation using project data supplied by a software development company. In order to deal with uncertainties that exist in initial project estimates, the concept of neural network simulation was developed and employed. This paper discusses this concept and comments on the results that were obtained when artificial neural networks were trained and tested on the data supplied.

The first abstract is presented (incorrectly) as a contents listing, while the second sets the scene for the article and identifies the content and contribution that the article is making. The first abstract is presented as a breakdown of the article's sections and it includes acronyms and references to papers that may be unfamiliar to the reader. The second article avoids these pitfalls and presents a much better overview of what the reader will gain by reading the article. It sets the scene by introducing the field in which the project resides. It then identifies some problems with the field before going on to state how the article attempts to fill this gap. When writing your own abstract, try to follow the structure and style of the second abstract presented here.

 ## 8.4 Data presentation

8.4.1 Introduction

In almost all projects, you will have to present data in one format or another – data you obtain from questionnaires or surveys, software test results, algorithm speed trials and so forth. While textual presentation of numeric results can often provide a rather 'dry' interpretation of the information gathered, pictures in the form of graphs and charts provide a far more pleasing, intuitive and holistic idea of what is going on. A 'diagram can often simplify quite complex data which could take a paragraph or more to explain' (Bell, 2005: 226).

Although a picture is worth a thousand words, you must ensure that the picture you are painting is the correct one and you are not presenting results in such a way as to hide their true meaning. Benjamin Disraeli (1804–1881) said that there are three kinds of lies: 'lies, damned lies and statistics', the implication being that you can make statistical results say practically anything you want them to say. Remember, when you compile your report, that you must be objective and present your results in a clear and honest way. This section deals with presenting information using charts and tables, presenting various examples of some of the most popular charts that are used and showing some instances where charts are used incorrectly.

8.4.2 Presenting charts and graphs

All figures and tables that you include within you report should be clearly and uniquely labelled with a number and a short description. The most common approach is to label each figure and table using consecutive numbers prefixed by the current chapter number. The approach used within this book, where we have, for example, 'Figure 8.1 *A chapter breakdown structure for this chapter*', is quite a common standard which you can follow. Note that it is permissible to label a table and a figure with the same number; for example, Table 8.1 and Figure 8.1 refer to two different items within a report. When labelling a figure it is usual to put the caption beneath the figure. When labelling a table, it is often better to place the caption above the table (because sometimes tables cover several pages). Above all, be consistent and don't change the way in which figures and tables are labelled from one chapter to the next.

Use figures and tables within your report only when they can add something of value; do not include them simply because you think they look nice. Figures and tables should help to clarify and support information you are presenting within the text of the report and should be included as close to their original reference point as possible, but not before. Take, as an example, Table 8.1. This table presents the final degree classifications of 100 students who completed their Computer Science course in 2009.

Table 8.1 presents these data in a much clearer way than you could hope to achieve using text alone. For example, compare this table with:

'Seven students obtained first class degrees, twenty three obtained an upper second, thirty eight achieved a lower second, seventeen received third class degrees, ten achieved only a pass degree, and five students failed'.

1st	2:1	2:2	3rd	Pass	Fail
7	23	38	17	10	5

Table 8.1 Degree classification of 100 students

Although Table 8.1 is easier to follow than the text presented above, it is not necessarily the best way of presenting these data. Figure 8.3 is perhaps a clearer way of interpreting these results and it provides a more 'holistic' view of the spread, pattern, or *distribution* of degree grades. Note that the distribution of data is only relevant when the data are of at least ordinal scaling. In other words, the categories into which the data are arranged represent an increasing magnitude of one kind of another (for example, the position of runners in a race; good, average or poor software quality and so on). Data that merely represent classes in which the order is irrelevant (for example, gender or religious belief) have no distribution as such and the order of the columns in these charts is unimportant. In this case the chart can only emphasise the difference between the number of items identified within each category.

Figure 8.3 is a *vertical bar chart* or *column chart*. These charts can also be presented horizontally, but generally the vertical representation is preferred. Bar charts are used to present categorical data and are useful for presenting the results of questionnaires which have used Likert-type scales. These scales 'indicate strength of agreement or disagreement with a given statement' Bell (2005: 219). For example, 'Do you think this software is poor, average, or good?' Note how, on this chart, the data have been split into columns with gaps between, both axes have been labelled and the chart has been uniquely titled as Figure 8.3 with a corresponding brief label.

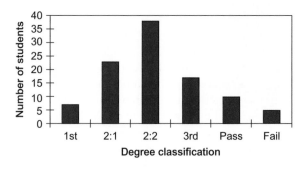

Figure 8.3 Bar chart showing degree classification of 100 students

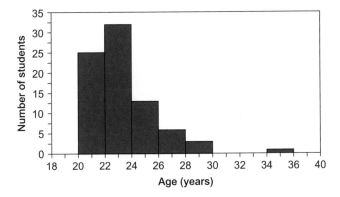

Figure 8.4 Histogram showing age of 100 students on graduation

For *continuous* data an alternative to the bar chart is required as the data are not arranged in distinct categories but can take any *real* value (for example, age, size, weight, etc.). In these cases, a *histogram* is used. Histograms present data in a similar way to bar charts in that columns are used to represent frequencies of occurrence of a particular data item. However, because histograms present continuous data, it is now up to you how you split the data into unique categories. Remember that bar charts have their categories defined for them based on the categories defined within the data they represent. As an example, Figure 8.4 presents a histogram showing the *age* of the 100 Computer Science students at graduation.

In Figure 8.4 the age of graduates has been split into ten unique categories; 18 to 20, 20 to 22, 22 to 24, 24 to 26 years old and so on. It has been assumed, in this case, that each category's upper boundary is actually one day before the year indicated, so that people whose even-numbered birthday (20, 22, 24, etc.) falls on the day of the survey will be placed in the next category up (i.e., 20 to 22 actually represents 20 years to 21 years 364 days old). Each column now represents the number of students that fall within the defined range. Notice how the bars in this chart are now touching. This highlights the fact that the data are continuous and there is no absolute break between the categories.

There is no reason why you could not, alternatively, have defined the categories as; 20 to 25, 25 to 30, 30 to 35, etc. This results in the histogram shown in Figure 8.5.

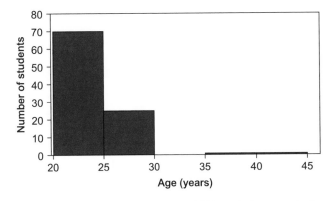

Figure 8.5 Histogram showing age of 100 students on graduation

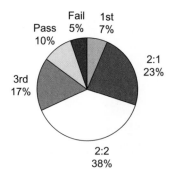

Figure 8.6 Pie chart showing degree classification of 100 students

Figure 8.5 provides a 'coarser' interpretation of the findings and, perhaps, provides a poorer overview of the spread of student ages at graduation. This figure emphasises the importance of carefully selecting appropriate categories for presenting continuous data in histograms. Splitting your data into too many categories can lead to a number of gaps, while splitting your data into too few categories can lead to broad, 'high' bars that provide little indication of the underlying distribution.

Another form of chart you may wish to use within your report is a *pie chart*. Pie charts are used to show *proportions* of categories within your data. Take, as an example, Figure 8.6 which presents the same data as those presented in Figure 8.3. While Figure 8.3 shows the *distribution* of degree classifications, the pie chart in Figure 8.6 shows the *proportion* of students with particular degree classifications. Which figure you use would depend on what you were trying to emphasise or explain within your report. You would use a pie chart to discuss proportions and a bar chart to discuss distributions.

Pie charts come in various shapes and sizes; three-dimensional, exploded, coloured, shaded, wheels, etc., and most spreadsheet packages provide these formats. How you present your charts is clearly up to you, but don't get so carried away with a chart's presentation that you obscure the real meaning of the data you are presenting.

While you could use several pie charts next to one another to compare proportions between two or more subjects, a *combined bar chart*, such as that shown in Figure 8.7, can be used to present this comparison more clearly. In this case the spread of degree

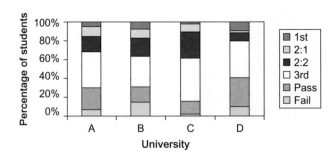

Figure 8.7 Comparison of pass rates at four universities

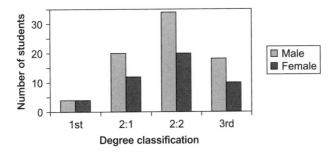

Figure 8.8 Degree classification and gender of 125 recent graduates

grades at four universities (A, B, C and D) is presented. Notice how a legend has been included in this chart to identify the shading used in the columns and how this legend and shading follow a logical top-down approach based on degree classification from First to Fail.

If you weren't interested in looking at proportions between categories but actual values, you could use combined bar charts such as that shown in Figure 8.8. In this figure you can see the number of students graduating in Computer Science categorised according to their gender. The bars are arranged in degree classification order and split according to gender, i.e., gender is identified within each degree classification.

Note that the bar chart in Figure 8.8 has been presented in a rather conventional format. These days you will quite often see three-dimensional plots, colours and shading used to enhance the attractiveness of such charts. Be careful that you do not obscure the true meaning of what you are trying to portray or hide insignificant findings behind elaborate diagrams and figures.

Figure 8.9 takes the data used in Figure 8.8 and transposes the groupings to present the results of Figure 8.8 in a slightly different way. This time the bars have been split into degree classification and these grades grouped by gender. Once again, how you present these data is up to you and will depend on what you are trying to emphasise. Figure 8.8 is concerned with showing how each individual grade is spread between men and women. Figure 8.9 is concerned with showing the spread of grades for all men and the spread of grades for all women.

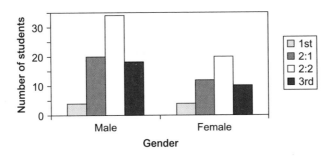

Figure 8.9 Alternative view of degree classification and gender of 125 recent graduates

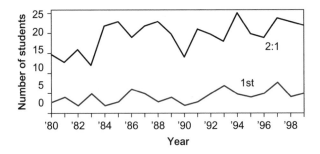

Figure 8.10 Trends in Firsts and Upper Seconds, 1980–1999

One drawback within Figures 8.8 and 8.9 is that the total number of male and the total number of female students differs. Ideally one would like to see the proportion of men obtaining Firsts, 2:1s, 2:2s, etc. and be able to compare this with the proportion of women obtaining these grades. For example, do women, on average, obtain more Firsts than men? Although you would need to perform a statistical analysis on your data to 'prove' this, the charts would present a clear, visual overview of the situation. Your y-axis in both of these cases would be relabelled as 'Percentage of students' as opposed to 'Number of students' and the charts would provide a better comparison of grade spread based on gender – if this is what you wanted.

Another form of chart you may find useful is a *line chart*. These figures are generally used to show trends over periods of time. Figure 8.10 presents such a chart, in this case showing the trend (if indeed there is one) of Firsts and Upper Seconds awarded between 1980 and 1999. Note that this only provides a visual interpretation of these data. The scale presents raw numbers rather than percentages so you would have to consider whether a change in student numbers over time was affecting the results (for example, if student numbers had risen 'significantly' during this time, the number of Firsts and Upper Seconds should have increased, too). You would need to perform some statistical analyses on your data to determine whether there was a significant trend or not. Statistical tests are beyond the intended scope of this book as there are numerous texts available that deal with these issues.

The last form of 'popular' chart to look at within this section is the *scatter diagram*. Scatter diagrams are used to show the relationship between two variables. For example, Figure 8.11 plots the assignment grades of 30 information systems students against the

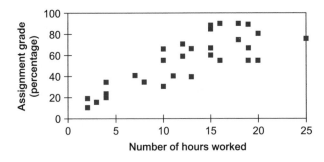

Figure 8.11 Relationship between assignment grade and hours of effort of 30 students

number of hours each student worked on their assignment. Notice how the chart shows a general upward trend, perhaps indicating that there is a relationship between these two variables. Although the strength and significance of this relationship would be calculated statistically, the chart provides a visual interpretation of this relationship which is perhaps easier to follow than some statistical calculations. This is not to say that you could omit any rigorous statistical interpretation of data that you obtain but that you can support these calculations and improve their presentation by use of **appropriate** figures and tables within your report.

8.4.3 Checklist

Saunders *et al.* (2007: 421) present a checklist of points that you should observe when you have completed tables and figures within your report. For both diagrams and tables, they recommend that you ask yourself the following questions:

- 'Does it have a brief but clear and descriptive title?'
- 'Are the units of measurement used stated clearly?'
- 'Are the sources of data used stated clearly?'
- 'Are there notes to explain any abbreviations?'
- 'Have you stated the sample size?'

For diagrams, the following checklist of questions are suggested:

- 'Does it have clear axis labels?'
- 'Are bars and their components in the same logical sequence?'
- 'Is more dense shading used for smaller areas?'
- 'Is a key or legend included (where necessary)?'

And for tables:

- 'Does it have clear column and row headings?'
- 'Are columns and rows in a logical sequence?'

8.4.4 Common mistakes

You should not include figures and tables within your report just for the sake of it. They should be there to support arguments you make within the text and to clarify, in diagrammatical form, data, results and interpretations you are making. This leads to the first common mistake that people sometimes make in using figures and tables – including them unnecessarily. Figure 8.12 is an example of just such a case where a pie chart is presented (sometimes even on a whole page) adding no value to the report whatsoever. In this case, as 100% of those questioned responded 'yes', the use of the pie chart, which normally shows proportions, is unnecessary and makes the report look as though it is being padded out because it has little of real value to say.

The second common mistake when using charts is to use the wrong kind when another type of chart would present your data more clearly. Figure 8.13 provides just such an

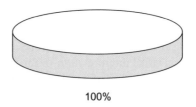

100%

Figure 8.12 100% of respondents said 'yes'

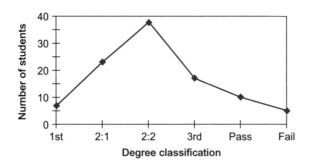

Figure 8.13 'Incorrect' use of a line chart

example – in this case, a line chart is being used when a trend isn't the focus of attention. Although one might be interested in trying to identify the shape of the underlying distribution of degree grades, a bar chart would be more appropriate in this case.

Another common mistake people make when including charts within reports is to scale them incorrectly. Sometimes this is done deliberately to hide the true meaning of the data presented. At other times it is done by accident when you are unsure about what your data are trying to tell you or what your data mean.

Figures 8.14 and 8.15 present a university department's spending between 1980 and 1999. Although both these figures present exactly the same data, using exactly the same type of chart, they both appear very differently. Figure 8.14 shows, perhaps, an alarming

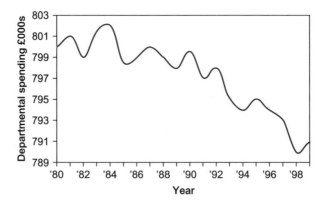

Figure 8.14 'Dramatic' decline in spending

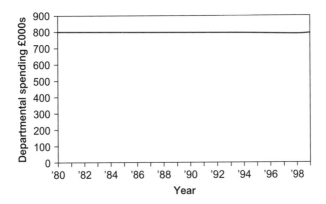

Figure 8.15 Less dramatic decline in spending

decrease in spending during this period; while Figure 8.15 puts this 'trend' into perspective and shows that spending has changed only very slightly over this period of time. However, Figure 8.14 provides a good view of the *detail* of the spending changes while Figure 8.15 provides little information on what has happened. In Figure 8.15, it appears, unless you look very closely, that spending has not changed at all throughout this period, but you know this is not the case. These two figures emphasise the importance of getting scales right. You need to decide what it is you are attempting to show, not what you are attempting to hide, and scale your charts accordingly.

8.4.5 Miscellaneous charts

Some less common charts that you might come across and wish to use are presented in Figures 8.16 to 8.19. Figure 8.16 is a three-dimensional bar chart which is used to enhance the appearance of 'bland' two dimensional charts. While these charts don't necessarily add anything significant to the presentation of the data, they do provide a more visually appealing diagram.

Figure 8.17 is a *polar* chart which is used to compare variables with several comparable factors. For example, each 'arm' of the polar chart would represent a particular factor

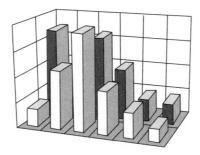

Figure 8.16 An example three-dimensional bar chart
(axes have deliberately not been labelled for clarity)

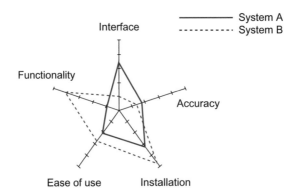

Figure 8.17 An example polar chart comparing two software systems

and each shape would represent the variable in which you were interested. Each shape would thus provide an indication of the similarities and differences of each variable for each of the factors presented on each axis. In the case of Figure 8.17, each arm represents a user's view of different aspects of two software systems (A and B). In this case, it is easy to see that the user, for example, prefers the interface of System A but they prefer the functionality provided by System B.

Figure 8.18 is a *doughnut chart*, another type of pie chart. The advantage of this representation is that you can now plot several pie charts together on the same figure to enable proportional comparisons between variables to be made.

Figure 8.19 is a factor analysis plot which presents the results of two combined factors from a factor analysis. This figure helps to show how variables are grouped together depending on a number of factors in two dimensions. While some of the variables may appear closely related to one another in this diagram; looking at other factors in other dimensions might show that they are not. Factor analysis is a statistical technique that can only really be performed using a statistical software package. The calculations are much too complex to be performed by hand.

8.4.6 Other data presentation

Not only will you be presenting data in the form of charts and graphs, there are other things you might wish to present, too – program listings, designs,

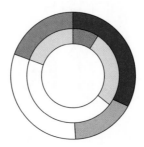

Figure 8.18 An example doughnut chart

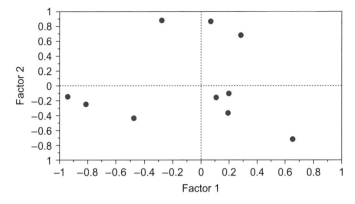

Figure 8.19 An example factor analysis plot

photographs, diagrams and more. When presenting these kinds of data, keep the following tips in mind:

■ As for charts and graphs, each figure should be uniquely numbered and labelled.

■ Try to keep figures and listings to one page. If code listings spread over several pages, consider moving the listing to an appendix and include only short extracts (of interesting algorithms/sections) in the main body of the report.

■ Consider alternative ways of presenting diagrams. For example, rather than including several figures showing the evolution of a system's interface design, you could include a photograph showing the preliminary sketches and interim designs next to one another – for example, see Figure 8.20.

■ Present pseudo code and designs in boxes rather than 'floating' amongst the text – for example, see Figure 8.21.

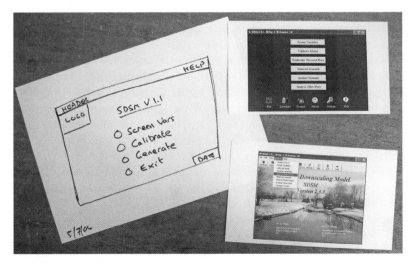

Figure 8.20 An example of preliminary and interim design presentation using a photograph

```
if      n<0
then  n ← 0
else
         if n>10
         then n ←10
         fi
fi
```

Figure 8.21 Pseudo code of an example algorithm

● 8.5 Referencing material and avoiding plagiarism

8.5.1 Introduction

'Nothing is said that has not been said before.'

Terence (ca. 195–159 BC), The Eunuch, Prol.

With Terence's statement in mind, it is important that you support the work you are presenting within your report by appropriate references. Much of what you present will have been touched on, discussed, written about or covered by other authors in the past – particularly for undergraduate projects. Thus, any arguments that you make within your report and, especially within your literature review, should be justified by referencing previous research (Saunders *et al.*, 2007: 58). Material is referenced within reports to:

■ **Avoid plagiarism.** In other words, you do not present other people's ideas, thoughts, words, figures, diagrams or results without referencing them, as if their work were your own; in other words, you must credit people with their ideas. Plagiarism can be performed accidentally or deliberately, but in either case it is deemed a serious academic offence. This is one reason why you should perform an extensive literature survey – to ensure that you are not merely repeating the work of others.

The concept of plagiarism and its significance varies between countries and cultures. For example, in the East, Confucianism embraces the concept of collective knowledge owned by society as a whole rather than individuals (Hirji, 2004). Hirji goes on to state that the idea of individuals acquiring knowledge and 'owning' that knowledge is frowned upon. In the West, plagiarism is looked upon more as the 'theft' of other people's ideas if we try to present them as our own.

There are a number of tools available to examiners that can be used to assess whether or not work has been plagiarised. One example is turnitin (see www.submit.ac.uk) which 'enables institutions and staff to carry out electronic comparison of students' work against electronic sources including other students' work'.

Generally speaking, you will be criticised (and penalised) in most institutions if you do not cite the work of others appropriately. One thing you should try to do is to carefully annotate your notes when you read articles so you can distinguish between direct quotes you have copied, ideas you have taken from other authors and your own ideas. When you come to write up your final report you will then know what requires referencing either directly or indirectly.

- **Identify context.** To place your work in context with other recognised publications. This will strengthen your report by showing how it builds and extends the work of others and how it resides within a recognised academic field of study.

- **Support and validate.** To support your own arguments and validate any statements that you make. If you are making certain claims you will have to support these with either research results or references to other authors.

- **Identify sources.** Provide people reading your report with a comprehensive list of related work that they can use to study your topic in more detail or take your work further. By identifying sources clearly, people reading your report will be able to locate the articles you have used.

Cornford and Smithson (2006: 107) identify a number of issues with referencing that appear in poor student reports. Poor reports often exhibit the following (so these are things you should avoid):

- A lack of references. What references there are refer to standard texts. You should refer to more than just the standard text books recommended on the first year of your course.

- A lot of references to old and obscure texts. This might indicate you have merely copied them from another source rather than reading around the subject and identify more contemporary sources.

- The references in the main body do not match with the list of references at the back of the report. This is sloppy and suggests 'a failure to recognise the importance of references'.

- The references are swamped with URLs rather than traditional sources. Although the Internet can provide a useful starting point for research, the content is largely unrefereed. A reference list dominated by URLs shows a lack of rigour in your literature search and an element of laziness. It also indicates that your work might not have a firm foundation but may be built on a number of opinions and ideas that have yet to be established.

There are two aspects to referencing. The first aspect to consider is how to use references correctly within the body of your report – in terms of their presentation and appropriateness – called *citing*. The second aspect is how to present these references correctly at the end of your report. Each of these aspects will be dealt with in turn.

8.5.2 Citing references

Generally speaking, there are two ways to cite references – the *Harvard System* and the *Numeric System* (also called the *Vancouver System*). There are numerous variations on these techniques that have their own idiosyncrasies (for example, *Chicago* is a form similar to Harvard; *MLA-style* and *CBE-style* are forms based on the numeric system). However, we will concentrate here on a general overview of a Harvard-type system. Harvard is the better system to use as the numeric system requires each reference to be identified by a unique number which needs updating every time you decide to add or remove a reference from your report. Quite often the numeric system also gives no indication of the author to whom you are referring and the reader has to search through the reference list at the back of your report to find this information.

These days, many word processing packages have reference management systems that enable you to maintain and update references within your report quickly and easily. Chapter 5 identified a software tool called Reference Manager that can help you manage your references. However, with or without such a system, it is recommended that you use the Harvard style of referencing which is more flexible and clearer than the numeric approach.

The Harvard-type system uses the name of the author(s) and the year of their publication to uniquely identify each reference within a report. For example, take the following extracts from an undergraduate project report:

It is often said that computing is an art not a science (Smith and Jones, 2009: 20).

or

It is often said that computing is an art not a science. This was first suggested by Smith and Jones (2009: 20) who justified their proposition by....

The article by Smith and Jones is identified by author name and its year of publication. If you are referring to more than one of their publications of the same year, you would append letters to the date (a, b, c, ...) to uniquely identify each article – thus (Smith and Jones, 2009a), (Smith and Jones, 2009b), etc. The page number (20), where the point in question was made, has also been identified. This is common when referencing books, which obviously have many pages, but not when referencing journal articles.

An alternative way of presenting this argument, supported by the same reference, could be:

Smith and Jones (2009: 20) state that 'computing has much more in common with the finer things in life, like art, than science or engineering'.

In the previous examples, Smith and Jones' ideas had been put into our own words so quotes were unnecessary. However, because their text has now been used verbatim, this text **must** be included within quotes to show that these are their words, not ours. If you are quoting a large block of text it is acceptable to present that text without quotes providing it stands out from your own text in some way. For example, you would either present that text in italics, in a different font to the one you were using or as a justified block of text between reduced margins in your report.

Berndtsson *et al.* (2008:41) point out that a common mistake when referencing large blocks of text (a paragraph) is to put the reference at the end of the paragraph. In this case, it might not be clear that the reference refers to the whole of the paragraph. It is therefore better to identify the source of the extract first.

According to Cornford and Smithson (2006: 165), there are only three occasions when you should quote other people's work verbatim:

■ where the original author has presented something 'more succinctly, elegantly or clearly' than you could;

■ 'where you need to prove that it was a particular author who wrote the words, or you are introducing some text in order to analyse it'; and

■ where there is no way of paraphrasing; for example, quoting lists.

You should also bear in mind that including too many direct quotes and references to other authors may *give away some authority* from your own work. In other words, you might include so much material from other authors that it is difficult for the reader to identify your contribution because much of the material presented is really the work of others.

Many articles are written by individuals. The Harvard system caters for single authors like this:

It is often said that computing is an art not a science (Johnson, 2007).

However, when there are more than two authors involved with the same article you generally omit all but the first author's name and use *et al* instead:

It is often said that computing is an art not a science (Peterson *et al.*, 2009).

When you wish to refer to more than one reference to support the arguments you are making in your report you would include them alphabetically:

It is often said that computing is an art not a science (Johnson, 2007; Peterson *et al.*, 2009; Smith and Jones, 2005: 20).

Sometimes you will want to present a reference to an article you haven't read (a *secondary* reference) which has been cited by another author. In this case you only need to list the article you've read in the list of references (the *primary* reference) and you should cite the reference like this (in this case you would only list the Markos *et al.* reference):

It is often said that computing is an art not a science (Johnson, 2007 cited by Markos *et al.*, 2008).

Finally, try to place references in your text in appropriate places so that the reader is not hindered by their presence. It is perhaps easier to read a sentence in which the reference is placed at the end than one which is broken up by having a reference embedded in the middle.

Before concluding, we will look briefly at the numerical referencing format for completeness. In this case, each reference is identified by a unique number:

It is often said that computing is an art not a science [1,2]. Or, it is often said that computing is an art not a science [1,2]. Or, Smith and Jones [2] state that 'computing has much more in common with the finer things in life, like art, than science or engineering'.

In this case, each time a new reference is used within your report it is given a new reference number. References are then listed at the back of your report in numerical, rather than alphabetical, order. Notice that if you decide to remove your reference to Smith and Jones, all subsequent references would need renumbering to replace the deleted reference. Similarly, inserting a new reference into your report would require all subsequent reference numbers to be incremented – something that can take a long time in terms of search and replace if your word processor doesn't have a reference management system. For these reasons, if you have a choice, it is recommended that you use the Harvard system for referencing material if at all possible.

Three abbreviations that you might use when referencing are:

■ op. cit. – *in the work already cited*

■ ibid. – *in the same place*

■ loc. cit. – *in the place cited*

Op. cit. is used to refer to an article you have cited before, earlier in your report, and is used when other references occur in between. You may have to provide the date if other authors of the same name exist. For example:

> It is often said that computing is an art not a science (Johnson, 2007: 22). Smith and Jones (2009) emphasise this point when they state that 'computing has much more in common with the finer things in life, like art, than science or engineering'. However, Johnson (*op. cit:* 34) goes on to discuss....

Ibid. is used when there are no intervening references. You must provide page numbers if required:

> It is often said that computing is an art not a science (Johnson, 2007). Intervening text here but no references.... Johnson *(ibid.)* states that computing can be defined in terms of romantic form....

Loc. cit. is used to refer to the same page of an article you have previously cited. You should provide the date as appropriate. For example:

> It is often said that computing is an art not a science (Johnson, 2007: 22). Smith and Jones (2009: 20) emphasise this point when they state that 'computing has much more in common with the finer things in life, like art, than science or engineering'. However, Johnson *(loc. cit.)* goes on to discuss....

While these abbreviations are often found in short articles and are useful when using a numeric referencing system, they should be used sparingly and with care in longer documents. Try to limit these abbreviations to references that occur on the same page or at most one page earlier in your report. Linking *ibid., op. cit.* and *loc. cit.* to a reference that occurred two or more pages beforehand makes it difficult for the reader to follow.

Above all, make sure from the way you have referenced material within your report that it is clear exactly to which article you are referring and you do not identify two articles in the same way. In addition, make sure that you use a consistent style – don't switch from Harvard form to numeric form and vice versa and try not to mix the two forms together like this[1] (Dawson, 2009).

8.5.3 Listing references

Generally speaking, the best place to list all the references you have used is at the back of your report, as opposed to footnotes at the bottom of pages or lists at the end of each chap-ter. This provides the reader with a single compendium of all relevant material that they can easily access. Articles you have used are presented under the heading of either *References* or *Bibliography*. References list only those articles that have been referred to within the report itself. A bibliography will list all the articles you have used in your project but are not necessarily referred to in the body of the report. Bibliographies are useful for the reader in that they identify all material that is relevant for taking your work forward or understanding it in more depth. For taught degree projects and books it might be more appropriate to include a bibliography, but for a research degree it would not. Your supervisor should be able to advise you on which approach to use.

How you present references will depend on the referencing system you are using – *Harvard* or *numeric*. Only the Harvard system will be discussed in detail as the numeric system is basically the same. The only difference with the numeric system is that each reference is presented in its numerical order and is presented with its numerical identifier first. For example:

15. Wilson, G. (2009) *The implications of art,* Gower, London.

16. Herbert, K. (2008) *The art of science,* Chapman Hall, Manchester, UK.

In the Harvard system, the use of italics, commas, colons, upper-case letters, abbreviations (such as Vol for Volume) and brackets may well be dictated by your own institution's 'in house' style or by a variation in the style used (for example, Chicago style). However, Harvard references should always be presented alphabetically with articles by the same author(s) presented chronologically. Examples are:

Books:

Anderson, J. Jones, J.P. and Peterson, K.K.L. (2008) *The implications of science* (2nd Edition), Pitman Publishing, London.
Benjamin, T. (2007) *Computer science made easy,* Arnold, Leeds, UK.

Note that it is not necessary to include terms such as 'Ltd', 'Inc', etc. for publisher's names as long as the publisher is clearly known from the information presented. The date that is presented represents the date on which that edition of the book was *first* published. This provides an indication of the age of the book which would not be apparent by referencing a reprint date which could be several years later. The country of publication is also included if it is not clear from the place alone. For example, cities like New York and London do not usually require USA and UK, respectively.

In cases where the author(s) is an editor of the cited work use (ed) or (eds) to denote this. For example:

Anderson, J. Jones, J.P. and Peterson, K.K.L. (eds) (2009) *The implications of science* (2nd Edition), Pitman Publishing, London.
Benjamin, T. (ed) (2006) *Computer science made easy,* Arnold, Leeds, UK.

Journal articles:

Brown, A. and Wesley, C.W. (2008a) 'An Investigation of the Hawthorne Effect', *Management Sciences Journal,* Vol 42(1), pp 47–66.

Brown, A. and Wesley, C.W. (2008b) 'Adaptation of Genetic Algorithms in Hawthorne Analysis', *Management Monthly,* Vol 28(2), pp 21–23.

Notice the use of letters (2008a, 2008b) to uniquely identify these two articles produced by the same authors in the same year.

Web addresses:

Gaynor, L. (2007) *Introduction to artificial intelligence,* <http://www.cai.com/ai/1086> (25 July 2008).

International Group on Complex Systems (2008), *Systems analysis,* Minutes of Second Meeting, 12 June 2008, <http://www.IGCS.com/Min/two.html> (25 July 2008).

References to Internet sites should include the **full** URL including *http,* etc. Make sure that you present the title of the page/article/site/author name where appropriate. These references should also include the date on which the site was accessed. Because the Internet is ever changing, these references may become outdated very quickly.

Trade or company publications:

IAEA (2008) *Guidebook on computer techniques in nuclear plants,* Technical Report Series No 27, International Atomic Energy Agency, Russia.

National Environment Research Council (2009) *Computers in hydrology report,* Vol II NERC, London.

Theses:

Hampson, J. (2008) *The effectiveness of AI in calcite modelling,* unpublished PhD thesis, Department of Computing, University of Strathclyde.

Conferences:

Jowitt, J.D. (2009) *Information Systems in a Progressive Society,* Applications of Information Systems XI, Cartwright, R.A. and Laurence, G. (eds), Rowntree Publications, Leeds, UK.

ISAIS (2008), International Symposium on Applications of Information Systems XI, proceedings of an international conference organised by the Society of IS, held London, 12–16 June 2008, Rowntree Publications, Leeds.

The first reference here (Jowitt, 2009) is for an article presented at a conference. The second reference refers to the conference proceedings themselves.

Television programmes:

The Information Programme (2008) Channel Four Television Corporation, broadcast 8.30pm Tuesday 18 November 2008.

Kay, S. (2007) *The World's a Stage,* BBC1.

The first reference here has no specific 'author' or presenter so is presented using the programme's title as a reference. The second reference is more vague and, perhaps, represents a secondary reference in which as much information as possible has been presented.

DVD/CD-ROM:

Katlen, P. and Rose, P. (2009) *Information systems in the 1990s,* CAROM DVD, Solar Information Systems, London.

Personal communication:

Sometimes people will say something to you that is useful to quote in your report. In these cases there is no physical record of the statement or source so you have to refer to the quote as a 'personal communication'. In your main text you would cite this as the following example shows – (Smith, pers comm) or Smith (pers comm). You would then list this reference using a Harvard-style as:

Smith, J. (2009) Personal communication, 12 July.

The references presented above are by no means comprehensive and you will undoubtedly come across an article, data or material from an obscure source that is not covered by these examples. However, unless your institution has specific guidelines to follow when referencing such material, you will have to present the reference in a way that you feel is appropriate. If your supervisor is unable to help you, remember two things. First, the reference should be clear enough in the body of the report so that anyone reading your report knows to which article you are referring and, second, you have provided sufficient information when listing the reference so the reader can trace that article easily if s/he wishes.

● 8.6 Documenting software

8.6.1 Introduction

People sometimes argue that it is more important to get a program's supporting documentation right than the program itself. They argue that it is always possible to mend 'bad' code that is well documented than it is to fix 'good' code that is poorly documented. This emphasises the importance of good documentation to support all software systems.

The documentation required to support a piece of software can be immense, covering a vast range of issues; from internal commenting of program code, systems analyses and design notes, figures and system documentation, to test plans and user guides. The following items are a list of topics and documentation you might be expected to cover and include in your project to support any software that you produce:

- An introduction/overview – simple introduction to the program, what it does, who is it for?

- Technical solution adopted – what technical solution has been implemented?; is this ideal?; is there an alternative?

- Design – systems analysis, systems design, human factors, story boards, etc.

- Software engineering information – structure, definition languages, test plans, etc.

- Development approach used – evolutionary delivery, build and fix, etc.
- Problems encountered – bugs, errors, uncompleted sections of code.
- Limitations – what limitations are there to the program; for example, can it only handle files of a certain size? Is it only calculating results to an accuracy of 10%, etc.? This can also include technical capabilities.
- Hardware/software requirements for running the program.
- Next stage – if you were to continue the project or somebody else was to take over from you, which parts of the software should be developed next? Which parts of the program could be enhanced with new features? Are the code, documentation, comments, etc. at a level whereby somebody could take over from you easily in the future?
- Evaluation of the software – how well does it do what it is supposed to do? Does it satisfy the user's needs?
- User guide – written at the right level of detail for the intended user.

Depending on the nature of your project, you will have to present more or less detail in each of these areas. How you complete documentation such as designs, analyses and test plans is beyond the scope of this book as it is dependent upon the development process, the methods employed and the type of project you have undertaken. For example, a pure software development project would require comprehensive analysis diagrams, test plans and system documentation, whereas a project in which you are merely developing a piece of code as a vehicle for presenting some ideas would not. The focus here is on commenting programs and writing user guides as these should be included with any piece of code you produce.

8.6.2 Commenting program code

Commenting program code is dependent on the programming language used (for example, a third or fourth generation language, an object oriented language, a formal language and so on), the style of code being developed and the requirements of your course and project. Having said this, there are a number of general guidelines you can follow when commenting your code:

- Understand the purpose of the program you are writing. Who is going to use it, maintain or enhance it, mark it? What is their level of knowledge? If you are merely writing a small program for your own use to test out some ideas you will not need as many comments as a program that is going to be used and enhanced by somebody else.
- Try to ensure you provide the right level of comments within your program – don't over-comment or under-comment and avoid comments on every single line of code. Comments should tell the programmer something that is not clear from the code itself and they are not there to explain the programming language used. For example:

$$X: = X + 1; \qquad \{add\ 1\ to\ X\}$$

This is an example of poor commenting; the comment (in brackets { }) tells the reader no more than they can deduce from the code itself (and the variable name could probably be more explicit too).

Provided you have used suitable variable names and a logical structure for your program then comments should be limited.

■ It is advisable to comment each function/procedure/object/block/screen, etc. (depending on the language used). This will explain, at the very least, what each component of your program does and may be the required depth of commenting for someone to understand how the program works and is structured.

■ Try to make comments stand out from your code so they don't become buried as a mass of text in your program. For example, tab each *in-line* comment (on the same line as a program statement) clear of the code to the right and keep line spaces around *full-line* comments (comments that have one or more lines to themselves).

■ Avoid long-winded explanations. Keep comments brief and clear – you are not writing an essay.

■ Avoid wasting time producing fancy borders, header styles and so on. Your comments are there to provide understanding and explanation to your program; they are not there to make it look pretty.

■ Make sure you include vital information at the start of your program such as author, date, version number, a description of what the program does and, possibly, a brief explanation of how it does it. These comments are often included as *block* comments – several lines of in-line comments providing more detailed explanation.

■ Try to make sure that you maintain and update program comments as you amend and develop your software. There is little point in keeping outdated comments in your code that refer to much earlier versions of your program.

In summary, it is probably a good idea to get guidance from your supervisor as to the style and level of comments required. Your department may have guidelines on what is expected in the form of program comments and there may be an 'in house' style you have to follow.

8.6.3 Writing user guides

There has been a lot of research in recent years into user guides; their structure, presentation, content, usability, 'trainability', minimalist training issues and so on, all of which are beyond the intended scope of this book. For the purposes of this book we are interested in user guides from a narrower perspective in that your guide is not going to be used by the 'masses' but within your own institution as part of your computing project and part of its assessment.

In this context any user guides you develop are likely to be presented within separate documents to your final report or included within its appendices. How you present user guides is up to you, but the longer they are the more sensible it will be to present them as a separate document. Whatever the case, a user guide should provide the user with at least these pieces of information:

■ an overview of the software – what does it do, who is it intended for?;

■ an idea of its hardware requirements – memory requirements, disk space required, additional hardware requirements such as sound cards, platform requirements (PC, Macintosh, Unix, etc.), operating system requirements, etc;

■ how to load/install the software;

■ how to start the software;

- how to end and perhaps uninstall the software; and
- details of any known problems and restrictions imposed by the program.

More broadly speaking, according to Rogerson (1989: 87), a user manual should satisfy three aims:

- 'to provide practical information about the software when help is not at hand';
- 'to help inexperienced users get started quickly and with least difficulty'; and
- 'to help experienced users become productive quickly'.

When writing user guides as part of your project, you should begin by identifying your target audience. Will you need a comprehensive guide so that complete beginners will be able to understand your software or will a simple overview of its functionality be sufficient as it will only ever be used by your supervisor?

User manuals tend to come in two different forms. First, as *training manuals* – where the user is taught how to use the software through a number of examples that build on one another. Second, as *reference manuals*, whereby experienced users can 'dip into' the manual at appropriate points for clarification/explanation of specific features of the program. How you structure your documentation will be based largely on your intended users. For experienced users a reference manual may be all that is required. However, for inexperienced users, evolutionary examples may be more appropriate. In addition, depending on the nature of your user you may have to provide detailed explanations describing simpler operating principles such as 'save as', 'page set-up', etc. It is also a good idea to include some screen dumps from your program in a user guide so users feel they are following your guide correctly when it appears that things aren't happening as they would expect. It also provides users with additional confidence to see things mapping out on the screen in the same way they are presented on paper. You might also wish to include a description of possible mistakes that could be made by a user and how the user can avoid or overcome them.

Quite a lot of user guides and help systems are embedded within programs themselves. While some of the points made earlier are relevant to these kinds of systems, their integration and technical implementation issues are beyond the scope of this book. You should consult with your supervisor and your client for advice and requirements on this issue.

● 8.7 Writing papers

 At undergraduate level it is unlikely that you will publish the results from your project unless you have made some significant findings and undertaking a research-based project. However, at postgraduate level it is pretty much expected that you will publish results from your research as either conference papers or journal papers. Getting work published is a significant milestone for PhD students as it shows that their research is making a contribution to knowledge. The advantages of writing papers while undertaking your postgraduate studies are numerous:

- Submitting a paper will provide valuable feedback from referees. From this feedback you will get an idea of the value of your work; you will get an alternative, external viewpoint on your research (other than yours or your supervisors); they may provide valuable pointers to other, similar studies; and you will receive valuable suggestions on how your work might be improved.

- It will help to improve your writing skills through practice at writing at an academic level.

- It will provide motivation – giving you a short term target at which to aim.

- When your paper is published it shows that your research is making a contribution to knowledge – showing that your PhD is at an appropriate level.

- It gives you an opportunity to start writing up your thesis early. By writing papers as you go along you may well find that your final thesis write-up is little more than a few changes to your already published works. You may be able to convert each of your papers into chapters (depending on the content) – reducing the final write-up significantly.

8.8 Summary

- When you begin to write your report, consider the reader and the purpose of your report. Use a top-down approach to structure your report and allow sections within your report to evolve over time. There is a particular order in which you should write your report and a specific way in which it should be structured. Look for ways of practising and improving your writing style.

- Your abstract should be one of the last things that you write. It should be clear and concise, and summarise the context, scope and contribution of your report. Avoid presenting your abstract as a contents listing.

- Charts and graphs can do much to enhance the appearance and content of a report. They should be used appropriately (in terms of necessity and type) and each one should be uniquely labelled and titled. You must also ensure that you scale them correctly in order to clarify the point you are trying to portray.

- A Harvard-style system is the most appropriate system to use for referencing material within your report. Each article should be uniquely identifiable and each reference should be complete so that the reader can trace the article which is referred to.

- Documenting software covers a multitude of topics – from commenting program code to writing user guides. In this chapter the development of user guides has been discussed including training manuals (with worked examples), or reference manuals (for more experienced users).

8.9 Further reading

Day, R.A. (2006) *How to write and publish a scientific paper* (6th Edition), Cambridge University Press, Cambridge, UK.

Gustavii, B. (2008) *How to write and illustrate a scientific paper* (2nd Edition), Cambridge University Press, Cambridge, UK.

Levin, P. (2005) *Excellent dissertations!,* Open University Press, Buckingham, UK.

Malmfors, B. Garnsworthy, P. and Grossman, M. (2003) *Writing and presenting scientific papers* (2nd Edition), Nottingham University Press, Nottingham, UK.

Montgomery, S.L. (2002) *The Chicago guide to communicating science,* University of Chicago Press, Chicago, USA.

● 8.10 Exercises

1. Write a short abstract of around 200 words for an article you have read recently. Compare your abstract with the article's abstract. Do you think your abstract is better or worse and why?

2. Collect some data from your library on your own institution – for example, number of students entering the university each year, their age, qualifications and so on. How are these data presented? Enter these data into a spreadsheet and present the data in a different way. Do you think that your presentation is better or worse? Why?

● 8.11 Action point

■ Produce a report breakdown structure for your own project.

CHAPTER 9

Presentation skills

Aims:

To introduce the skills needed to present and defend your project effectively in oral form.

Learning objectives:

When you have completed this chapter, you should be able to:

- Understand how to structure, plan and present effective oral presentations.
- Demonstrate your software professionally.
- Produce an attractive poster for such presentations.
- Understand the purpose of, and be able to plan for, viva voce examinations.

  - Section 9.2 is appropriate for those projects requiring oral presentations.
  - Section 9.3 is aimed at students who have to produce posters of their work – for either assessment (at undergraduate level) or conferences (at research degree level).
- Section 9.4 is appropriate for students undertaking software development projects who need to demonstrate their programs.
- Section 9.5 is particularly relevant to research degrees and also to undergraduate projects that have viva voce examinations.

● 9.1 Introduction

One of the most important aspects of any project is being able to present your findings to others. There is no point in performing an excellent piece of research if the results cannot be disseminated. While dissemination usually takes place through written reports and articles (see Chapter 8), quite often you will be called upon to make oral presentations of your work. This chapter will cover the skills needed to make effective oral presentations: how to best prepare, structure and deliver them.

As a computing student, you might well be involved with the development of a software system. Presenting and demonstrating software falls within the theme of this chapter and is discussed in detail in Section 9.4.

You may also find that, as part of your course, you will have to attend a viva voce or oral examination. How to prepare for and conduct yourself, during this kind of examination is discussed in Section 9.5.

● 9.2 Oral presentations

9.2.1 Introduction

Oral presentations are an essential part of many degree courses these days. They are frequently used to assess students' understanding of their work and their abilities to present their findings to others in oral form.

For many people, their only involvement or encounter with you and your project will be at your oral presentation. They may be interested in your work from a professional or personal viewpoint or they may be part of the assessment team evaluating your work. Whatever the case, the goal of your oral presentation should be to interest and inspire your audience, and to emphasize your own interest and enthusiasm in your project.

Two types of oral presentations you might be involved with, particularly at the postgraduate level, are conference presentations and internal departmental presentations. Quite often, postgraduate students will be expected to present at internal seminars and, for PhD students, submitting and presenting a conference paper may be compulsory during the course of their studies.

An oral presentation can be compared with an iceberg: most of it is hidden from view. Like an iceberg, your audience will only see around 10% of the work in your presentation – the delivery itself. They will not see the other 90% of effort that you put in to preparing it. In addition, of all the material you obtain and the results you acquire during the course of your project, you might only have time to present the more interesting and most important 10% of detail.

A number of considerations go into the development of an oral presentation: preparation, content, visual aids, the delivery of the presentation itself and dealing with questions. This chapter deals with each of these elements before offering a few final tips to help you present your project successfully. For more information on giving presentations, three books devoted entirely to this topic are: Etherington (2006), Hall (2007) and Reynolds (2008).

9.2.2 Preparation

The first stage of any oral presentation is preparation. During this stage you clarify your presentation's objectives, taking into account the audience who will be attending and the time you have available (including time for questions). If you don't know these things, it is important to clarify them as soon as possible as they will have a significant bearing on how you create your presentation.

Objectives

Begin by clarifying the objectives of your presentation – what do you hope to achieve and what should your focus be? Will you be discussing the project itself rather than its outcomes (for example, its problems, solutions, how you performed the project and so on)? Alternatively, you may be presenting the technical outcomes of your project to a more scientific audience (a conference presentation, for example). In this case, you might address such points as how the work was performed, the supporting research and its context, what you discovered and what your results were. You should also consider the assessment criteria being applied to your presentation (this is not relevant for conference presentations but is important if the presentation forms part of your project's assessment). In this case, are the examiners interested in the presentation itself rather than the content? Are they interested in how you form your arguments or state your case? This will clearly influence the way in which you put your talk together.

Cryer (2006: 178) identifies some additional possibilities that might represent the main purpose of your presentation:

- to explain what you have achieved and, if applicable, what you intend to do next;
- to obtain advice and feedback;
- a forum for learning and mutual support; or
- as part of your assessment or as a monitoring process.

Time

You will probably find that your presentation needs to last anywhere from ten minutes to one hour. Quite clearly, with only ten minutes for a presentation, you will have to get straight to the point; with an hour to play with, you will be able to cover more background and build up to the main point of your talk.

It's important to first clarify how much time is available for your presentation and for questions. Will you be able to decide on the proportion of time allocated for the presentation and the questions or is this specified? How flexible is this time – is it fixed to within one or two minutes or can you over- or under-run to a much greater extent?

Audience

The number and type of people who will be attending your presentation will have a significant bearing on its style and content. Ask yourself these questions: Will your audience be assessing you? Are they your peers? Are you hoping to inspire them with your work and persuade them to become involved with it? What do they already know? What do you want to teach them? What do you want to show them?

Now that you have an idea of the objectives, time and audience of your presentation you can move on to preparing the presentation itself. If you are struggling with ideas on what to include, begin by brainstorming ideas and writing them down on a piece of paper. Annotate each of these ideas onto a single piece of paper or peel-off sticker. You can then go about arranging your material into a logical structure – don't just expect to write a few notes down at random and expect to *ad-lib* your way through them on the day. Remember that your presentation should have a beginning, middle and an end, and the points you are trying to get across may need some build-up or explanation first. For example, if you wanted to discuss the application of artificial intelligence techniques to air traffic control scheduling, you would do well to provide some background on these two subjects separately first, before focusing on the main point of your talk – the overlap of these two topics.

The next stage of your preparation will be to develop visual aids. Rogerson (1989: 94) states that people retain only 10% of what they hear but 50% of what they see. Thus, visual aids are important for getting your message across and help your audience remember what you have presented. Visual aids can include over-head transparencies, slides, white boards and blackboards, computer-based presentation packages and physical objects that you wish to show or pass around the audience. Preparation of these visual aids is discussed in more detail in Sections 9.2.4 and 9.2.5.

With your talk physically prepared, the last stage of preparation is to compose yourself mentally by rehearsing your talk again and again (sometimes in front of a mirror). You may well find that you have developed too much material or are trying to cover too much detail, so you should prune your presentation to the time available. You must also familiarise yourself with the room and equipment you will be using. Make sure you can answer the following questions:

- If you are using an overhead projector, do you know how to operate it (and can you access the spare bulb)?
- For PowerPoint®-type presentations, do you know how to operate the hardware (the laptop and the projector) for projecting computer images?
- Do you know how the slide projector works if you are using one? Can you focus it and go forward and back through the slides?
- Do you know which way to insert slides into the slide projector or which way transparencies should be placed on the overhead projector?

You can begin initial rehearsals in the privacy of your own room or in front of a mirror to monitor issues like timing, structure and flow. If possible, rehearse your presentation in front of one or more people as well as on a stage. Other listeners will be able to spot silly mistakes or places where they feel you aren't explaining yourself clearly. Finally, try to rehearse your presentation in the room you will actually be using for the presentation – you might be able to do this the evening before for a conference presentation or book the room in your department if it is an internal presentation. Make sure you can use all the equipment there.

One cautionary note: oral presentations can suffer from *over* preparation. Presentations can appear stilted; the off-the-cuff remarks sound too well rehearsed, the talk doesn't flow naturally or the speaker appears to be reading from a script rather than having a conversation with the audience. Try not to fall into this trap by learning your presentation word for word. The audience expect to be spoken to as people, not read to from a script. Remember they are all individuals and expect to be spoken to as such rather than an amorphous group.

9.2.3 The presentation content

All presentations should have three main sections: the beginning, middle and end. The purpose of the beginning is to set the scene and tone for the audience and provide them with information about your presentation's content. To cover all the points necessary for your introduction, tell your audience *who, what, how, why* and *when:*

- *Who* are you – what is your affiliation, why are you there?
- *What* are you going to talk about?
- *How* long will the presentation last?
- *Why* should they listen to you – why is what you are going to say important and timely?
- *When* can they ask questions – during the talk or at the end?

It is useful to have an introductory slide for these points. You might then like to set the scene in more detail by identifying the specific topics you will be discussing. A slide listing the structure and content of your talk is also useful here (see Section 9.2.5).

Having set the scene for your presentation, you can move to the main body of your talk. What you include in your presentation will depend on the points discussed earlier – your objectives, the audience and the time allotted. A common approach for most talks of any reasonable length (20 minutes or more) is to cover three main points in their main body. People can easily retain three main ideas; any more than that and they may become confused.

You should always conclude and summarise your presentation; never end abruptly. Try to summarise what you have covered: what main points do you want people to remember? What are the conclusions from your work? How do you feel the work can be developed in the future? Try to end your presentation on a high. Many people 'switch off' during the main body of a presentation, listening mainly to the introduction and the conclusions. Try to emphasise the main contributions you have made.

To make sure your audience remembers your talk, give them something to take away. This could be a copy of some of your slides but, more importantly, something distinctive about your talk they will remember – an unusual diagram, an explosive demonstration or some earth-shattering results.

9.2.4 Visual aids

As noted earlier, visual aids come in various types: overhead transparencies, slides, flip charts, white boards, blackboards and computer-based presentation packages. The two most common are the overhead transparency and computer-based presentations based on tools such as Microsoft PowerPoint®. Although computer-based packages can produce neat, colourful and dynamic images, without adequate projection equipment they can be useless. The rules for presenting computer-based presentations are much the same as for producing overhead transparencies. However, three other points are worth noting with respect to these kinds of presentations:

- Will a laptop or PC be available or must you provide your own?
- What medium should you bring your presentation on – memory stick, for example?
- Will you have a back-up delivery method available if something goes wrong? For example, will you take overhead transparency slides of your presentation just in case?

Although white boards and blackboards are used extensively within teaching environments, they are not always well suited to presentations. You will find yourself continually turning your back to the audience to draw or write something; you may find yourself talking to the board rather than the audience and if your handwriting isn't particularly neat, your jottings may be illegible. However, white boards and blackboards can be useful if you have previously drawn or written something on them before you start your presentation, or if you plan to develop an idea or a list with audience participation. Having said this, unless you are confident with these media, it is best to avoid the use of white boards and blackboards during presentations.

For presentations using overhead transparencies or a computer program like PowerPoint, keep in mind these simple considerations:

- **Detail.** Make sure your slides are not too detailed or too sparse. Rogerson (1989: 95) suggests 40 to 50 words per transparency can be absorbed in one go, while Berndtsson *et al.* (2008: 95) suggest a maximum of seven lines of text with no more than seven words per line. Avoid long paragraphs. Figure 9.1 gives an example of a slide that is too detailed and contains too much text. Figure 9.2 shows a better example, following the advice of Berndtsson *et al.,* and presenting the information as a bulleted list the presenter can talk around.

- **Pictures.** Remember that *a picture paints a thousand words.* Try to strike a balance between images and text in your presentation. People are more likely to focus on and remember images than long textual explanations.

- **Font.** Use a clear font and, in general, avoid fonts with serifs (the added strokes at the ends of letters). Make sure the text is large enough to be read easily from the back of the room. To decide on a suitable font, try out a sample in the room beforehand. In a smaller room you might get away with 24-point text, but in larger auditoriums you will need at least 36 point for the text and 48 point for the headlines.

- **Colour.** Be careful when using colour in your slides. Some colours clash quite badly and others do not show up well when projected. Once again, experiment to find out which combinations are most suitable. As a general rule, bold, deep colours stand out best of all and contrasting colours between foreground text and background should be used. Computer-based presentations can usually get away with more varied colours than those based on transparencies as the projection equipment used is normally more powerful.

- **Hand writing.** If at all possible, avoid using hand-written or hand-drawn diagrams on transparencies. Word-processed and computer-generated transparencies look far more professional and appear much clearer.

- **Multimedia.** If you are delivering a computer-based presentation, consider including video clips, sound, computer graphics and music in your presentation. These can take time to prepare and they can also 'pad out' your presentation when the audience has really come to listen to you. However, there are certain aspects of student projects that can be presented in a better way through multimedia. For example, a video clip of a software system being used in the field; a short animation of some graphics generated by your software package and so on. Be careful when using these multimedia systems (make sure they are portable and will work on the presentation laptop) but be aware that they can 'spice up' otherwise dull presentations.

Advantages of Artificial Neural Networks

The attractiveness of Artificial Neural Networks (ANNs) to flood forecasting is threefold.

- First, ANNs can represent any arbitrary non-linear function given sufficient complexity of the trained network.

- Second, ANNs can find relationships between different input samples and, if necessary, can group samples in analogous fashion to cluster analysis.

- Finally, and perhaps most importantly, ANNs are able to generalise a relationship from small subsets of data while remaining relatively robust in the presence of noisy or missing inputs, and can adapt or learn in response to changing environments.

AI Conference   2

Figure 9.1 A slide with too much detail

Advantages of Artificial Neural Networks

- Representation of any arbitrary non-linear function;

- Finding relationships between different input samples;

- Generalise relationships from subsets of data;

- Robust with noisy or missing inputs;

- Adapt to changing environments.

AI Conference   2

Figure 9.2 A clear slide

- **Orientation.** It is often argued that transparencies should be presented in landscape rather than portrait format. This will clearly depend on the content of the transparency. Try to be consistent and stick with a landscape layout if possible.

- **Bullet points.** Some of the clearest slides are like the one depicted in Figure 9.2, with only a few bullet points that you 'speak to' during your presentation. These points provide focus for the talk but are not so detailed that the audience spends more time reading the slide than listening to you.

■ **Style.** Try to produce a consistent style for your slides – a consistent background, text colour and font; and a border style perhaps including your name, affiliation and presentation title. A consistent style looks more professional and the audience members don't have to keep 'acclimatising' themselves to ever-changing formats. If you are using a computer-based system like PowerPoint, you can set up a 'slide master' that applies a consistent style across all the slides you produce.

■ **Curling.** Although not a problem with computer-based presentations, transparencies can often curl when placed on the hot surface of overhead projectors. To alleviate this problem, transparencies can be 'framed' with cardboard. However, others, particularly those on which you have left a paper strip attached, curl almost in half. The solution is simply to carry a few coins to place on the edges of the transparency to weigh it down or, alternatively, use a pen.

■ **Slide transitions.** If you are using a presentation program like PowerPoint, you can vary the transition from one slide to the next as the program offers dozens of choices. There are no rules regarding which transitions are 'best', so select the one or ones that seem most professional to you. You might consider varying the transitions from one slide to the next to make it more interesting for the audience, or stick with one style. The important thing is, don't overdo the transition effects. Audiences tire of an endless parade of different effects. Remember, keep it simple.

Two other aids you might wish to consider are handouts and objects that can be passed around the audience. Before you pass out handouts you should be aware of their purpose. If the audience will need to refer to the handouts during your presentation, you should pass them out before you begin. If not, it is best to leave them until the end as they can cause a lot of distraction to you and the audience during your presentation. Handouts of your presentation can easily be generated with computer-based systems like PowerPoint®. They allow you to put two, four or six copies of your slides on a single sheet of paper (or even note-based pages that have copy of the slide and a space for annotating notes). Be careful that your audience members do not lose interest in your talk because they have all they need on the handouts. To avoid this you might like to give the copies of your slides on handouts after your talk is completed.

Passing around objects (for example, circuit boards) is quite interesting for the audience as it gives them a hands-on, close-up view of what you are talking about. They can, however, cause an unwelcome distraction so be careful as to the number of objects you pass around (especially if they are fragile!) and when you do it. Try to hand objects around during less intense periods of your talk, when the audience's complete attention is not required.

9.2.5 Slide content

Organise your presentation into three distinct components:

1. **Introduction.** One or two slides that introduce you and your talk.
2. **Main body.** The slides that constitute the bulk of your presentation and cover the main points that you wish to get across. How many slides you use within this section will depend on the length of the presentation and the information you wish to convey.

3. **Summary/conclusion.** A few slides that summarise your presentation and perhaps identify areas of further work.

The introduction to your presentation usually involves two slides (although this can be compressed into one slide for presentations of less than ten minutes). The first slide should present (as a minimum) the title of your talk, your name, your affiliation and the date. You might add the name of your supervisor(s) if you feel this appropriate and any co-authors of the work. Consider also including sponsors and organisations/companies involved with the project.

Be sure to number your slides so that people can refer to them after the presentation when they are asking questions and, for transparencies, if you drop them you can soon sort them back into order. Sometimes people also include the total number of slides with the slide number (for example, '1/12' or '1 of 12'). This gives the audience an idea of how much of your talk is left to go at any stage (which sometimes helps and sometimes does not!). You might also consider adding the date or, in the case of conferences, the name of the conference somewhere innocuous at the foot of each slide. These can make the slides appear more 'personal' to the audience – they have been produced just for them at this conference (despite the fact that you are re-using the slides from another talk you gave some time ago!).

Figure 9.3 presents a typical example of a title slide. Note that the presentation title, the presenter and his affiliation are listed (and also, in this case, the name of the conference in the bottom left and slide number in the bottom right). You will use this slide to

Figure 9.3 A title slide

introduce these points as these are things that are easy for you to remember and it helps you to settle into your talk.

The second slide usually presents an 'agenda' or the structure of your talk as a bulleted list. A typical example of such a slide appears in Figure 9.4. This is another slide that is fairly easy to 'talk to' and should also help you settle into your stride.

Your talk then moves into the main body of the presentation. Berndtsson *et al.* (2008: 93) suggest the following slides for the main body of a presentation lasting around 20 minutes:

■ Background
■ Arguments
■ Aims and objectives
■ Approach
■ Results.

The *Background* allows you to introduce the project to the audience. The *Arguments* support the *Aims and objectives,* which are introduced next. The next slide discusses the *Approach* (and methods) used for the research. The *Results* are

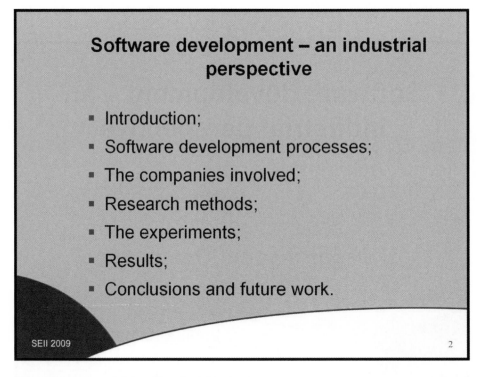

Figure 9.4 A second slide outlines the talk's structure

the last element of the main body. As noted earlier, the content of the main body depends largely on the purpose of your presentation. For a software-development project you might be presenting the requirements, designs, some implementation issues and so on. For a PhD you would want to concentrate on your main contribution and will probably be presenting a highly technical presentation. Whatever the case, discuss the content of your presentation with your supervisor and take his or her advice.

The summary or conclusion is the last stage of your presentation. You may need up to four slides to do this, or you may be able to summarise in a single slide. Short presentations may not need a summary slide, but for presentations over 30 minutes, a summary is useful to bring everything back together for the audience. A second slide might be used to highlight the conclusions of your work – for example, what have you discovered, developed and contributed? A third slide could be used to present ideas for future work – how your work may be developed going forward and what direction you feel the research should go. This *future work* slide is also a useful starting point for the questions and discussion that inevitably follow a talk. The last slide you might consider using is an *Any questions?* slide. An example is presented in Figure 9.5. This is used to complete your presentation; it might provide your contact details again if people are interested and it invites the audience to start asking you questions about your presentation.

Figure 9.5 An 'Any questions?' last slide

9.2.6 Delivery

Although you might be well prepared and your visual aids stunning, a poor delivery can ruin your presentation. Rogerson (1989: 97) identifies a number of factors that can distract the audience from what you are saying during delivery:

■ talking with your back to audience or mumbling. Lots of 'mmms' and 'errs';

■ not scanning the audience as a whole but focusing on one part of the room only;

■ wild gesticulation – people focus on this rather than what you are saying;

■ irrelevant information or sidetracking from the main point; or

■ extraneous noise.

In addition, you are likely to lose the audience's attention if you are trying to cover too much detail in a particular area – perhaps presenting lots of statistics, detailed equations and so on. Figure 9.6 illustrates an audience's attention during a presentation. As you can see, many people remain focused only at the beginning, when they are wide awake, and towards the end, when they wake up and try to catch up on what you are saying. Your delivery has a distinct affect on the audience's attention during the main body of your presentation.

Following are some tips for successful delivery:

■ **Scanning.** Make sure that you scan around all the audience during your presentation and remember to talk to people, not just their faces. Quite often you will see two or three people paying close attention to what you are saying, perhaps nodding in agreement or taking notes. You will tend to find that you focus in on these people. It then feels as if you are almost talking to one person at a time, not a large group and this can help reduce your nerves.

■ **All clear?** When you put slides onto the overhead projector or you project slides from your computer, make sure that they are clear. Make sure that you are not standing in the way, the slides are the right way up and everything is in focus.

■ **Handovers.** If you are involved with a joint presentation, for example, as part of a group project, make sure that the handovers to each other are rehearsed and you know the sequence in which each of you is speaking. It looks very unprofessional to see people end their section abruptly and ask the rest of the group, 'Who's next?'

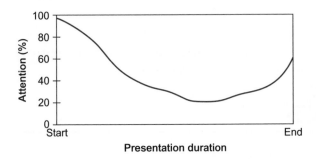

Figure 9.6 An audience's attention level during a presentation

- **Voice.** Make sure that you maintain a clear, confident voice throughout your presentation and don't mumble. Take deep breaths, slow down and pause to compose yourself if you have to.

- **Timing.** Make sure that you keep to your allotted time during your presentation. Keep a watch or a clock within sight and know what time you are due to finish. As a general rule-of-thumb, you would expect each slide to take at least one minute to present – so, for a 20-minute presentation, 20 slides would be more than enough.

- **Pauses.** Pauses can be used for good effect during a presentation. The audience will pay close attention to what you have to say after a pause, so use them only before you have something important to say. Try not to use too many pauses or they will lose their impact.

How should you use your notes? Many people use a series of cards with points set down on each of them covering the content of their talk. Quite often, however, people get ahead of themselves and are often seen rummaging through their cards to see what they are supposed to be talking about next. Alternatively, if you use transparencies, write your notes on the backing sheet of each transparency. These might direct you towards the points that you want to make for that transparency. Another approach is to have one or two sheets of paper nearby with the main points and structure of your talk noted down to prompt you, possibly with lines and arrows to direct you.

How much detail should you include on your note cards? That is up to you. With practice, just a few prompting words should be sufficient. At the other extreme, you might want to write out your talk word for word in case you dry up and have to read it. However, this is ill advised. Although you should make the notes detailed enough so that you know what to say, they shouldn't be so detailed that you have to stop your presentation to read them. A cursory glance should be all that is required for a well-rehearsed presentation.

9.2.7 Dealing with questions

Although you might complete your presentation satisfactorily, quite often the hardest part of an oral presentation is fielding the questions at the end. This is the part over which you have little control. In some circumstances, particularly if your presentation forms part of your assessment, questioners know the answer to the questions they pose. They are probing your depth of knowledge and ability to convey that knowledge. They are also interested to see how you handle questions and how well you can 'think on your feet'.

Following are a few points to help you deal with questions:

- **Preparation.** Try to think beforehand what kinds of questions you might be asked: will they be technical or more general? What kinds of answers will you be expected to give – extended answers or short answers? Will you be expected to justify or defend parts of your project?

- **Plants.** It is not uncommon for presenters to 'plant' questions with colleagues in the audience. This can help to relax you because you have the prepared answers, and can take up time that might otherwise have been filled with more difficult questions.

- **Repeat the question.** Sometimes the audience doesn't hear the whole question when it is asked (particularly if the room is large and only you have access to a microphone), so repeat the question for the entire audience before you begin to answer it. This technique will also give you a moment to collect your thoughts before you frame an answer.

- **Confidence.** At all times try to remain confident. You have been asked to speak for a reason, so you are justified in being there and people feel you are worthy to be asked a question.
- **Brevity.** Try to keep your answers brief and to the point.
- **Conflict.** Avoid conflict with the audience. Admit that differences do exist, discuss alternative interpretations and opinions and try to address things from a higher level. In addition, avoid apportioning blame. If some results came out unexpectedly or some aspects of your project didn't conclude satisfactorily, explain why this happened from your perspective. Don't blame person x or person y – your project is your responsibility so justify it from this angle.
- **Clarification.** You should always ask for clarification if you haven't understood a question. Don't try to answer what you think was asked or the question you would like to answer. The questioner will usually probe you further until they receive the response they are looking for.
- **Offer to speak to the questioner later.** If you are really struggling with a question or really don't understand it you can offer to speak to the questioner in more detail later.
- **Address the audience.** When you answer questions, make sure that you address your answer to the whole audience. Your presentation isn't over and you still have a responsibility to speak to the entire audience rather than entering an intimate conversation with one individual.

In conference situations, the chair of your presentation's session will often step in if questioning becomes hostile. This is very rare but it does happen on occasions. If you feel you are being victimised or insulted, you should ask the chair to intervene on your behalf.

9.2.8 Presentation tips

Following are a few tips to improve your oral presentations.

- **Time.** If you have difficulty keeping to time (either over- or under-estimating), have some spare slides you can 'drop in' or take out of your presentation depending on how time is progressing.
- **Pointers.** Try to avoid using laser pointers. They are never clear and wobble all over the screen. A much better way is to use a pen or pointer on the overhead projector or at the screen. If you are nervous, place the pen down against the point you are referring to and leave it there. If you are using a computer-based presentation, you could use the mouse pointer as a pointing device.
- **Movement.** Many people fidget and move around alarmingly when they are giving a presentation. With practice you can suppress these urges and learn to avoid annoying habits such as jangling keys in your pocket. If you are going to make a movement, try not to make it an exaggerated one unless you need to do so for emphasis and to

demonstrate your enthusiasm. If you want to stop yourself from walking around, place a finger on the nearest desk or chair – subconsciously your body will want to remain fixed where you are.

■ **Nerves.** Everybody suffers from nerves to some extent or another. While nerves are never totally eliminated, they do ebb as you become more and more used to giving presentations. The 'secret' here is to give as many presentations as possible and keep on practicing. The more presentations you do, the easier it becomes. And remember, without a few nerves, you would not have enough adrenalin to deliver an exciting presentation. If you are shaking you could perhaps switch the overhead projector off as you change slides.

■ **Technical failure.** Overhead projectors are not infallible (the bulbs do blow in them quite frequently) and laptops linked to projectors do go wrong from time to time. Quite often, projectors have spare bulbs within them that you can switch to; so learn how to do this. Alternatively, have a contingency plan such as using transparencies if you have a computer-based presentation or moving to a white board or referring to handouts of your slides if you are using an overhead projector. Usually, however, if the there is a major technical failure, your session chair will step in to assist you.

Above all else, be *enthusiastic*. Enthusiasm can do a lot to hide nerves and perhaps even some content lacking from your presentation. The audience will be on the edge of their seats when they see how interested you are in your work and will become motivated and supportive of you as well.

● 9.3 Poster presentations

9.3.1 Introduction

Instead of students doing software demonstrations or oral presentations, some institutions arrange poster sessions as part of the assessment process. At the postgraduate level you may have to produce a poster for other reasons. Your department may hold a poster competition for its postgraduate students – encouraging them to share their work with others. Alternatively, a poster presentation might be a good first step to getting your work published at an international conference – giving you a chance to meet others in your field and discuss your ideas with them.

In some ways, poster sessions are better than oral presentations. You can interact more with people who are interested in your work (as they discuss the content of your poster with you) rather than having to follow a predefined presentation; they are less stressful (it is easier to stand by your poster and discuss your work than to present a talk to a roomful of people); you can selectively view the work of others (rather than having to sit through many presentations you might not be interested in); and you can focus on aspects of your work that you feel are most important as you discuss your poster face to face with others.

Because typically many posters are on display during poster sessions, you need to find a way to make your poster stand out so that people will be attracted to it and take an interest in your work. People tend to spend three different phases of time in front of posters – it is important to attract their attention in the first instance and then maintain their attention as they progress through different levels of detail on the poster. A viewer will form an impression of your poster in the first couple of seconds they look at it (phase 1). Some questions that instinctively go through a viewer's mind when looking at your poster are these:

- Is it the right subject material for me?
- Is it at the right level of detail?
- Is it presented in such a way that I can easily understand the main points or principles?
- Is it interesting?

If your poster passes the phase 1 scrutiny and the viewer decides to read your poster rather than move on, he or she will generally spend another 10 to 15 seconds on the second phase of assessment. If a viewer is still interested after this stage, he or she will tend to be willing to read the whole poster and ask questions of the presenter (phase 3).

In the following sections we look at some ways you can make your poster look good, keep people interested to phase 3 of viewing and provide some examples of good and bad poster design. The main areas to consider are the poster's content, size and shape, layout, font (size and style) and colour scheme.

9.3.2 Content

You need to have some idea of what to cover, what will go into your poster and how large the poster should be before you can start putting it together. The first thing to consider is the audience. Are you producing the poster for an international conference, so the audience will be largely informed researchers in the field who will be interested in the detail of what you have done; or is the poster forming part of your final assessment and will be viewed largely by colleagues and examiners who might be more interested in a general overview of what you have achieved? The type of project you have undertaken will also influence its content. For a research-based project, you might want to focus on information such as research methodology, your findings, results and conclusions. For a software development project, you might want to discuss the requirements, designs, implementation issues, user feedback and the like.

Regardless of your project topic, include these essential sections in your poster.

- Title. Normally, this is your project title (or title submitted to the conference). The title should be catchy and not overly long. Make sure it is presented in sentence case (Like this, Not Like This or LIKE THIS).
- Name and affiliation/course details/contact details as appropriate.
- Introduction/overview/summary. This shouldn't be an abstract but an introduction to what your project is about – providing the audience with a general idea of what you have achieved and what the poster is about.
- Conclusions. What are the main findings from your work, what is its contribution?

- Acknowledgements.
- References. Include these if appropriate but don't list so many that they take up a large area of space.

The rest of the poster's content is clearly influenced by the project type, the intended audience and the project's contribution. It would be usual to include sections such as Results, Further Work, Methodology; but what goes into these sections is clearly dependent on the poster's purpose. Bear in mind that a poster should have only enough content so that the average reader could read the entire poster in ten minutes maximum.

9.3.3 Size and shape

Make sure you know how large the poster should be when planning what to put in it. Usually posters are printed in at least A1 size (84cm × 54cm) but A0 is more usual (around 119cm × 84cm). It doesn't really matter how big you print your poster (as long as it is within suggested guidelines) as the larger the poster is, the further people stand away from the poster to take it all in anyway.

Note that posters are normally produced in landscape rather than portrait format but it doesn't matter which orientation you use as both forms are usually acceptable. When you come to print out your poster, will you have access to a large printer that can print this size of poster or must you print out a number of smaller sheets and stick them together (which will look much less professional)?

9.3.4 Layout

Start by drafting your poster on paper – getting an idea of the layout, where each section will be placed and how much space each section will be allocated. What graphs, figures and tables do you plan to include and where will they be placed? Use sticky notes to plan where things will go and move these around as your ideas and the poster evolves. Posters tend to be easier to read when split into three or more columns . Having all the text arranged in one block like a report does not work well. The content should be arranged so that it progresses, firstly down columns and, secondly, from left to right in a logical sequence. Whether you have long columns or smaller sectioned columns depends on how much information is going into each section. A suggested content for posters is that around 25% of the poster should be text, 45% graphics (figures, pictures, etc.) and 30% should be white space.

Figure 9.7 shows some sample layouts for posters. Both have a section at the top where the poster's title and the author's name would go. Both are split into a number of columns, the height and size varying according to the content. The poster on the right-hand side has been split so that supplementary information (not part of the main content of the poster) – such as acknowledgements, logos, email addresses, references, etc. – is presented in a number of boxes at the bottom of the poster.

Another way to design your poster is to use a template. If you search for 'poster template' on the Internet you will find a number of predefined templates produced for different software packages. These can be tailored to your own needs and provide some interesting ideas on layout, colour schemes and fonts. Another useful resource is

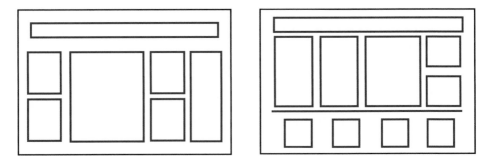

Figure 9.7 Sample poster layouts

http://www.ePosters.net (the online journal of scientific posters). This site allows you to view other people's posters and upload your own for comment.

9.3.5 Font

Use a proportional sans serif font for your poster – particularly for the title and headings, which need to be clear. Earlier in this chapter, we mentioned that serifs are the small strokes on the ends of the letters. As its name suggests, a sans-serif font does not have serifs. In a proportional font, the letters take up different widths of space depending on their size/shape. For example, 'i' takes up less space than 'w' in a proportional font. Graphic design experts believe proportional fonts are easier to read than non-proportional (also called monospaced) fonts in which each letter takes up the same amount of space, irrespective of its size (for example, Courier is a monospaced font). Try to use the same font throughout your poster (although headings and titles could be in a different font to smaller blocks of text) – don't chop and change from one section to another (even on figures and charts). This consistency adds a professional touch to your poster. Arial is a good, readable font to choose for posters as it is proportional and sans serif. You may use a serif font for the smaller text on your poster if you believe, as some people do, that such fonts are easier to read than sans-serif fonts when reading large blocks of text – but stick to a sans serif font for headings and titles.

In terms of font size, as a general rule of thumb, never use 12-point type or smaller for a poster. The minimum type size for poster text is 14 points, while titles and section headings will obviously need to be much larger.

9.3.6 Colours

The choice of colours can make or break your poster. While you may have got the content, layout and font correct, choosing clashing, garish colours or colours that do not contrast very well can make your poster unreadable.

Softer colours tend to work well for backgrounds, while foreground text should be presented in bold colours to make it stand out. Make sure that the colours you choose for backgrounds and foregrounds contrast well – there is no point, for example, in having a pale yellow text on a white background or white text on a pale pastel background – it will be too difficult to read. However, don't go for white text on a dark (black) background either. While these colours may contrast well, the overall appearance of the poster can be daunting and difficult to read.

9.3.7 Examples

Figures 9.8 and 9.9 provide two example posters from a student project that aimed to develop a web site to statistically analyse various kinds of data. Ignoring the content of the posters, they provide a contrasting example of bad and good poster design. While both posters are based on the same project and say much the same thing in terms of content, the way they have presented this information is vastly different. Figure 9.8 shows a badly designed poster. The layout is poor – consisting of a number of sections of text. There are no images or diagrams to break up the poster. There is little white space. There are spelling mistakes (notably in the title). The poster uses a number of different fonts and font size is too small in many cases. Perhaps worst of all is the colour scheme – the white on black text is intense and the section with the white on pale blue is unreadable.

In contrast, Figure 9.9 shows a better presentation of the same material. The layout has been split into three columns with a header section (containing the title and author). A consistent font (Arial) is used throughout and 20-point type has been used for the smallest text. The main title is produced in 110-point type while the sub-headings are in 100 point. The background is generally pale with the text presented in a contrasting dark

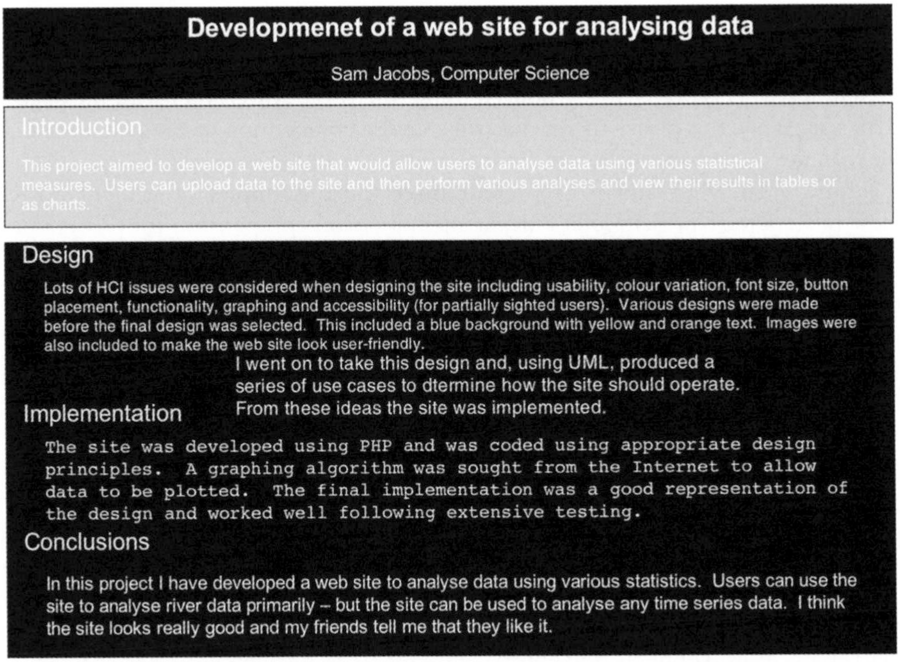

Figure 9.8 Example of a badly designed poster

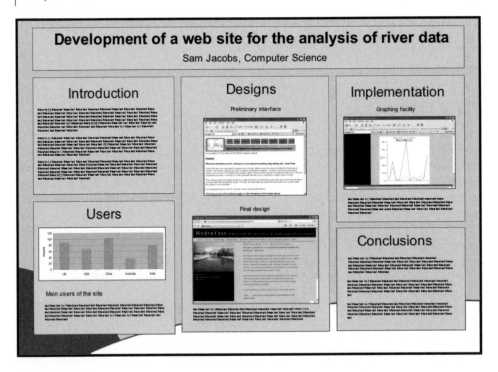

Figure 9.9 Example of a three-column poster with a coloured background

type. Figures and pictures are used to make the poster more appealing and there is plenty of white space. This poster was produced using Microsoft PowerPoint with the page set to A0 size. While this poster might not win a design competition, it is much more readable than the previous version.

Figures 9.10, 9.11 and 9.12 present three more examples of student posters. These posters were presented at a departmental poster competition for postgraduate students. Of the 30 or so posters presented at the competition, these three caught the eye most. The first is very clear in its layout and flow; the second provides a lot of detail but has some interesting images to break up the text and the third (which won the poster competition) has a very interesting, clear layout with a themed presentation style.

9.3.8 Software

There are a number of software packages available to produce posters. You can use specialist desktop publishing packages such as QuarkXpress, Adobe InDesign and Microsoft Publisher. Alternatively, use graphics or drawing packages to piece together your poster. Examples include CorelDraw, OmniGraffle, FreeHand, and SmartDraw. A less sophisticated approach might be to develop your poster in a word processing package such as Microsoft Word. The examples in this chapter used Microsoft PowerPoint. This allowed text and graphics to be inserted on the page,

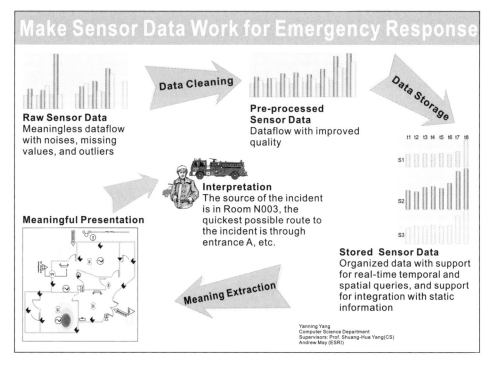

Figure 9.10 Example of a postgraduate poster

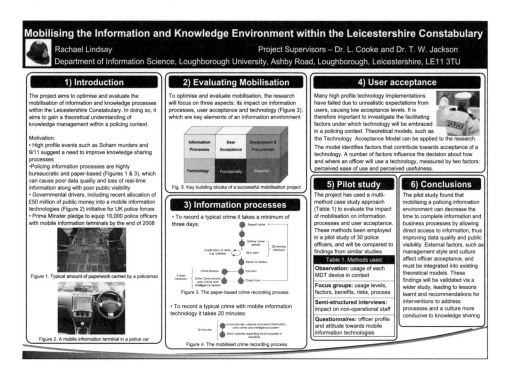

Figure 9.11 Example of a postgraduate poster

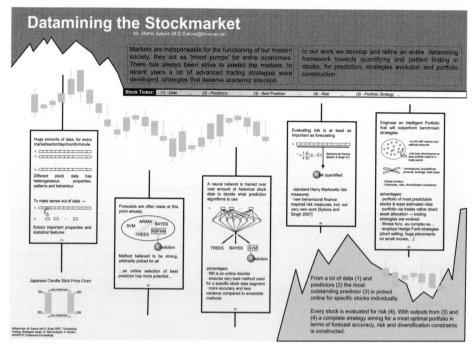

Figure 9.12 Example of a postgraduate poster

colours to be set, lines to be drawn and, importantly, spelling to be checked. Most students will use a package such as PowerPoint as this is readily available and relatively easy to use.

9.3.9 Poster preparation tips

■ Use boldly coloured text and more subtle background colours. Don't choose clashing colours or colours that makes people's eyes hurt. Contrasting colours are important. Take the following two examples in Figure 9.13 and Figure 9.14. Both of these posters have exactly the same content but have been presented in a slightly different way. Figure 9.13, while split into four columns, has no distinguishing border or outline to these columns. In contrast, Figure 9.14 has placed the entire poster on a darker background so that the columns stand out more. You might want to consider which one you feel looks best.

■ Use non-shiny paper (do not laminate the poster). Shiny posters are often difficult to read as the light catches them.

■ Depending on the context (conference, final assessment, etc.), consider providing handouts – perhaps A4 copies of the poster, a summary page, etc.

■ Do not use smaller than 14-point type and use a consistent font throughout.

■ Make sure the poster is structured logically – flowing down through columns and from left to right.

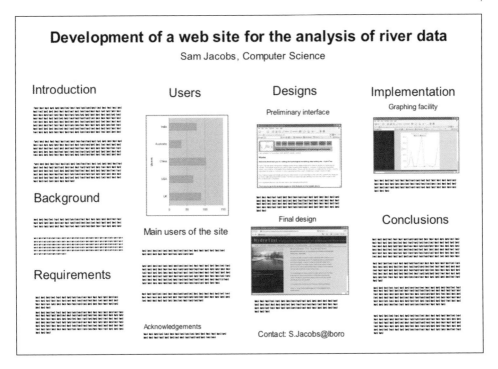

Figure 9.13 Example of a four columned poster with a plain white background

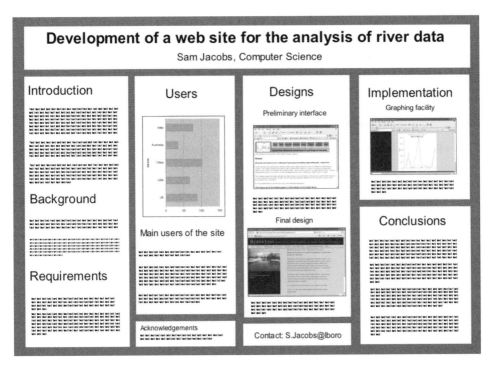

Figure 9.14 Example of a four columned poster with white column background and darker overall background

- Keep equations to a minimum.
- For variety, use figures, tables, charts and other visuals. A poster made up entirely of text will not be engaging or attractive.
- Be careful when using clip art or images in your poster. Sometimes, when the poster is printed out full-size, the images will become pixillated and appear blurred.
- Make sure all graphs and charts are correctly labelled and can be read in isolation (for example, you don't have to read through the text to determine the map scale or what the axes on a graph represents).
- Where figures and pictures are used, applying a border can enhance their appearance. Consider Figures 9.15 and 9.16. In Figure 9.15 a picture is shown with and without a border. In Figure 9.16 a chart is shown with and without a border. By encapsulating the images within a border they appear to stand out from the page more.
- Check your spelling. Spelling mistakes look a lot worse when blown up to large scale on a poster.
- Avoid large blocks of text – probably up to ten sentences at most in any one section.

Figure 9.15 Example of a photograph with and without a border

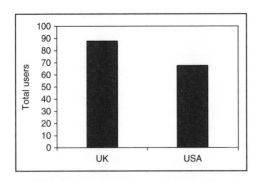 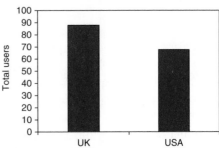

Figure 9.16 Example of a chart with and without a border

- Don't try to pack too much into your poster – remember to leave sufficient white space on the poster. Be selective in which results you are presenting and focus on those charts and figures that convey the main contribution of your work.

Once you have produced your poster, it is a good idea to get feedback from friends or colleagues. Although you may think you have chosen an interesting design and appropriate colour combination, they may have other opinions. You are unlikely to produce a perfect poster on your first attempt – so be prepared to draft and redraft until you get it right.

9.4 Demonstrating software

9.4.1 Introduction

As a student on a computing course of one kind or another, there is a strong chance that you will have developed a piece of software at some stage. Whether this software is the main component of your project or merely a vehicle for testing out and presenting some ideas, you may well have to demonstrate this software to your tutor, your examiner, your peers, a client or some other interested parties. This section discusses ways to prepare for such a presentation, some considerations you should make before your demonstration and some tips that will assist you.

9.4.2 Preparation

You should prepare for a software demonstration in much the same way as you would prepare an oral presentation. You should decide on your demonstration's purpose, then plan, prepare and rehearse your demonstration.

When deciding on your demonstration's purpose, ask yourself what you hope to achieve. What do you hope to show and get across to the audience?

Your demonstration should also be planned thoroughly. Structure the demonstration beforehand – don't just expect to 'play around' with your program on the day. Like an oral presentation, it should have a beginning, a middle and an end. You should also decide how you want the demonstration to be performed:

- **Solo running.** You run through a particular, planned sequence of tasks on your own with no interruptions or audience interaction. This approach is not advisable as it might appear that you are 'protecting' your program's weaknesses by merely demonstrating some simplistic features. In other words, any variations to the sequence or the data you are entering might cause your program to crash. Although this might not be the case, this is how it might appear to the audience.
- **Rolling demonstration.** The software runs itself through a predetermined demonstration that cannot be interacted with. This might be a demonstration package you have developed rather than the software package itself.
- **Audience participation.** You allow the audience to request things or suggest examples as you run through the program in a relatively free manner. This is the most common approach to software demonstrations where you have an approximate idea

of the functions and options you wish to demonstrate but expect to be directed at times by audience requests.

■ **Audience running.** You permit the audience to play with the software with you guiding them. This approach is suitable for a software tool that is demonstrating usability and ease of learning.

■ **Supporting presentation.** When students perform software demonstrations they sometimes use two machines. One is for the demonstration of the software; the other is for a short PowerPoint-style presentation that introduces the demonstration – the project, the client, the format of the demonstration and so on. You can run the presentation and the demonstration on the same machine but there is a risk that your software won't load and run smoothly while the presentation package is still running in the background.

When you prepare your demonstration, keep in mind the *time,* the *audience* and the *focus.*

■ **Time.** How much time is available? You do not want to overrun or underrun your demonstration so careful preparation and timing of actions during rehearsal is important. If you are overrunning, think about parts of the program that don't really need demonstrating. Can you go straight to the part of the program you really want the audience to see and skip any introductory screens or messages?

■ **Audience.** Know who the audience will be – what do they know, want to see/ learn? Are they staff, students or a client? What will you have to explain? What is the audience likely to ask you? Will you need to justify primary things such as the choice of programming language used, the algorithm you have decided to use and so on?

   It may be that you are presenting your software to your tutor but the software is actually for somebody else – an industrial client, for example. Your tutor, therefore, may be more interested in your design, interface development and so on, whereas the client may be more interested in learning how the software works and its functionality and limitations.

   The size of group will also have a bearing on your presentation. According to Rogerson (1989: 103), a software demonstration 'to a large group will be more generalised and more high level than that to a smaller group when the interests can be identified and the demonstration tailored accordingly'. The size of audience will also have an effect on the choice of hardware you will need to use. For three or four people a single monitor might be suitable, but for larger groups you will have to consider using a projection system of some kind or another.

■ **Focus.** Concentrate and focus on the good points of your software – not just basic functions such as loading and saving files, printing and so on. Similarly, try to focus the demonstration towards the purpose of your project. For example, if your project aimed to explore human computer interaction issues, concentrate on the software's screen designs, layouts and navigation routes. If it was to implement and test a particular algorithm, focus on the results and outputs from the software and its efficiency.

Before you actually perform your demonstration, rehearse it thoroughly – preferably on the hardware system you will be using on the day. Make sure that your software will work on the system you will be using – is it the right hardware configuration, does it need a graphics card and so on?

9.4.3 Demonstration tips

The following points will help you prepare and present effective software demonstrations. This list is not exhaustive and the effectiveness of individual tips will depend on the type of demonstration you are performing, the programming language you have used and the audience.

- If possible, try to set up as much as you can beforehand. People hate to wait around while you load software, set up overhead projectors and so on. If this is not possible, try to practice loading your software somewhere else so that you can load it as quickly and easily as possible. Although your presentation may not yet have started, people can be put off your program before they have even seen it working because it appears to need half an hour and a PhD to install! Alternatively, be prepared to give a small anecdote, story or some additional information about your program to help pass the time while it loads.

- Make sure that all the audience can see the screen clearly. Is there any reflective light on the screen? Is the monitor clear of smudges and finger marks?

- Know your software's limitations, bugs and faults so that you don't try to do something that your software can't handle. This is also useful if you are to demonstrate a particular aspect of the code in which there are problems so you don't look embarrassed or surprised when things go wrong. In this case, you can explain that a particular section is still under development or hasn't been thoroughly tested yet. You can also joke that the fault/bug is known and is documented on page 52 of the report!

- Know how your software works and how it is structured. This will enable you to explain these points if asked and will demonstrate your deeper understanding of the code.

- If your software is well written and well structured, it is likely to consist of a number of *stubs*. These stubs are sections of code (components and functions) that haven't been completed but will be developed in the future. Developing a program using a top-down approach to identify its components and functions is a recognised practice and is acceptable providing that the system doesn't crash when it accesses these stubs (see Chapter 6 for more discussion of this development approach). In these cases it is usual for each stub to return a message such as 'This function is still under development'. Developing your program in this way improves its maintainability, readability and structure.

- Highlight some additional features you have included that may not be apparent from a straightforward demonstration. For example, if the software asks the user to enter a month number, the software might check that the value is between 1 and 12 (not apparent if they entered 6). These kinds of checks, although included, are not normally evident from a demonstration unless pointed out or questioned.

- Never say 'Oh, that shouldn't have happened', or 'What's happening now?'

- Be aware of similar software packages. Know the competition and understand how your software compares with (and improves upon) them. Section 5.3 provided some guidance on where to look for software relevant to your project.

- Practice beforehand. The main point to emphasise is rehearsal. You don't want to run out of time having only demonstrated half of your program and you don't want to come across unexpected bugs.

9.5 Viva voce examinations

 Not only must students often present their projects in oral presentations, they also have to 'defend' their project during a viva voce examination (*vivas*). This form of examination is more common at the postgraduate level and is compulsory for PhDs.

A *viva* is an oral 'interview' conducted by one or more examiners. Sometimes it is used merely to check that the work of the project is your own and has not been done by someone else. Sometimes it is used to clarify some points you made in your report that are vague or unclear. It is more commonly used to assess your understanding, depth of knowledge, confidence and ability to present your project in an examination situation. You should be prepared to defend your project during the examination; justifying why it is important and timely. You should also be able to explain and discuss the contribution your project is making. You will not be expected to know your report/dissertation word for word (for example, what is on page 10, paragraph 2) so you should be able to refer to your report during the examination.

In some cases the viva is used only to upgrade your mark; for example, at the undergraduate level, if you are a borderline case, the examiner might be looking for a good reason to increase your final mark. At postgraduate level the viva is used as an additional way of examining your understanding of your project and the subject area and provides further evidence to support your project.

The nature of your course will affect the duration and content of any viva you might have to attend. Vivas can last anything from five to ten minutes to several hours or even two or three days in the case of some PhDs. For open-ended vivas, generally speaking, the shorter they are the more confident the examiners are with the quality of your work and the less they feel they need to probe you on your understanding.

Who conducts the examination will also be dictated by your course's requirements. At one extreme it might be little more than a brief chat with your supervisor. For research degrees it is more than likely that external examiners will conduct the viva, with internal examiners and possibly your own supervisor in attendance. Sometimes examining committees are involved and sometimes the examination is held in public (this is common in Europe). For undergraduate projects, external examiners are unlikely and your own supervisor or another academic within your department will conduct the interview.

Whether your viva is a short interview with your supervisor, or the more formal postgraduate viva, you should still prepare for it thoroughly;

■ Make sure that you read your report thoroughly beforehand so that it is fresh in your mind. For postgraduate projects there can often be a gap of several months between the time you submit your dissertation and the time you attend your viva.

■ Try to identify any errors, omissions and perhaps shortfalls with your work, so that you are prepared to defend these points in the examination. If an examiner identifies a shortfall with your work of which you were unaware, it can catch you off-guard and leave you struggling. If, however, you have identified any problems beforehand, you can perhaps be prepared to discuss why you didn't do something in a particular way or feel that such-and-such a method was inappropriate in your case. You could then move on to emphasise some of the more important findings you made.

- Be aware of the things you left out of your report – references, data, methods and so on. Be prepared to defend your reasons for omitting them.

- Be prepared to discuss future developments to your work. Where do you feel your research is heading? What do you think is the future of your subject area? What topics do you feel are suitable for further research and development? If you are unable to do this you might give the impression that your project has been merely a vehicle for obtaining your degree and you have no motivation towards the work or enough interest to care how it is developed in the future.

- Cryer (2006: 249) notes that you should be prepared to answer quite general questions about your project; 'What did you enjoy most about your work?', 'What would you do differently if you were starting out all over again?', and so on. These kinds of questions can often cause more problems than the highly technical questions on specific aspects of your project that you understand in detail and can talk about for hours. They might also be used by examiners to probe 'how well you can appraise your own work and your personal development as a researcher and scholar' (Cryer, ibid).

- Make sure that you understand the broader subject area in which your project resides. This will allow you to emphasise the contribution that your project is making and enable you to discuss its context within wider issues.

During the examination:

- Make sure you defend your project positively. In other words, don't criticise the work of others but focus on the contribution your own project is making. Cryer (2006: 252) states that you should show that you do take the work of others seriously even if you disagree with them.

- Be prepared to answer open questions and give extended answers; not just simple 'yes' or 'no' answers. Ricketts (1998: 25) presents some typical questions you might encounter in your viva that require extended answers. Typical questions include:

  - What related research did you locate and draw on?
  - What do you feel was the most challenging part of your project?
  - What was the most interesting part of your project?
  - What is the main contribution your project is making?
  - What would you do differently next time?
  - What makes you think your project is the right level (in terms of scope, breadth, depth, quality) for your course?
  - What parts of your work could be published?
  - Why did you **not** use methods X, Y or Z? Why **did** you use methods P, Q or R?

- Avoid confrontation. Don't argue with the examiners but try to explain your point of view and why you feel things are the way you see them. The examiners will expect you to argue your case, but not aggressively.

Cryer (2006: 251–252) presents some additional guidelines for conducting yourself during your viva:

- Take a notepad and pen to the viva if you feel this will help.

- Take your own copy of the report/dissertation with you to refer to during the examination. You might also wish to include some annotated notes to provide yourself with prompts – for example, why you did things in particular ways, why you chose this method, how you implemented this algorithm and so on. However, Ricketts (1998: 26) points out that you should try to avoid reading directly from your report during the viva.

- Remain composed. Be pleasant and polite and sit squarely on the chair.
- Listen attentively to the examiners and ask for clarification if you need it.

Cryer (2006: 251) also presents some suggestions on how you should dress for an oral examination. She suggests that you should 'choose clothes that are smart and businesslike, to show that you appreciate the importance of the occasion'. However, you shouldn't try to upstage your examiners and in certain circumstances casual dress would be quite acceptable but confirm this with your supervisor beforehand.

Overall, remember not to panic during your viva. The examiners are not trying to catch you out but merely trying to probe your understanding about your work and clarify some of the ideas and points you have made. Bear this in mind and think of your viva as an *opportunity* to put forward your own views on the subject and support the work you have accomplished.

● 9.6 Summary

- Oral presentations are quite common within most computing degree courses. You must prepare for such presentations thoroughly. Begin by deciding on the objectives of your presentation and make sure you know who the audience will be and how much time you have available. Make sure that your presentation has a logical structure with a beginning, a middle and an end. Make sure all your visual aids are clear and that you rehearse your presentation well. A number of tips were presented on preparing slides, delivering your presentation and fielding questions.

- When preparing posters you need to consider the audience, content, layout, font and colour scheme. Make sure that the poster is structured into columns, it has figures as well as text and there is sufficient white space. Use light-coloured backgrounds and contrasting dark colours for text.

- Prepare software demonstrations in the same way that you would prepare an oral presentation. Decide on the demonstration's purpose then plan, prepare and rehearse it thoroughly. Be aware of your audience, the time you have available and what you want to focus on.

- It is not uncommon for computing students to sit viva voce examinations. Make sure that you are well prepared for such an examination – read through your report beforehand and try to think of, and prepare for, any questions that may be asked. Know about the strengths and weaknesses of your report and understand how it fits into its wider context. During the examination you should avoid confrontation and be prepared to defend your work. You should also be able to discuss how you feel your work could be developed further in the future.

● 9.7 Further reading

Etherington, B. (2006) *Presentation skills for quivering wrecks,* Cyan Books, London.

Hall, R. (2007) *Brilliant presentations: What the best presenters know, say and do,* Prentice Hall, Englewood Cliffs, USA.

Nicol, A.A.M. and Pexman, P.M. (2003) *Displaying your findings: A practical guide to creating figures, posters and presentations,* American Psychological Association, Washington, USA.

Reynolds, G. (2008) *Presentation Zen: Simple ideas on presentation design and delivery,* New Riders, Indianapolis, USA.

● 9.8 Action points

- Prepare a presentation of around 20 minutes based on the lessons you have learnt within this chapter. Try to identify slides that could be skipped or added if you are overrunning or underrunning.

- Prepare a poster based on your project and try to get some feedback on it from your colleagues.

- Prepare a software demonstration. Rehearse it thoroughly and try it out on some of your colleagues first.

- Prepare for a viva voce examination. Try to think of some questions that might be asked and prepare your response to those questions.

The future

Final considerations

Aims:

To discuss life after your project is handed in.

Learning objectives:

When you have completed this chapter, you should be able to:

- Understand how examiners will be marking your project.
- Understand ways in which you can develop your project further in the future.
- Recognise the skills you have acquired from doing your project and understand how you can apply these skills in the future.
- Develop your project into publishable material.

- This chapter is relevant for postgraduate and undergraduate projects.

● 10.1 Introduction

Now that your project is coming to an end, there are a number of things you will want to consider. How will your project be examined? What does the future hold for you? Are you going to stay on in academia or move on to pastures new and go into industry? Do you wish to forget all about your project or take it further? Will the successful completion of your project lead to further qualifications and professional recognition? What have you learnt from doing your project and how will these skills be useful in the future?

This chapter brings together answers to these questions and shows you how you have gained knowledge and benefited from the project you have undertaken. You should be proud of the work you have put into your project and view it as a stepping-stone to the next stage of your career – be it in academia or industry. This chapter concludes with a list of top ten tips for completing your project successfully. This list draws together ideas that have been covered in earlier chapters.

● 10.2 Examiners and the marking of your project

10.2.1 Introduction

How your project will be assessed depends on the type of project you have undertaken, its level (undergraduate or postgraduate) and the regulations within your institution. For example, at undergraduate level you may have undertaken a software development project so you will be assessed on the system you have developed, its supporting documentation, your evalu-ation of the software and processes used, feedback you have received from the client/user(s) and comparisons you have made with other similar systems. At undergraduate level there may be explicit *learning outcomes* for projects against which you will be assessed. These might range from your ability to plan and manage a project to your ability to undertake research and complete a report. At Loughborough University the Intended Learning Outcomes (ILOs) for final year projects in Computer Science (taught bachelor's degree) have been split into the following four areas:

- **Knowledge and understanding.** This covers all aspects of the project and includes taught and self-taught knowledge.
- **Cognitive abilities.** This covers the student's abilities in planning the project, analysing requirements, application and judgement.
- **Practical abilities.** This covers skills in the development of software systems using appropriate techniques, methods and tools. It can also include skills such as applying appropriate research methods for those projects that do not involve software development.
- **Transferable skills.** What has the student learnt that can be used in other work (for example, information retrieval skills, report writing or use of IT)?

At research degree level, particularly PhD, you will be assessed on the *contribution* your project has made. Quite clearly, if you have published some journal and/or conference articles during the course of your studies, you will satisfy this particular requirement by the time the examiners come to read your dissertation. In some countries this is compulsory; for example, you may be expected to have published at least five first-author journal papers by the time you submit your thesis.

The nature of regulations at your institution will also dictate how the examiner(s) will be involved in the assessment of your work. At taught degree level the examiner might simply be your supervisor or another academic member of staff in your department who will simply read your report. At research degree level the assessment will be more rigorous and may involve external examiners from other universities or countries interviewing you (viva voce examinations, discussed in Chapter 9) or an examining committee questioning you in a public defence.

It would take too long to cover all assessment processes, methods and marking schemes individually, so this section provides a general overview of the possible considerations examiners might be looking for. You should look through the following points and decide which of these issues the examiners will be looking for in your own case.

10.2.2 Assessment criteria

As a starting point, we will look at the assessment criteria Berndtsson *et al.* (2008: 7–8) identify for evaluating student projects. They split the assessment criteria into the following four areas for undergraduate projects:

1. **General.** Examiner(s) will look at the relevance and appropriateness of the topic you have studied, the significance of the findings and the amount of contribution you have achieved (rather than the contribution of your supervisor).

2. **Report.** Examiner(s) will look for clarity, consistency, an appropriate use of arguments, a clear differentiation between your own work and that of others in the literature and appropriate referencing (in terms of style and references used).

3. **Defence.** Examiner(s) will assess the types of arguments you have made to support and defend your claims and conclusions. They will also look for your own insight and understanding in the work you have presented.

4. **Other.** Examiner(s) will review the administrative issues of your project. For example, have you followed the regulations correctly? Have you provided the right documentation at the right time?

While some of these issues are relevant to postgraduate projects, it is worth looking at some specific criteria used to assess research degrees. In this case, Chinneck (1999) identifies four things that examiners look for when examining postgraduate dissertations:

1. What was the research question?

2. Is it a 'good' question? This involves a comprehensive literature review to ensure that the question is 'useful' – i.e., worth answering. Through the literature review the student will show the context of the question, that the question has not been answered before and the extent to which others may have partly answered the question in the past.

3. Has the student answered the question adequately?

4. Has the student made an adequate contribution to knowledge?

These two sets of criteria go some way to emphasise the diversity of elements that examiners are looking for when assessing student projects. The lists are by no means exhaustive, so a criterion is now presented that attempts to capture most of the issues. This criterion has been split into four areas.

1. *General* considerations (cf Berndtsson *et. al.,* 2008). These considerations occur in all types of projects at all degree levels.

2. *Foundations* of your project – is its existence justified within other literature in the field?

3. The project *approach* from a technical perspective (i.e., not a project management viewpoint). Were the correct methods used? Were appropriate data gathered?

4. *Results* and *contribution* of the project. This is particularly important at postgraduate level where the ultimate contribution of the work is the quality measure used.

The four areas are presented below with a list of criteria that may be assessed within them. You will not be assessed on all of these criteria (and indeed, you may not be assessed in all four areas) but you should be aware of which points are relevant to your project. Those marked with the *mortarboard and certificate* symbol (🎓) are particularly important at postgraduate level.

1. General project considerations (subject independent)

- How well did you plan and control the project?
- Did you manage your time effectively?
- How did you conduct yourself throughout the project? How motivated were you? How much effort did you put in?
- How clear is your report? Is it well written and well laid out? 🎓
- How well did you defend your work orally? 🎓
- Did you handle trade-offs effectively during the course of your project?
- To what degree is your project completed? For example, is some software you were developing only 80% complete?
- Have you fulfilled all the regulations required? 🎓
- What evidence is there of learning and development?
- Is the subject matter of the project suitable for the qualification you are pursuing?
- Have you identified a clear aim and set appropriate objectives?

2. Literature review/project foundation

- How effectively have you managed the information you have acquired for the project?
- How effective have your information retrieval skills been?
- How well do you understand and comprehend the subject area of the project? 🎓
- What is the extent and depth of the literature survey undertaken? 🎓
- Does the literature survey provide a firm theoretical basis for the report/dissertation? 🎓
- What new knowledge has been acquired by you and the reader? 🎓
- Does your literature survey set your project in context?

3. Project approach/methods

- For software development projects questions will include: Have you used appropriate development processes, methods and techniques? Have you used these processes/methods/techniques correctly? Have you justified your choice of these processes/methods/techniques?
- Have you used appropriate research methods in your project? Have you justified your choice of particular methods? 🎓

- Have you undertaken appropriate data collection for your project? Are the data adequate for your hypotheses? Have the data been processed in an appropriate way?

- Have you selected, and used effectively, appropriate hardware and software during the course of your project (programming languages, software tools, statistical packages, multimedia, etc.)? Have you justified your choices?

4. Results and contribution(s)

- How well have you interpreted the results of your project? Have you used appropriate techniques for evaluating these results?

- Have you clearly identified future work from you project? Have you made any recommendations as to where the work should go next?

- What is the overall contribution of your project? Who will benefit from your contribution?

- What is the scope of your project? For example, has it applied existing techniques to new areas? Have you developed innovative solutions?

- Can your work/results be applied in other areas? What are the limitations of this application?

- How does it fit in/support/consolidate existing work?

- Have you critically evaluated your own solution/approach/method/development?

- Have you evaluated your work with respect to your original aims and objectives?

While examiners will look for these points, it might also help you to know why some projects do not fare well (so that you can avoid these issues). Cornford and Smithson (2006: 190) identify a number of reasons why projects might be awarded poor marks:

- There is no link between the work performed and other literature in the field.

- The report is long-winded, ill-structured and poorly presented.

- The report includes a number of generalisations that do not have appropriate supporting evidence.

- There is a lack of meaningful conclusions.

Other reasons for poor marks (and things you should avoid) include:

- **Misplaced focus within the report.** The student has focused on the minutiae when the overall contribution of the project has been weak or misplaced. Try to take a step back from your project and consider it within its wider context. The fact that some small part of your project has been done really well may be immaterial if the project achieves little overall.

- **Poor software evaluation.** This usually stems from the lack of any real client or user. In software development projects those that are done well usually have a real client. Those students who undertake projects without a real client or without considering who might benefit from their software generally perform badly.

- **Not taking the work far enough.** Although some reports go some way to addressing a particular problem, they sometimes do not go far enough – usually due to lack of time. It can be annoying for examiners to see that you have only really gone so far with your project; there may have been a straightforward 'next step' that you could have taken that would have rounded off your project nicely.

■ **Poor evaluation.** While the student may have undertaken a sound piece of work, the report's final conclusions are weak. There is little evaluation of all aspects of their work and little indication that the student has thought about any wider issues.

■ **Lack of justification.** The student has failed to include any justification for anything he or she has chosen to do. For example, there is no justification of the research methods chosen, the hardware platform used, the development process followed, the programming language used and so on.

■ **Poor presentation.** The report is badly presented and/or is aimed at the wrong level of reader (novice readers, for example). Sometimes students spend a long time explaining something trivial for novice readers when they should be focussing on more academic matters that the examiner will be interested in. Make sure you write your project report at the right level.

■ **Lack of evidence** that the student has applied skills from their course during the project. For example, if the student has been taught database design techniques there should be evidence that the student has used these skills appropriately in their project if they have to design a database.

■ **The conclusions are no more than a summary of the rest of the report.** The conclusion does little more than say what has already been reported. There is no critical evaluation, justification or identification of further work.

Overall, it is impossible to say precisely what examiners will be happy with and unhappy with in projects they are assessing. Examiners are individuals and they all have their own opinions, preferences and ideas on what is right and appropriate within projects at different levels. Even within departments, academic staff will disagree on what is a good project and what constitutes a poor project. For example, using some of the elements listed above a project may look good; against another subset of these criteria, that project may appear poor. What you can do is try and find out a little bit more about your examiner(s) beforehand. You may find they have particular interests or preferences that you can work towards. Speak with your supervisor as well; s/he should advise you on which aspects of the report to focus and may also have some ideas on the preferences of the examiners.

● 10.3 Taking your project further

10.3.1 Introduction

When you complete your project, hand it in and crack open the champagne, you will probably have one of two feelings about it. You will either be so fed up with the sight of it that you never want to see it again and you want to burn all your books and notes. This, however, is not advisable as you may need to attend a viva or rework some of your project if things didn't go quite according to plan and you have to resubmit your report.

Alternatively, you might be so enthusiastic about what you have achieved that you can't wait for your 'A' grade and you can't wait to get back to your work and develop your great ideas further.

Developing your project further can result in a number of things. You may wish to develop a commercial software package from a program that you wrote as part of your project. If you have completed an undergraduate project, you might want to develop your ideas further into an MPhil or PhD. You might want to write a paper on your work to share your ideas with the academic community. You might want to patent your work or you might want to seek some kind of funding so that you can develop your work further. Some of these issues will be discussed in the following few sections.

10.3.2 Seeking funding

Obtaining project funding is not an easy task, even for experienced academics and managers. As a newly qualified graduate with little track record and probably few, if any, publications, you stand little chance of obtaining funding on your own. You also have the problem of not knowing whom to turn to for funds and how to appropriately apply and complete any required forms and paperwork. In short, you will probably not obtain funding on your own. One way around this is to try to forge links with research groups and industry. Your own department might have a research group with internationally recognised researchers who might be interested in your work and wish to involve you with theirs. Your supervisor may wish to keep you on as a research student or a research assistant. You may be lucky and have developed some software for a local company as part of your project so it might be worth liaising with them for further funds. Whatever the case, you will need to work with somebody else and learn from experience.

Applying for research funding and obtaining grants is not discussed widely and there are few texts devoted to this topic. However, two books that you may find useful to help you are Browning (2005) and Peters (2003), which provide a useful overview of this topic.

10.3.3 Developing commercial software packages

Because of the nature of your course it is possible that you might have developed a software system as part of your project. You might feel that this software has some commercial value and you might wish to market it as such. This may require a lot more development work or it may simply mean packaging the software in an appropriate way for delivery. Once again, this kind of project advancement is not easy to do on your own.

You may have to establish some commercial links to market your product. You might have to obtain some kind of funding or financial backing to get your ideas off the ground. You might also find there are difficulties with patents and intellectual property rights over work you have done for your project. These problems might be even more pronounced if your project involved working with an organisation or company and they wish to stake some claim over your work.

Whatever the case, perhaps the best place to start to resolve these issues is with your project supervisor. S/he should be able to help you or know whom you should contact to address these issues. Having been closely involved with your project thus far, your supervisor might also be keen to be involved with any future developments that you make. Your supervisor should also be able to advise you on another important, related issue – copyright and patents, discussed next.

10.3.4 Copyright and patents

Who owns the rights to your project when you have finally submitted it for assessment is a 'grey area' within universities. Some institutions openly recognise that you have *intellectual property rights* (IPR) over any work you produce as part of your course. The copyright for everything you produce thus belongs to you. This means that, while your institution would require copies of your work to retain for assessment purposes, you would be able to sell patent and copyrights for your work as you wished. You would also be entitled, for example, to develop and sell any software that you had produced as part of your course.

While this level of recognition of student ownership represents one extreme, other institutions will claim to own all rights to any student work produced during, and as part of, an academic course. In addition, where collaborative projects have been undertaken with industry, the company may retain ownership of anything you produce. It can also be argued that your supervisor has some (perhaps a lot of) investment in your project. The supervisor may have suggested the project in the first place, provided invaluable advice and guidance during the course of the project, and so on. In these cases, your supervisor is entitled to some of the ownership of your project too.

If you wish to take your work further or develop something commercial from it, check to see what rights you have over what you have produced. Check your own institution's guidelines and rules on matters of this nature – there is usually a department that will deal with these issues. Patent and copyright laws are extremely complex and you may well find that you end up going round in circles and generate more questions than answers. For more information on IPR, refer to Bainbridge (2008), an entire book devoted to the subject of intellectual property. The following web sites also provide some useful information on copyright and patent issues:

- The United States Patent and Trademarks Office: http://www.uspto.gov/
- The UK Patent Office/Intellectual Property site: http://www.patent.gov.uk/
- The European IPR helpdesk: http://www.ipr-helpdesk.org/

● 10.4 Publishing your work

Your project may have gone so well that you wish to publish your work. Your supervisor may be closely involved with this idea and will certainly advise you. Writing for publication is not as simple as cutting and pasting a few sections from your report. It must have a logical structure and show clear evidence of a contribution. Getting work published can also be a rather long-winded process – for example, it is common for some journal articles to be published well over a year after they have been submitted.

There are number of places that you might consider publishing your work, the most respected being an academic journal. Journals have guidelines on the type of work they accept and how the work should be submitted (including the paper's layout and format). While journals are the most respected source of perceived wisdom, some are more respected than others (and are consequently more selective). If you do submit your work to a recognised journal, one thing is sure: through the review process you will receive useful feedback on your work from experts in the field. Sometimes it is worth submitting your work to a 'high-class' journal simply to obtain feedback. You might then consider making the changes the reviewers suggest before resubmitting your work to a less-recognised publication.

Conferences are a good route to presenting your work if you have only preliminary findings to discuss. There will be deadlines you need to adhere to for conferences, including quite strict regulations on the layout of your paper (camera-ready). Like journals, conferences come in varying degrees of quality but they do provide a useful way of meeting and discussing your ideas with like-minded people. Having discussed your work with others through a conference publication, you may wish to develop your work into a journal paper. One point to bear in mind with conferences is that they do cost to attend – registration, travel and accommodation. Make sure you (or your department) have the funding available to support a conference publication before you submit a paper or poster. You might also wish to consider other routes into publication through submitting internal reports within your own department or by writing brief summary papers or articles in more popular journals and newspapers.

Some books can advise you on writing for publication. Five such texts on this topic are Day (2006), Day (2008), Gustavii (2008), Lester and Lester (2008), and Malmfors *et al.* (2003). Refer to one or more of these text if you are thinking of writing an academic article for the first time. Shaw (2003) also provides some interesting information on writing papers within the field of software engineering.

● 10.5 Additional topics

While this book has covered probably all the topics you will require to complete both undergraduate and postgraduate computing projects successfully, there are a number of subjects that have only been mentioned in passing and may be relevant to your project. This section briefly summarises these topics and provides you with some pointers towards further reading that you may find useful.

- **Statistics.** Part of your project may require some form of statistical analyses. For example, from running some software speed trials, is an algorithm you have developed *significantly* better than an existing algorithm? If you have conducted a survey, are any of its responses significant?

  The number of statistical tests available is enormous and beyond the scope of this book. In addition, there are a wealth of books on the subject. Some that you may find useful are Kanji (1999), which summarises a number of statistical tests and defines their application; and Gibson (2007) and Larsen and Marx (2005), which provide a reasonable introduction to elementary statistics.

- **Qualitative analysis.** Qualitative data are those data you gather that are not expressed in absolute arithmetical terms. They represent opinions, observations and ideas and are generally culled from questionnaires, surveys and interviews. Reviewing, analysing, evaluating and summarising these data often occurs in sociological studies. This may, for example, form part of an information systems project that aims to obtain user feedback on human interface issues. Two texts that cover this subject in detail are Mason (2002) and Silverman (2004).

● 10.6 The future

10.6.1 Your new skills

This section discusses briefly how you will be able to apply the skills you have learnt from your project in the future. As an undergraduate, you might find yourself moving on into industry or staying on within the academic community to pursue your studies further; for example, for an MPhil or PhD. As a postgraduate, you may wish to remain in academia as a lecturer, a research assistant or fellow, or you too might decide to move into industry. The following points relate to a number of skills you should have developed during the course of your project, whether at the undergraduate or postgraduate level:

■ **Independence.** One of the objectives of your project was to develop your skills as an independent worker. Quite often, institutions refer to student projects as *Independent Studies,* which emphasises this point. Being able to work on your own without detailed supervision is certainly a skill worth cultivating and it should be one of the skills you developed during the course of your project. Industry expects independence from graduates, and postgraduate research degrees will require this skill as a matter of course. Be prepared to show initiative and independent thinking in your chosen career and be able to take charge of situations rather than having to be told what to do and be directed all the time.

■ **Thinking.** Your project should have taught you how to think about things more critically and in a deeper way. Independent thought and ideas represent a maturity of understanding that does not develop from merely attending lectures and tutorials. Your project should have furnished you with these kinds of skills. Once again, being able to look at things in new ways, showing deeper understanding and imagination, are skills that postgraduates are expected to have.

■ **Learning.** Your project should have taught you how to learn. As part of your project, you should have had to learn new skills, new ways of looking at things and new ways of thinking. This 'learning' would not come from lectures and tutorials but from your own independent research and study. You have, therefore, understood and developed the skill of independent learning – a skill that will be useful both in industry and postgraduate work.

In addition, your project may also have provided an underpinning theoretical grounding in a number of areas rather than a specific technical skill. This is important as it means you can often develop and learn new skills more quickly from this firm base than you could otherwise have done by merely learning a particular tool, language or technique. For example, although you might not be able to program in a particular programming language, your underpinning theory of languages will mean that you can learn a new language very quickly. You are thus more flexible and adaptable to change than you would otherwise be with a purely technical background.

- **Technical skills.** You might also have picked up some technical skills during the course of your project. You may have learnt how to use a particular software package or apply particular analysis and design methods. While you may never use these particular technical skills again, they can provide you with a basis on which to learn similar techniques and tools in the future and they also help to bolster your CV!

- **Communication skills.** Both written and verbal communication skills are a vital part of any degree project. Improving your skills in these areas will certainly be useful, whether you go into industry or continue with postgraduate work. Verbal communication skills will be useful in industry as you will have to liaise with all kinds of people; managers, customers and clients, your own staff, consultants and others. You might also be expected to give presentations and demonstrations and will certainly be expected to produce reports that must be clear and concise.

  At postgraduate level, you will encounter many new people and situations that require both your written and verbal communication skills. You might have to attend conferences or give seminars. You may be required to do some teaching or support tutorials and laboratory sessions. You will certainly have to produce written reports, transfer documents, articles and, ultimately, a thesis.

- **Time management.** During the course of your project, you will have needed to make a number of trade-offs, you will have had to meet a number of deadlines and you will have needed to balance your project against other commitments. Undertaking your project will have helped you to develop your time management skills (discussed in Chapter 7). These skills will be invaluable to you in the future as you try to juggle work, family and social commitments.

10.6.2 Your new job

While the above issues represent developments to your own portfolio of skills, this section will look briefly at how things might be done differently in your new career.

- **Industry.** Going to work in industry for the first time can be quite a culture shock. Where in the past you might have looked at things from a purely academic viewpoint because they interested you, within industry your primary concern will be **cost.** The work you do and projects you undertake will be performed only if financially viable. The software you produce must do what it is supposed to do and what was asked for – there will be little need to justify it or place it within a wider context. You will also feel even more pressure to complete work on time. While your project was your own responsibility and you were the only one who would suffer if it was handed in late, in industry many people will be relying on you to get the job done.

  Another area that may appear alien to you within industry is the politics. An academic environment usually has an 'open door' policy whereby you can speak to people (administrators, professors, technicians and others) as and when you require. The more structured hierarchy in industry, however, sometimes means you cannot talk directly to the person you need to communicate with. Instead, you may have to go through your own manager for permission to speak to another manager. This can seem quite frustrating when, in an academic environment, everyone has been approachable and easy to contact.

■ **Higher degrees.** If you are moving from an undergraduate bachelor's degree to a higher-level course – an MSc, MPhil or PhD – you will have to adapt your way of thinking to some extent. MScs usually contain a project as a significant part of their assessment. MPhils, on the other hand, are represented almost entirely by a research project. In both of these cases, your depth of understanding and critical evaluation will have to be far more mature than at bachelor's level.

The nature of the PhD is also very much different to a taught degree project. It will need justification and contextualisation and it will certainly have to make a contribution to knowledge. These days, timing is also more critical. Departments are sometimes penalised by funding bodies if you take longer than you should to complete your PhD, so pressure will be on you from sources outside yourself to complete your thesis on time. You might also need to diversify your work into articles and papers for publication. As mentioned earlier, you might also have to do some teaching or help out with tutorials. An excellent book that can help you with the transition from a first degree to a PhD is Phillips and Pugh (2005), which provides some interesting information on doing a PhD.

10.6.3 Professional accreditation

Completing your degree may open professional doors to you. For example, when you start work you might wish to join a professional body that supports your particular field. Examples are the British Computer Society (BCS) in the UK and the Institute of Electrical and Electronic Engineers (IEEE) and the Association for Computing Machinery (ACM) in the United States. To become a member of the IEEE and ACM you will be required to hold some formal qualifications. To become a full member of the BCS, you will either have to complete some Society examinations or show that you have completed an academic course approved by the BCS.

Check with your institution to see what level of exemptions or accreditations, if any, apply to your own particular course and which professional bodies are involved. You may find, for example, that while one course within your department is fully exempt or recognised, another is not.

These Internet links will provide additional information on appropriate professional bodies:

■ The British Computer Society: http://www.bcs.org/
■ The IEEE: http://www.ieee.org/
■ The Association for Computing Machinery: http://www.acm.org/
■ The Engineering Council UK: http://www.engc.org.uk/
■ European Federation of National Engineering Associations: http://www.feani.org/

● 10.7 Top ten tips for successful projects

As a summary of the main points of this book, this section presents my top ten tips for completing student projects successfully. Although these tips will not guarantee that you achieve top marks for your project, they should ensure that your project is completed well. The tips are not presented in any particular order as no tip is better than any other and the extent to which you follow their guidance is up to you, your project and your circumstances.

- Choose a project that interests you (Section 3.2). It is difficult to motivate yourself and produce a good project if you have little interest in the topic area. If you choose a project that interests you, you will be far more committed to it and keen to undertake the work than you would otherwise be.

- Have a clear goal and objectives (Section 4.2). If you understand clearly in your own mind the ultimate goal of your project (and can define some intermediate milestones, objectives or sub-goals to achieve this aim) you will know where you are going with your project and what you should be doing.

- Try to get a client for your project. At an undergraduate level, projects that have real clients (for example, for a software system you are developing or a case study you are undertaking) generally turn out better than those which do not (for example, developing a web site for an imaginary company, etc.). A real client will provide you with more motivation and perhaps clearer requirements than you could obtain from your supervisor alone. In addition, a real client (and users) will provide valuable feedback when your project nears completion. Although your project may have been suggested as an academic exercise by your supervisor you could still make the effort to find a client for the project yourself. You could use friends, relatives, industrial placement contacts, etc. to help identify a suitable client.

- Put together a project plan and follow it (Chapter 4). There is an old saying – 'fail to plan, plan to fail'. With a project plan in place you will have some idea on what you should be doing on your project and some means of tracking and controlling your progress. However, do not spend so long planning your project at intricate levels of detail that you fail to get on with any real work. You should spend no longer than around 10% of your effort on project management activities.

- Identify risks to your project and put contingency plans in place (Section 4.4). You should have some idea of the key risks to your project (and risk triggers) and their impact on your project. Make sure that you are aware of these risks and have some ideas on how you will deal with those risks if they should occur. Don't assume that everything will go well – consider problems that might occur and be prepared to deal with them.

- Be well organised. Put together a project folder, establish a working area and good working practices, keep your references up-to-date and organised, arrange data and files on your computer logically and make regular back-ups. Failure to follow these guidelines will lead to sloppy work and inefficiency as information is lost and you are unable to keep track of everything you are doing.

- Start to write early. Get into the habit of writing up notes and work you have completed as you go along. This will prevent you having to write your report/thesis from scratch towards the end of your project when time is limited. It will also get you into habit of writing and will improve your writing skills.

- Undertake a literature survey (Chapter 5). Make sure you have 'read around' your subject area thus ensuring you do not complete your project in a vacuum and you are aware of the subject areas that it draws from and the context in which it resides. At postgraduate level this is essential but it can also be important for undergraduate projects too (although many undergraduates ignore this point). This will enable you to show what contribution your project is making, show that it is not repeating the work of others, assist you with different aspects of your project and provide justification for any decisions that you make.

■ Have regular meetings with your supervisor. Your supervisor is there to help you and they are experienced – so make sure you use this resource as much as possible – and follow any advice s/he gives you. Students who rarely see their supervisor often fail.

■ Aim to finish your project early. It is always a good idea to aim to complete your project one or two weeks before the actual hand-in date (for a six month project this should be achievable). This will provide you with some contingency time that may be needed if things don't go quite according to plan.

● 10.8 Summary

■ Although you have finished your project, there are still ways to continue your work further in the future; seeking funding for further research, developing commercial software from your project, seeking patents and copyright on the material you have produced and publishing your work in academic journals and conferences.

■ You should have learnt a number of skills from your project that will come in useful in the future – for either a job in industry or further academic work: independence, the ability to 'think', learning skills, technical skills and communication skills.

■ Your degree course and project may provide you with exemption from and accreditation for membership in such professional bodies as the IEEE or the British Computer Society and Engineering Council. Your own department will be able to advise you on this.

● 10.9 Further reading

Browning, B.A. (2005) *Grant writing for dummies* (2nd Edition), John Wiley, New York.
Day, A. (2008) *How to get research published in journals* (2nd Edition), Gower, Aldershot, UK.
Day, R.A. (2006) *How to write and publish a scientific paper* (6th Edition), Cambridge University Press, Cambridge, UK.
Gustavii, B. (2008) *How to write and illustrate a scientific paper* (2nd Edition), Cambridge University Press, Cambridge, UK.
Lester, J.D. and Lester, J.D. (2008) *Writing research papers a complete guide* (12th Edition), Pearson Education, Essex, UK.

Malmfors, B. Garnsworthy, P. and Grossman, M. (2003) *Writing and presenting scientific papers* (2nd Edition), Nottingham University Press, Nottingham, UK.

Peters, A.D. (2003) *Winning research funding,* Gower, Aldershot, UK.

Phillips, E.M. and Pugh, D.S. (2005) *How to get a PhD: A handbook for students and their supervisors* (4th Edition), Open University Press, Buckingham, UK.

10.10 Action points

- Think about how you could develop your project further in the future.
- Write down what you have learnt by doing your project. How have you changed and developed as a result?

References

Bainbridge, D. (2008) *Intellectual property* (7th Edition), Longman, New York.

Barker, S. and Cole, R. (2007) *Brilliant project management: What the best project managers know, say, do*, Prentice Hall, Englewood Cliffs, USA.

Barnes, M. (1989) *Have project, will manage*, BBC2.

Belbin, M. (1993) *Team roles at work*, Butterworth-Heinemann, Oxford, UK.

Bell, J. (2005) *Doing your research project: a guide for first time researchers in education, health, and social science* (4th Edition), Open University Press, Maidenhead, UK.

Benington, H.D. (1956) 'Production of large computer programmes', Proceedings ONR, Symposium on Advanced Programming Methods, pp 15–27.

Berndtsson, M. Hansson, J. Olsson, B. and Lundell, B. (2008) *Thesis projects A guide for students in Computer Science and Information Systems* (2nd Edition), Springer-Verlag, London.

Blaxter, L. Hughes, C. and Tight, M. (2006) *How to research* (3rd Edition), Open University Press, Maidenhead, UK.

Boehm, B.W. (1979) 'Software Engineering: R & D trends and defense needs', *Research Directions in Software Technology*, (Wagner, P. ed.), Cambridge, MA, MIT Press.

Boehm, B.W. (1981) *Software engineering economics*, Prentice Hall, Englewood Cliffs, USA.

Brace, I. (2008) *Questionnaire design: how to plan, structure and write survey material for effective market research* (2nd Edition), Kogan Page, London.

Bradburn, N.M. Sudman, S. and Wansink, B. (2004) *Asking questions: The definitive guide to questionnaire design*, JosseyBass, John Wiley, New York.

Browning, B.A. (2005) *Grant writing for dummies* (2nd Edition), John Wiley, New York.

Chinneck, J.W. (1999) *How to organize your thesis*, <http://www.sce.carleton.ca/faculty/chinneck/thesis.html> (7 October 2008).

Cornford, T. and Smithson, S. (2006) *Project research in information systems a student's guide* (2nd Edition), Palgrave Macmillan, Basingstoke, UK.

Cryer, P. (2006) *The research student's guide to success* (3rd Edition), Open University Press, Maidenhead, UK.

Czaja, R. and Blair, J. (2005) *Designing surveys a guide to decisions and procedures* (2nd Edition), SAGE Publications, London.

Davis, A.M. Bersoff, E.H. and Comer, E.R. (1988) 'A strategy for comparing alternative software development life cycle models', *IEEE Transactions on Software Engineering*, Vol 14 (10), pp 1453–1461.

Dawson, C.W. and Wilby, R. (1998) 'An artificial neural network approach to rainfall-runoff modelling', *Hydrological Sciences Journal*, Vol 43(1), pp 47–66.

Dawson, R.J. (2004) Personal communication, 5 July.

Day, A. (2008) *How to get research published in journals* (2nd Edition), Gower, Aldershot, UK.

Day, R.A. (2006) *How to write and publish a scientific paper* (6th Edition), Cambridge University Press, Cambridge, UK.

Dochartaigh, N.O. (2007) *Internet research skills: How to do your literature search and find research information online* (2nd Edition), SAGE Publications, London.

Dodd, P. (2008) *The 25 best time management tools and techniques: how to get more done without driving yourself crazy*, Capstone, Oxford, UK.

Etherington, B. (2006) *Presentation skills for quivering wrecks*, Cyan Books, London.

Evans, C. (2008) *Time management for dummies*, John Wiley, New York.

Fearn, H. (2008) 'The long and the short of it', *Times Higher Education*, 2 October, pp 30–37.

Ferner, J.D. (1995) *Successful time management* (2nd Edition), John Wiley, New York.

Flay, B. Bull, P. and Tamahori, J. (1983) 'Designing a questionnaire for Polynesian and Pakeha car assembly workers', in Bulmer, M. and Warwick, D. (eds), 'Social research in developing countries: surveys and censuses in the Third World', John Wiley, Chichester, UK, pp 167–172.

Forster, M. (2006) *Do it tomorrow and other secrets of time management*, Hodder & Stoughton, London.

Gall, M.D. Borg, W.R. and Gall, J.P. (2002) *Educational research: an introduction* (7th Edition), Longman, New York.

Gerring, J. (2006) *Case study research principles and practice*, Cambridge University Press, Cambridge, UK.

Gibson, H.R. (2007) *Elementary statistics* (2nd Edition), Kendall Hunt, Dubuque, USA.

Gill, J. and Johnson, P. (2002) *Research methods for managers* (3rd Edition), SAGE, London.

Gleeson, K. (2003) *The personal efficiency program: How to get organized to do more work in less time*, John Wiley, New York.

Greenfield, T. (ed) (1996) *Research methods guidance for postgraduates*, Arnold, London.

Groves, R.M. Fowler, F.J. Couper, M.P. Lepkowski, J.M. Singer, E. and Tourangeau, R. (2004) *Survey methodology*, Wiley Blackwell, Oxford, UK.

Gustavii, B. (2008) *How to write and illustrate a scientific paper* (2nd Edition), Cambridge University Press, Cambridge, UK.

Hall, R. (2007) *Brilliant presentations: What the best presenters know, say and do*, Prentice Hall, Englewood Cliffs, USA.

Haywood, P. and Wragg, E.C. (1982) *Evaluating the literature*, Rediguide 2, University of Nottingham School of Education, Nottingham, UK.

Helmer-Heidelberg, O. (1966) *Social technology*, Basic Books, New York.

Herbert, M. (1990) *Planning a research project*, Cassell Educational, London.

Higher Education Academy (2008) 'Personal development planning', <http://www.heacademy.ac.uk/ourwork/learning/pdp> (2 April 2008).

Hirji, P. (2004) 'Cultural aspects of plagiarism', *Teaching and learning innovation*, Professional Development publication, Vol 2(2), Loughborough University, UK.

Hughes, R. and Cotterell, M. (2006) *Software project management* (4th Edition), McGraw-Hill, Maidenhead, UK.

Intute (2008) *The best web resources for education and research*, <http://www.intute.ac.uk/>, (10 October 2008).

Jones, K. (1998) *Time management the essential guide to thinking and working smarter*, Marshall Publishing, London.

Kane, E. (1985) *Doing your own research*, Marion Boyars, London.

Kanji, G.K. (1999) *100 Statistical tests* (2nd Edition), SAGE Publications, London.

Knott, R.P. and Dawson, R.J. (1999) *Software project management*, Group D Publications, Loughborough, UK.

Larsen, R.J. and Marx, M.L. (2005) *An introduction to mathematical statistics and its application* (4th Edition), Pearson Education, Essex, UK.

Lester, J.D. and Lester, J.D. (2008) *Writing research papers: A complete guide* (12th Edition), Pearson Education, Essex, UK.

LevelA Software (2005) 'Software life cycle models', <http://www.levela.com/software_life_cycles_swdoc.htm> (11 October 2008).

Levin, P. (2005) *Excellent dissertations!*, Open University Press, Buckingham, UK.

Levine, H.A. (2002) *Practical project management: tips, tactics and tools*, John Wiley, New York.

Lock, D. (2007) *Project management* (9th Edition), Gower, Aldershot, UK.

Loughborough University (2008) *Questionnaire design*, University Library study advice publication.

Maciaszek, L. (2007) *Requirements analysis and systems design* (3rd Edition), Addison-Wesley, Wokingham, UK.

Malmfors, B. Garnsworthy, P. and Grossman, M. (2003) *Writing and presenting scientific papers* (2nd Edition), Nottingham University Press, Nottingham, UK.

Mason, J. (2002) *Qualitative researching* (2nd Edition), SAGE Publications, London.

Mayo, E. (1933) *The human problems of an industrial civilization*, MacMillan, New York.

Montgomery, S.L. (2002) *The Chicago guide to communicating science*, University of Chicago Press, Chicago, USA.

Munger, D. and Campbell, S. (2006) *What every student should know about researching online*, Longman, Harlow, UK.

Nicol, A.A.M. and Pexman, P.M. (2003) *Displaying your findings: A practical guide to creating figures, posters and presentations*, American Psychological Association, Washington, USA.

O'Sullivan, T. Rice, J. Rogerson, S. and Saunders, C. (1996) *Successful group work*, Kogan Page, London.

Oetiker, T. Partl, H. Hyna, I. and Schlegl, E. (2008) *The not so short introduction to LaTeX 2ε*, <http://www.ctan.org/tex-archive/info/lshort/english/lshort.pdf> (13 October 2008).

Ohio State University Library (2008) *Evaluating web sites > overview - key ideas*, <http://liblearn.osu.edu/tutor/les1/> (10 October 2008).

Orna, E. and Stevens, G. (1995) *Managing information for research*, Open University Press, Buckingham, UK.

Orna, E. and Stevens, G. (2009) *Managing information for research* (2nd Edition), Open University Press, Buckingham, UK.

Ould, M. (1999) *Managing software quality and business risk*, John Wiley, Chichester, UK.

Peters, A.D. (2003) *Winning research funding*, Gower, Aldershot, UK.

Phillips, E.M. and Pugh, D.S. (2005) *How to get a PhD a handbook for students and their supervisors* (4th Edition), Open University Press, Buckingham, UK.

Phillips, S. (2002) *Time management 24/7: How to double your effectiveness*, McGraw-Hill, London.

Post, G.V. and Anderson, D.L. (2006) *Management information systems solving business problems with information technology* (4th Edition), McGraw-Hill, New York.

Pym, D.V. and Wideman, R.M. (1987) 'Risk management', in *The revised project management body of knowledge*, Project Management Institute.

RAE (2008) *Research assessment exercise*, <http://www.rae.ac.uk/> (23 April 2008).

Reynolds, G. (2008) *Presentation Zen: Simple ideas on presentation design and delivery*, New Riders, Indianapolis, USA.

Ricketts, I.W. (1998) *Managing your software project a student's guide*, Springer-Verlag, London.

Robertson, S. and Robertson, J. (2006) *Mastering the requirements process*, Addison-Wesley, Wokingham, UK.

Robson, C. (2002) *Real world research* (2nd Edition), Blackwell, Oxford.

Roethlisberger, F.J. and Dickson, W.J. (1939) *Management and the worker*, Harvard University Press, Cambridge, USA.

Rogerson, S. (1989) *Project skills handbook*, Chartwell-Bratt, Sweden.

Rooney, K. (ed) (2004) *Steps to success manage your time: How to work more effectively*, Bloomsbury, London.

Rudestam, K.E. and Newton, R.R. (2007) *Surviving your dissertation* (3rd Edition), SAGE Publications, London.

Saunders, M. Lewis, P. and Thornhill, A. (2007) *Research methods for business students* (4th Edition), Prentice Hall, Essex, UK.

Sharp, J.A. Peters, J. and Howard, K. (2002) *The management of a student research project* (3rd Edition), Gower, Aldershot, UK.

Shaw, M. (2003) 'Writing good software engineering research papers', Position paper for Proceeding of International Conference on Software Engineering, Portland, Oregon, USA.

Silverman, D. (2004) *Doing qualitative research: A practical handbook* (2nd Edition), SAGE, London.

Tracy, B. (2008) *Eat that frog! 21 great ways to stop procrastinating and get more done in less time* (2nd Edition), Berrett-Koehler, San Francisco, USA.

Tuckman, B.W. (1965) 'Developmental sequence in small groups', *Psychological Bulletin*, Vol 63, pp 384–399.

Turla, P. and Hawkins, K.L. (1994) *Time management made easy*, Penguin Books, New York.

Turner, J.R. (1993) *The handbook of project-based management*, McGraw-Hill, London.

University of Derby (1995) *Literature searching for computing*, University of Derby, internal library publication.

University of Derby (1999) *Independent studies guidance: notes for postgraduate students*, internal publication.

University of Warwick (1994) *Graduate student handbook 1994/95*, University of Warwick, Department of Continuing Education, UK.

Verma, G.K. and Beard, R.M. (1981) *What is educational research?*, Gower, Aldershot, UK.

Wells, D. (2006) *Extreme programming*, <http://www.extremeprogramming.org/> (11 October 2008).

Weiss, J.W. and Wysocki, R.K. (1992) *5-Phase project management: A practical planning and implementation guide*, Addison-Wesley, Reading, USA.

Yin, R.K. (2008) *Case study research design and methods* (4th Edition), SAGE Publications, London.

Index